Firebug 1.5: Editing, Debugging, and Monitoring Web Pages

Arm yourself to destroy UI and JavaScript bugs

Chandan Luthra

Deepak Mittal

BIRMINGHAM - MUMBAI

Firebug 1.5: Editing, Debugging, and Monitoring Web Pages

Copyright © 2010 Packt Publishing

All rights reserved. No part of this book may be reproduced, stored in a retrieval system, or transmitted in any form or by any means, without the prior written permission of the publisher, except in the case of brief quotations embedded in critical articles or reviews.

Every effort has been made in the preparation of this book to ensure the accuracy of the information presented. However, the information contained in this book is sold without warranty, either express or implied. Neither the authors, Packt Publishing, nor its dealers or distributors will be held liable for any damages caused or alleged to be caused directly or indirectly by this book.

Packt Publishing has endeavored to provide trademark information about all the companies and products mentioned in this book by the appropriate use of capitals. However, Packt Publishing cannot guarantee the accuracy of this information.

First published: April 2010

Production Reference: 1300310

Published by Packt Publishing Ltd.
32 Lincoln Road
Olton
Birmingham, B27 6PA, UK.

ISBN 978-1-847194-96-1

www.packtpub.com

Cover Image by Filippo Sarti (filosarti@tiscali.it)

Credits

Authors
Chandan Luthra
Deepak Mittal

Reviewers
Balaji D Loganathan
Michael Ratcliffe
Michael Sync

Acquisition Editor
Dilip Venkatesh

Development Editor
Dilip Venkatesh

Technical Editors
Gaurav Datar
Rukhsana Khambatta

Copy Editor
Sanchari Mukherjee

Indexer
Hemangini Bari

Editorial Team Leader
Gagandeep Singh

Project Team Leader
Lata Basantani

Project Coordinator
Poorvi Nair

Proofreader
Aaron Nash

Graphics
Geetanjali G. Sawant

Production Coordinator
Adline Swetha Jesuthas

Cover Work
Adline Swetha Jesuthas

About the Authors

Chandan Luthra is a Software Development Engineer with IntelliGrape Software, New Delhi, India—a company specializing in Groovy/Grails development. He is an agile and pragmatic programmer and an active participant at local open source software events, where he evangelizes Groovy, Grails, Jquery, and Firebug. Chandan is a Linux and open source enthusiast. He also involves himself in writing blogs and is an active member on various tech-related mailing lists. He has developed web applications for various industries, including entertainment, finance, media and publishing, as well as others.

He loves to share his knowledge and good coding practices with other team members in order to hone their development skills. In his free time, he loves to contribute to open source technologies.

Chandan also loves to code in jQuery and Firebug, which makes development very easy for him. He is a very fond user of Firebug and has been using it since 2007.

I would like to thank my family for their love and support during my far-flung adventures into esoteric nonsense. Thanks also to all my cooperative colleagues at IntelliGrape for their feedback and suggestions. I would also like to thank Deepak Mittal for co-authoring and motivating me to write this book. Finally, I wish to thank Dilip Venkatesh (Acquisition Editor at Packt), Poorvi Nair (Project Coordinator at Packt), Micheal Sync (Reviewer), Micheal Ratcliffe (Reviewer), and Balaji Loganathan (Reviewer) for giving a perfect shape to this book. Special thanks to S. Vivek Krishna for his help on the Preface of the book.

Deepak Mittal is a software developer based in New Delhi, India, and he has been involved with software engineering and web programming in Java/JEE world since the late 1990s. Deepak is a Linux and open source enthusiast. He is an agile practitioner and speaks about open source, agile processes, and free software at various user group meetings and conferences. He has designed and built web applications for industries including pharmaceutical, travel, media, and publishing, as well as others. He loves to explore new technologies and has been an early-adopter of quite a few mainstream technologies of today's world.

In early 2008, he co-founded IntelliGrape Software, an agile web application development company focused on Groovy and Grails. At IntelliGrape, he has been occupied with building world class applications on Grails and also mentors and trains other team members.

Deepak is a veteran user of Firebug and has been using it since 2006.

I want to thank all my colleagues at IntelliGrape for their valuable feedback and suggestions, my family for putting up without me for weeks, and all the contributors of Firebug. My special thanks go to Dilip Venkatesh (Acquisition Editor at Packt), Poorvi Nair (Project Coordinator at Packt), Chandan Luthra (my co-author), and all the reviewers of the book.

About the Reviewers

Balaji D Loganathan has 10+ years of experience in the software field, is a CEO and Co-founder of Spritle Software—a software development company in Chennai, India. Balaji is an Agile Guru specializing in Agile Offshore, a Certified Scrum Master. Balaji has a Master's degree in IT from the RMIT, Australia and a Bachelors Degree in Engineering from the Annamalai University, India.

When **Michael Ratcliffe** was 9 years old he saw a movie called "Wargames". Like many kids his age he became very interested in computers. A few weeks later he was playing "Roland in the Caves" on a friend's Amstrad CPC 464 when the game crashed and the command prompt displayed "Illegal Operation." Believing that he had hacked something, he decided that he wanted to become a full time hacker and therefore became much more determined to learn how computers work and what can be done with them.

At 12 years of age, his parents bought him an Acorn Electron Microcomputer as a Christmas present. Within 6 months he had written his first game, Wargames, in BBC Basic. By the time he was 14, he was regularly writing programs in 6502 Assembly language and would regularly send pokes (infinite lives, invulnerability, and so on) to computer magazines to help people with their new games.

At 15 years of age, he started work in IT as a support engineer. His use of programming languages extended to Turbo C, C++, Pascal, Delphi, C#, VB, VBScript, VB.NET, HTML, JavaScript, ASP, PHP, Perl, and so on. Some years later he discovered that he was spending a large amount of time writing tools to help his colleagues with their work and decided that he should get the paper qualifications he would need. He started as a computer science major but, after receiving a ton of job offers in the field, he just dropped out of university and has been professional ever since.

Michael is currently working for Comartis AG, Switzerland on e-Learning software called i-qbox Human Performance Suite. He works daily with VB.NET, C#, and JavaScript but prefers JavaScript, claiming that its quirks just make the language more fun. As the "JavaScript Guy" he uses Firebug to get his work done properly. In 2008 he began logging Firebug issues and soon began spending lots of time fixing bugs to make his work easier. He worked for a time on Firebug Lite but spends most of his "spare time" now working on improving the Firebug Inspector, which he likes to think of as "Aardvark on Steroids."

He would like to thank his wife Sabine for her patience during the many hours spent performing technical reviews on this book.

Michael Sync has lately been associated with Memolife as a Solution Architect, responsible for building their products using Silverlight and other .Net technologies.

Prior to venturing into this, he was creating a niche in Web Application Development using ASP.NET, AJAX, JavaScript, and so on.

He had always believed in the concept of "Sharing Knowledge", which is the key to building his in-depth understanding of the technology. That's the main reason why he always tries to participate in public forums and local newsgroups for helping fellow technologists; benefits are also received, as learning is a two-way process.

Being a member of Microsoft WPF/Silverlight Insider team, he really enjoys playing with early drops of Silverlight and giving his feedback to the team.

Table of Contents

Preface 1

Chapter 1: Getting Started with Firebug 7

What is Firebug? 7

The history of Firebug 8

The need for Firebug 8

Firebug capabilities 9

Installing Firebug on different browsers 9

Installing Firebug on Firefox 10

Installing Firebug on non-Firefox browsers 10

Opening and closing Firebug 11

Firebug modes 11

Dock view 12

Window mode 12

Summary 13

Chapter 2: Firebug Window Overview 15

Console tab 15

Command line JavaScript 16

Errors and warnings 17

Status bar error indicator 18

Errors can be descriptive and informative 19

Executing JavaScript commands 19

HTML tab 20

The hierarchy of DOM nodes (the HTML source panel) 21

Options for HTML source panel 22

Editing HTML on the fly 23

Editing an existing attribute of HTML element 23

Editing an HTML element 24

Logging events 26

CSS tab 29
CSS inspector 29
List of CSS files 30
Modifying CSS 30
Script tab 34
DOM tab 36
Net tab 38
Summary 40
Chapter 3: Inspecting and Editing HTML 41
Viewing source live 41
Seeing changes highlighted 43
Modifying the source on the fly 44
How to modify the value of an HTML attribute 45
How to add a new attribute to an existing HTML element 46
How to delete an HTML element 47
How to modify the source for an HTML element 47
Inspecting page components, editing, and reloading 48
Searching within an HTML document 50
Finding an HTML element on the page 51
Copying HTML source for an HTML element 52
Setting breakpoints on HTML element 52
Summary 54
Chapter 4: CSS Development 55
Inspecting cascading rules 55
Preview colors and images 57
Tweaking CSS on the fly 58
Enabling and disabling specific CSS rules 60
Inspecting our stylesheet 62
Modifying CSS from Firebug's UI 62
Inspecting and tweaking the box model 65
Searching under the CSS tab 65
Summary 66
Chapter 5: JavaScript Development 67
The command line API 67
$(id) 67
$ $$(selector) 68
$x(xpath) 69
dir(object) 70
dirxml(node) 71
clear() 72

inspect(object[, tabName]) 72
keys(object) 73
values(object) 74
debug(fn) and undebug(fn) 74
monitor(functionName) and unmonitor(functionName) 74
monitorEvents(object[, types]) 76
unmonitorEvents(object[, types]) 76
profile([title]) and profileEnd() 77
Columns and description of the profiler 78
The console API **79**
console.log(object[, object, ...]) 79
console.debug(object[, object, ...]) 80
console.info(object[, object, ...]) 80
console.warn(object[, object, ...]) 80
console.error(object[, object, ...]) 80
console.assert(expression[, object, ...]) 81
console.dir(object) 81
console.dirxml(node) 81
console.trace() 81
console.group(object[, object, ...]) 81
console.groupCollapsed(object[, object, ...]) 81
console.groupEnd() 81
console.time(name) 82
console.timeEnd(name) 82
console.profile([title]) 82
console.profileEnd() 82
console.count([title]) 82
JavaScript debugging **82**
Steps to debug JavaScript code with Firebug 83
Conditional breakpoints 85
Summary **89**
Chapter 6: Knowing Your DOM **91**
Inspecting DOM **91**
Filtering properties, functions, and constants 93
Modifying DOM on the fly **96**
Auto-complete 97
Losing the starting element 97
Adding/removing the DOM elements' attributes **98**
Removing attributes 98
Adding attributes 100

JavaScript code navigation **102**
Summary **103**

Chapter 7: Performance Tuning Our Web Application **105**

Network monitoring **106**
Description of information in the Net panel 107
Load-time bar color significance 108
Browser queue wait time 110
Breaking down various requests by type **110**
Examining HTTP headers **112**
Analyzing the browser cache **113**
XMLHttpRequest monitoring **116**
How to find out the download speed for a resource **117**
Firebug extensions for analyzing performance **118**
Summary **118**

Chapter 8: AJAX Development **119**

Tracking XmlHttpRequest **120**
Request/response headers and parameters 120
GET/POST request 125
Viewing live modifications on DOM **128**
Debugging AJAX calls using properties of a console object **130**
console.debug(object[, object, ...]) 130
console.assert(expression[, object, ...]) 133
console.dir(object) 134
Summary **135**

Chapter 9: Tips and Tricks for Firebug **137**

Magical cd() **137**
The hierarchical console **141**
Configuring Firebug to our taste **143**
Summary **145**

Chapter 10: Necessary Firebug Extensions **147**

YSlow **148**
Firecookie **151**
Pixel Perfect **153**
Pixel Perfect options menu 155
Firefinder **155**
FireQuery **157**
CodeBurner **159**
SenSEO **160**
Page Speed **162**
Summary **166**

Chapter 11: Extending Firebug 167
Setting up an extension development environment 167
Setting up the development profile 168
Development preferences 169
Getting started with a small "Hello World!" extension of Firebug 173
The chrome.manifest file 173
The install.rdf file 174
The helloWorldOverlay.xul file 175
The helloWorld.js file 176
Packaging and installation 177
Taking "Hello World!" to the next level 180
The "prefs.js" file 181
The "helloWorld.js" file revisited 181
Summary 183
Appendix: A Quick Overview of Firebug's Features and Options 185
Keyboard and mouse shortcuts reference 185
Global shortcuts 185
HTML tab shortcuts 186
HTML editor shortcuts 186
HTML inspect mode shortcuts 186
Script tab shortcuts 187
DOM tab shortcuts 187
DOM and watch editor shortcuts 187
CSS tab shortcuts 188
CSS editor tab shortcuts 188
Layout tab shortcuts 188
Layout editor shortcuts 189
Command line (small) shortcuts 189
Command line (large) shortcuts 189
Console API reference 190
Command line API reference 191
Firebug online resources 193
Features expected in future releases of Firebug 193
Firebug 1.6 193
Some improvements in this version 194
Firebug 1.7 196
Separate modules and panels 196
Components replaced by SharedObjects 197
Recode TabWatcher/DOMWindowWatcher 197
Sandboxed extension loading 198
Memory panel 198
Index 199

Preface

Firebug is a free and open source tool, available as a Mozilla Firefox extension, which allows debugging, editing, and monitoring of any website's CSS, HTML, DOM, XHR, and JavaScript. Firebug 1.0 beta was released in December 2006. Firebug usage has grown very quickly since then. Approximately 1.3 million users have Firebug installed as of January 2009. It is a very popular tool among web developers to aid during web application development.

The book begins with the steps to install Firebug, followed by an overview of the Firebug window. We will get the basic idea of Firebug and movement across the different panels and tabs within Firebug.

From there, we will make our way towards more advanced usages of each tab, such as CSS development, JavaScript development, and DOM modification. This will aid us during client-side development and debugging of RIAs. We will also learn to use Firebug for performance tuning our application on the browser. We have also dealt with the tracking of XMLHttpRequest and XMLHttpResponse during AJAX development, which is also an integral part of RIAs. We will also learn a few tips and tricks for Firebug that will help us in configuring Firebug according to our taste and make it a pleasurable experience to work with it.

Once we are comfortable with the usage of Firebug, we will learn to install and use some popular Firebug extensions. This will be followed by a discussion on how to develop our own Firebug extension.

What this book covers

Chapter 1: Getting Started with Firebug gives a quick introduction to Firebug, its origin and history, who should use Firebug, and a glimpse of Firebug's main features, hoping that this will spark your interest in both Firebug and the rest of this book.

Chapter 2: Firebug Window Overview explains Firebug's tabs and what they are used for.

Chapter 3: Inspecting and Editing HTML provides an understanding of using Firebug to inspect, edit, search, and play with the HTML source of the document.

Chapter 4: CSS Development aims to help the reader to understand the useful tools and utilities provided by Firebug for CSS development.

Chapter 5: JavaScript Development explains command line API, console API of Firebug, and debugging JavaScript in detail.

Chapter 6: Knowing your DOM gives a small introduction to DOM as well as discussing how to modify/edit values of properties and constants of any DOM object using Firebug.

Chapter 7: Performance Tuning Our Web Application explains various ways to analyze the performance of your web application on the browser.

Chapter 8: AJAX Development discusses how to track XmlHttpRequest and XmlHttpResponse as well as debugging AJAX calls.

Chapter 9: Tips and Tricks for Firebug discusses a few tips and tricks that can be very useful while debugging and developing. We have explained how to play with the features that Firebug provides and what other things you should know about Firebug.

Chapter 10: Necessary Firebug Extensions explains some of the Firebug extensions, such as YSlow, FireCookie, Page Speed, and so on. They are useful for development and performance tuning.

Chapter 11: Extending Firebug discusses the steps to develop a Firebug extension. We have also discussed how to set up a development environment, along with file and directory structure for the extension.

Appendix, A Quick overview of Firebug's features and options gives a quick reference for various Firebug features and options.

What you need for this book

We will need Mozilla Firefox v 3.5 - 3.6 installed on our systems. We also need Firebug 1.4 - 1.5 installed on top of it. The latter is not a prerequisite as we will discuss how to install it during the course of the book.

Having an Internet connection would be an added advantage as the examples provided run on top of live websites. This will also help us in learning to install and use Firebug extensions.

Who this book is for

The target audience is front-end web developers who are building software and pages using HTML, CSS, JavaScript, and AJAX, and want to learn Firebug. The book assumes that the reader has a very basic knowledge of HTML, JavaScript, and CSS. The examples in the book can be understood by someone who has just been introduced to web development.

Conventions

In this book, you will find a number of styles of text that distinguish between different kinds of information. Here are some examples of these styles, and an explanation of their meaning.

Code words in text are shown as follows: "We can include other contexts through the use of the `include` directive."

A block of code will be set as follows:

```
<body>
<font face="monospace">
Enter a number to calculate its factorial
   <input type = "text" name="searchBox"
          onkeyup="calculateFactorial(this.value,event)"/>
</font>
</body>
```

When we wish to draw your attention to a particular part of a code block, the relevant lines or items will be shown in bold:

```
initialize: function() {
 Firebug.Panel.initialize.apply(this, arguments);
    },
```

```
getOptionsMenuItems: function(context)
```

Any command-line input or output is written as follows:

```
/Applications/Firefox.app/Contents/MacOS/firefox-bin -no-remote -P dev
```

New terms and **important words** are shown in bold. Words that you see on the screen, in menus or dialog boxes for example, appear in our text like this: " If we want the information to persist, then we can click **Persist** button on the **Console** tab.

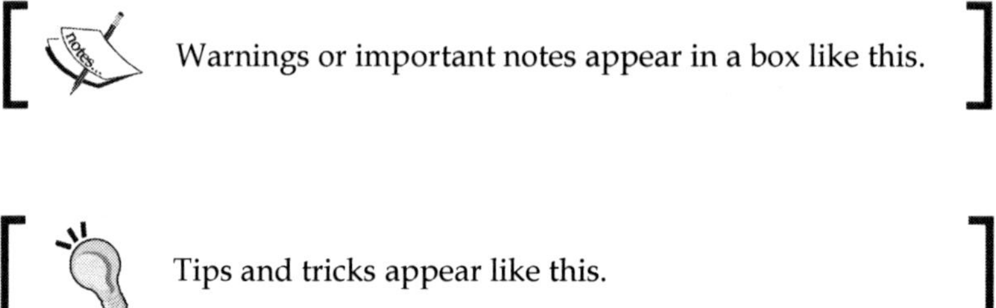

Warnings or important notes appear in a box like this.
Tips and tricks appear like this.

Reader feedback

Feedback from our readers is always welcome. Let us know what you think about this book—what you liked or may have disliked. Reader feedback is important for us to develop titles that you really get the most out of.

To send us general feedback, simply drop an email to `feedback@packtpub.com`, and mention the book title in the subject of your message.

If there is a book that you need and would like to see us publish, please send us a note in the **SUGGEST A TITLE** form on `www.packtpub.com` or email `suggest@packtpub.com`.

If there is a topic that you have expertise in and you are interested in either writing or contributing to a book, see our author guide on `www.packtpub.com/authors`.

Customer support

Now that you are the proud owner of a Packt book, we have a number of things to help you to get the most from your purchase.

Downloading the example code for the book

Visit `http://www.packtpub.com/files/code/4961_Code.zip` to directly download the example code.

The downloadable files contain instructions on how to use them.

Errata

Although we have taken every care to ensure the accuracy of our contents, mistakes do happen. If you find a mistake in one of our books—maybe a mistake in text or code—we would be grateful if you would report this to us. By doing so, you can save other readers from frustration, and help us to improve subsequent versions of this book. If you find any errata, please report them by visiting `http://www.packtpub.com/support`, selecting your book, clicking on the **let us know** link, and entering the details of your errata. Once your errata are verified, your submission will be accepted and the errata added to any list of existing errata. Any existing errata can be viewed by selecting your title from `http://www.packtpub.com/support`.

Piracy

Piracy of copyright material on the Internet is an ongoing problem across all media. At Packt, we take the protection of our copyright and licenses very seriously. If you come across any illegal copies of our works in any form on the Internet, please provide us with the location address or website name immediately so that we can pursue a remedy.

Please contact us at `copyright@packtpub.com` with a link to the suspected pirated material.

We appreciate your help in protecting our authors, and our ability to bring you valuable content.

Questions

You can contact us at `questions@packtpub.com` if you are having a problem with any aspect of the book, and we will do our best to address it.

1
Getting Started with Firebug

In this chapter, we will have a quick introduction to Firebug—its origin and history, who should use Firebug, and a glimpse of Firebug's main features. Hopefully this will spark your interest in both Firebug and the rest of this book. We will also look at how to install Firebug on several browsers and the different modes in which Firebug can be opened.

In this chapter, we will look at the following:

- What is Firebug
- The history of Firebug
- The need for Firebug
- The capabilities of Firebug
- Installing Firebug on different browsers
- Opening and closing Firebug
- Firebug modes

What is Firebug?

Firebug is a free, open source tool that is available as a Mozilla Firefox extension, and allows debugging, editing, and monitoring of any website's CSS, HTML, DOM, and JavaScript. It also allows performance analysis of a website. Furthermore, it has a JavaScript console for logging errors and watching values. Firebug has many other tools to enhance the productivity of today's web developer.

Firebug integrates with Firefox to put a wealth of development tools at our fingertips while we browse a website. Firebug allows us to understand and analyze the complex interactions that take place between various elements of any web page when it is loaded by a browser.

Firebug simply makes it easier to develop websites/applications. It is one of the best web development extensions for Firefox. Firebug provides all the tools that a web developer needs to analyze, debug, and monitor JavaScript, CSS, HTML, and AJAX. It also includes a debugger, error console, command line, and a variety of useful inspectors.

> Although Firebug allows us to make changes to the source code of our web page, the changes are made to the copy of the HTML code that has been sent to the browser by the server. Any changes to the code are made in the copy that is available with the browser. The changes don't get reflected in the code that is on the server. So, in order to ensure that the changes are permanent, corresponding changes have to be made in the code that resides on the server.

The history of Firebug

Firebug was initially developed by Joe Hewitt, one of the original Firefox creators, while working at Parakey Inc. Facebook purchased Parakey in July, 2007.

Currently, the open source development and extension of Firebug is overseen by the Firebug Working Group. It has representation from Mozilla, Google, Yahoo, IBM, Facebook, and many other companies.

Firebug 1.0 Beta was released in December 2006. Firebug usage has grown very fast since then. Approximately 1.3 million users have Firebug installed as of January 2009.

The latest version of Firebug is 1.5. Today, Firebug has a very open and thriving community. Some individuals as well as some companies have developed very useful plugins on top of Firebug.

The need for Firebug

During the 90s, websites were mostly static HTML pages, JavaScript code was considered a hack, and there were no interactions between page components on the browser side.

The situation is not the same anymore. Today's websites are a product of several distinct technologies and web developers must be proficient in all of them—HTML, CSS, JavaScript, DOM, and AJAX, among others. Complex interactions happen between various page components on the browser side. However, web browsers have always focused on the needs of the end users; as a result, web developers have long been deprived of a good tool on the client/browser side to help them develop and debug their code.

Firebug fills this gap very nicely—it provides all the tools that today's web developer needs in order to be productive and efficient with code that runs in the browser.

Firebug capabilities

Firebug has a host of features that allow us to do the following (and much more!):

- Inspect and edit HTML
- Inspect and edit CSS and visualize CSS metrics
- Use a performance tuning application
- Profile and debug JavaScript
- Explore the DOM
- Analyze AJAX calls

Installing Firebug on different browsers

Firebug is developed as a Firefox add-on and can be installed on Firefox similar to all other add-ons. In order to make Firebug work for non-Firefox browsers, there is a JavaScript available from Firebug that makes available a large set of Firebug features.

Based on your browser version, we can install the corresponding Firebug version.

Firebug version	Browser version
Firebug 1.5	Firefox 3.5 and Firefox 3.6
Firebug 1.4	Firefox 3.0 and Firefox 3.5
Firebug 1.3	Firefox 2.0 and Firefox 3.0
Firebug Lite	IE, Safari, and Opera

Installing Firebug on Firefox

To install Firebug on Firefox, we will follow these steps:

1. Open Firefox browser and go to `https://addons.mozilla.org`.
2. In the search box of the site, type **Firebug** and hit *Enter* or click on the **Search for add-ons** button.
3. In the search results, click on **Add to Firefox** button.
4. A pop up will appear asking whether we want to continue with the installation. We will now click **Install now**.
5. After installation is complete, let's restart Firefox.

When the browser comes up, it will prompt us by saying a new add-on has been installed. Now we are all set and ready to play with Firebug.

Installing Firebug on non-Firefox browsers

Firebug is an extension for Firefox, but that doesn't mean it works only on Firefox. What happens when we want to test our pages against Internet Explorer, Opera, or Safari? **Firebug Lite** is the solution for this. It's a product that can be easily included in our file via a JavaScript call, just like any other JavaScript, to support all non-Firefox browsers. It will simulate some of the features of Firebug in our non-Firefox browsers.

To use Firebug Lite on non-Firefox browsers, we should include the following line of code in our page:

```
<script type='text/javascript'
  src='http://getfirebug.com/releases/lite/1.2/firebug-lite-
                                                    compressed.js'>
</script>
```

For more information and updates on Firebug Lite, refer to `http://getfirebug.com/lite.html`

If we don't want to modify the source code of our page and still want to use Firebug Lite on a non-Firefox browser, we can run Firebug as a bookmarklet by creating a bookmark with the value of the URL as the following JavaScript code:

```
javascript:var firebug=document.createElement('script');
firebug.setAttribute('src','http://getfirebug.com/releases/lite/1.2/
                                        firebug-lite-compressed.js');
document.body.appendChild(firebug);
```

```
(function()
{
if(window.firebug.version)
    {firebug.init();}
else
{setTimeout(arguments.callee);}
})();
void(firebug);
```

We can inject Firebug into any page by running the bookmarklet created with the preceding URL.

Opening and closing Firebug

Opening and closing Firebug is very easy. We can open as well as close Firebug by pressing the *F12* key or by clicking the (bug) icon on the right-hand side of the browser's status bar.

Undock Firebug

By default Firebug opens in a dock view. If we want to open it in its own window, we can accomplish this by either clicking on the icon on the upper right corner of Firebug or by pressing the keys *Ctrl+F12*.

Firebug modes

Firebug can be opened in the following two modes:

- Dock view
- Window mode

In the dock mode, the Firebug opens the document in the browser's window while in the window mode the Firebug opens in its own window, which is separate from the browser window.

Dock view

Most often we use the dock view mode of Firebug while developing. In this mode, the inspection and CSS tweaking can be done more easily than in window mode. The advantage of this mode is that the user can view the rendered page while simultaneously working on Firebug.

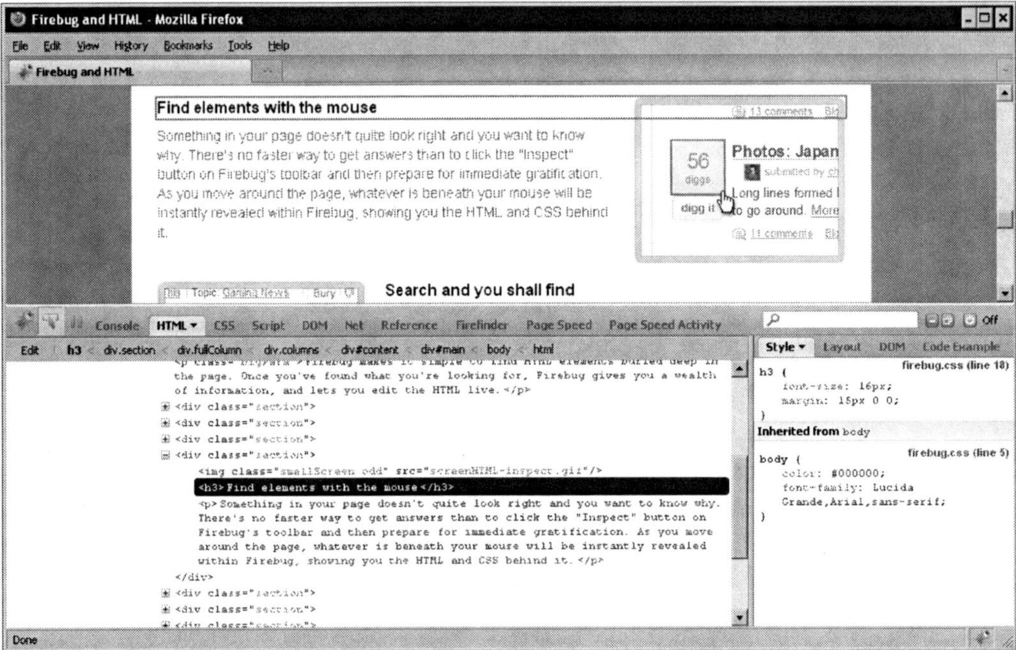

Window mode

The window mode is useful when we use its **Console** tab or **Net** tab. When we execute a large JavaScript code, we expect a large area where we can write easily. Similarly, the results shown by the **Net** tab require a big screen to examine it easily. Window mode is the best solution in this case.

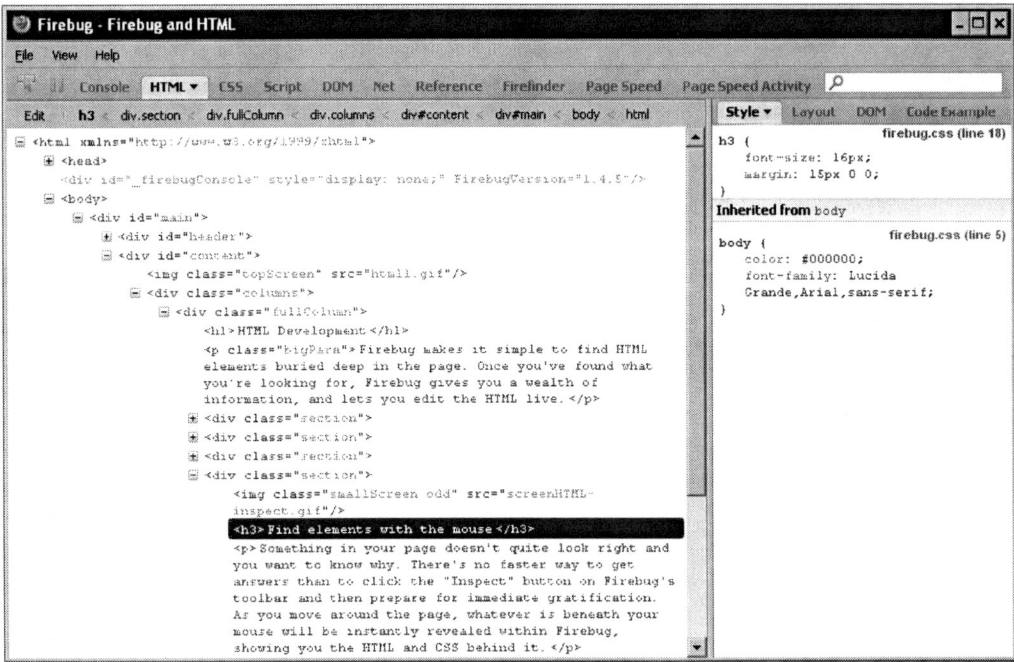

Summary

Firebug is an extremely useful web design and development tool that integrates seamlessly with Firefox. Firebug has a huge worldwide user base along with a very open and thriving eco-system.

We now have an idea of how to install Firebug on Firefox and Firebug Lite on non-Firefox browsers. Installing Firebug is as simple as installing any other add-on or extension of Firefox. We have also seen some of the ways of opening, closing, and undocking Firebug, and learned when to use dock view and when to use window mode for different purposes.

2

Firebug Window Overview

This chapter gives a brief introduction to the different tabs, subtabs, and menu options provided by Firebug.

Firebug is not about fixing the bugs and tweaking CSS; it consists of many tools that can be of great help to a web developer and designer. Firebug is like a golf club bag. Each club (tab) in Firebug is a powerful tool for web developers. Like a golf player, a web developer has to choose a club (tab) for different situations. The tools are:

- Console tab
- HTML tab
- CSS tab
- Script tab
- DOM tab
- Net tab

Console tab

Firebug also provides a console panel with a command line to view warnings, errors, info, logs, debug messages, JavaScript profiler output, XmlHttpRequest/ XmlHttpResponse, and many others, just like any other console output screen (for example C, C++, or Java). Firebug gives us a good, old-fashioned command line for JavaScript with an autocode completion feature and modern amenities. This feature of Firebug is a boon for JavaScript developers.

There are two main questions that come to anyone's mind while working with **Console** tab:

1. What do we do when we want to include a JavaScript on the web page to give it a dynamic functionality?

   Answer: We just type a few lines of JavaScript code wrapped within a `<script>` tag and then wait for the browser to execute that code to show us the output.

2. What do we do if that code has errors?

   Answer: We repeat the same process; we try to debug that code in our traditional style by inserting a few `alert` statements between the lines of code.

Somehow we manage to figure out the problems and bugs, we fix them, and also remove the unused code (`alert` messages).

Command line JavaScript

Command line JavaScript is a very powerful tool of Firebug. This feature provides us with the power to execute JavaScript files and commands on the fly, without even reloading the document. We love to execute complex JavaScripts using this feature. Most of the time we execute commands and code snippets of **jQuery**, a framework over traditional JavaScript, against the document to test whether the script that we have written is running.

This tab is our favorite one as, before integrating any JavaScript on our page, we first validate and execute it on a command line JavaScript provided under this tab.

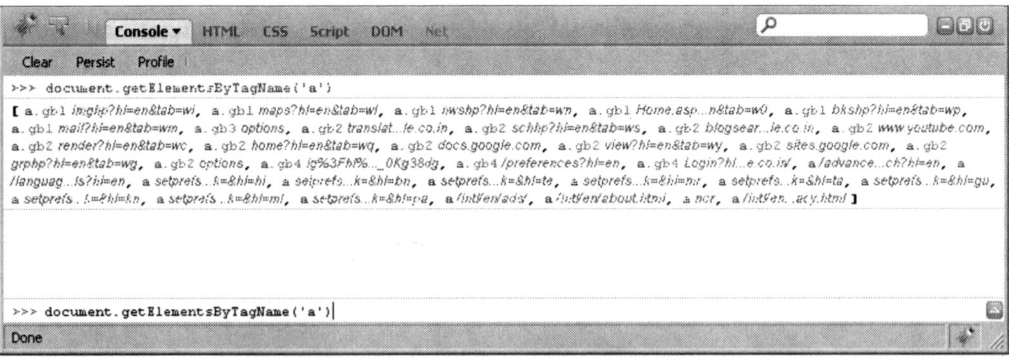

The preceding screenshot shows the **Console** tab. The **Console** tab is highlighted, showing that we are under this tab. There are three buttons under this tab—**Clear**, **Persist**, and **Profile**.

- **Clear**: This is used to clear the console
- **Profile**: This is used to profile our JavaScripts
- **Persist**: This will make sure that the errors, warnings, and information on the **Console** tab persists even if the page is reloaded or refreshed in the browser

JavaScript profiler (as shown in the following screenshot) is used to find out how much time (**Avg**, **Min**, and **Max**) a function or script consumed to execute on the browser. We'll discuss the profiler in more detail later in Chapter 5, *JavaScript Development*.

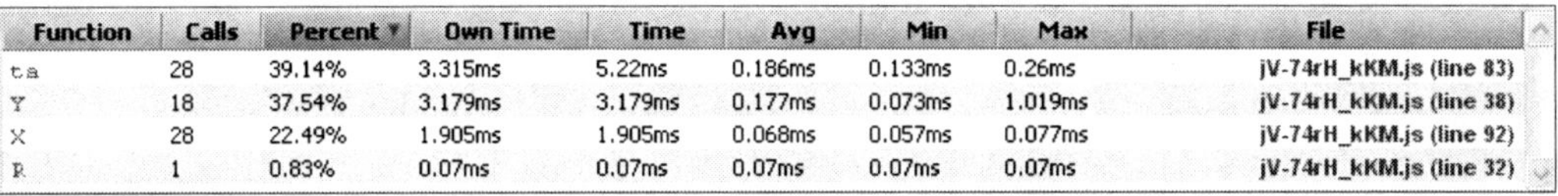

Function	Calls	Percent	Own Time	Time	Avg	Min	Max	File
ta	28	39.14%	3.315ms	5.22ms	0.186ms	0.133ms	0.26ms	jV-74rH_kKM.js (line 83)
Y	18	37.54%	3.179ms	3.179ms	0.177ms	0.073ms	1.019ms	jV-74rH_kKM.js (line 38)
X	28	22.49%	1.905ms	1.905ms	0.068ms	0.057ms	0.077ms	jV-74rH_kKM.js (line 92)
R	1	0.83%	0.07ms	0.07ms	0.07ms	0.07ms	0.07ms	jV-74rH_kKM.js (line 32)

Errors and warnings

When something goes wrong, Firebug lets us know the details and relevant information:

- JavaScript errors and warnings
- CSS errors
- XML errors
- External errors
- Chrome errors and messages
- Network errors
- Strict warnings
- **XHR** (**XMLHttpRequest**) information

The following is the representative screenshot showing JavaScript and CSS errors:

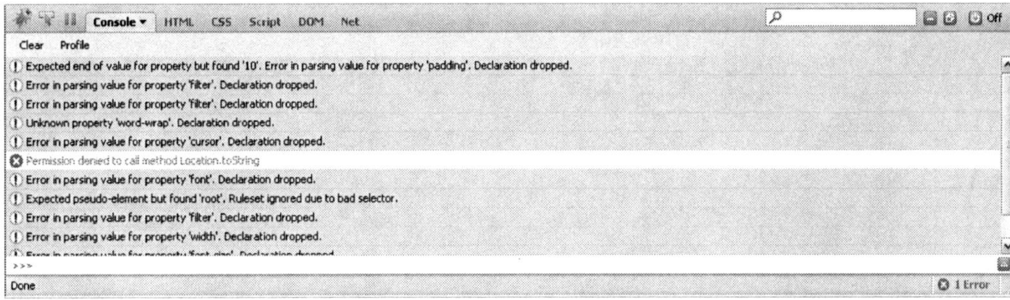

The lines that have an '!' (exclamation) icon at the beginning are warnings and lines with '**X**' (cross) icon are errors.

Status bar error indicator

When a JavaScript error occurs, Firebug will display a red **X** icon on the bottom right-hand side of the Firefox browser in the status bar. This is Firebug's way of telling us that things are not correct and something has gone pear-shaped.

Click the **X** icon to open the Firebug error console, which will show us all of the JavaScript errors that have occurred on the page.

The screenshot under the *Errors and warnings* section shows the expanded firebug error console, which opened when we clicked on the **X** icon.

I don't want JUNK

These include errors and warnings associated with each page we have ever visited. Firefox is better than those because it has Firebug; by default it shows us the errors and warnings only for the page that we're looking at. If we want the information to persist, then we can click the **Persist** button on the **Console** tab. When the **Persist** button is clicked, the console will copy information from old to new console when we reload the page.

Errors can be descriptive and informative

With Firebug we have the power to easily find out the types of errors—JavaScript errors, CSS errors, or XML errors.

Firebug shows very informative errors, which makes them easier to debug and fix. JavaScript errors include a wealth of information about what went wrong. It includes error description, the file and the line number, and the line of source code that caused the error. Firebug shows the stack trace for JavaScript errors, which helps the debugging of JavaScript to be easier and faster. The following screenshot gives an example of how Firebug shows the informative and descriptive JavaScript and CSS errors:

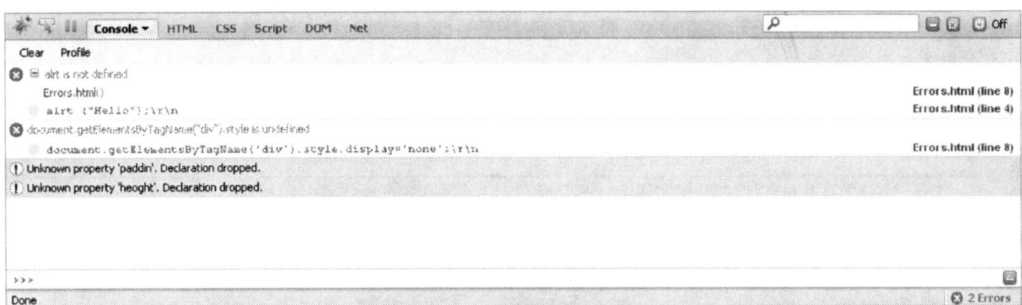

Executing JavaScript commands

If we execute the following lines of JavaScript code in Firebug's command line JavaScript console, we will get the output shown in the succeeding screenshot. The command line is at the bottom of the **Console** tab; it starts with **>>>** and accepts commands in JavaScript. The results of our JavaScript, if there are any, are then displayed on Firebug's console. The following code explains debug, info, warning, and error messages:

```
console.debug('This is a Debug message');
console.info('This is an Information');
console.warn('This is a Warning message');
console.error('This is an Error message');
```

To execute the preceding JavaScript code on Firebug's command line JavaScript console, just follow these steps:

1. Open Firebug with the *F12* key.
2. Click on the **Console** tab.

3. Type the code in the box that is next to the **>>>** symbol, as shown in the next screenshot, and then press the *Enter* key.

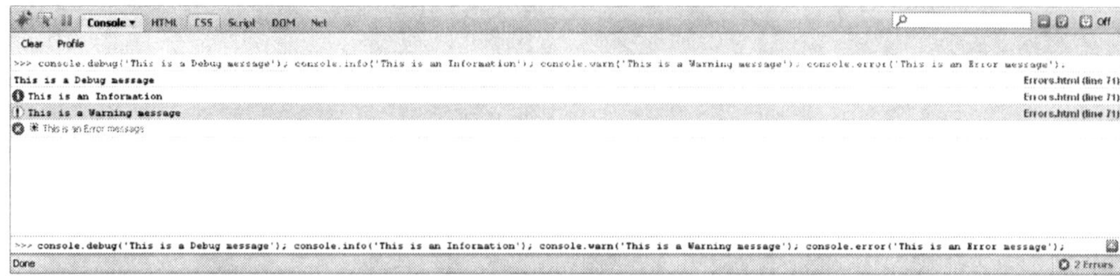

HTML tab

The **HTML** tab is the next tab of Firebug's **Console** tab, which allows us to edit HTML on the fly and play with our HTML DOM in our Firefox. There is an HTML source panel to the left-hand side. The right-hand side contains four subtabs or panels—**Style**, **Computed**, **Layout**, and **DOM**.

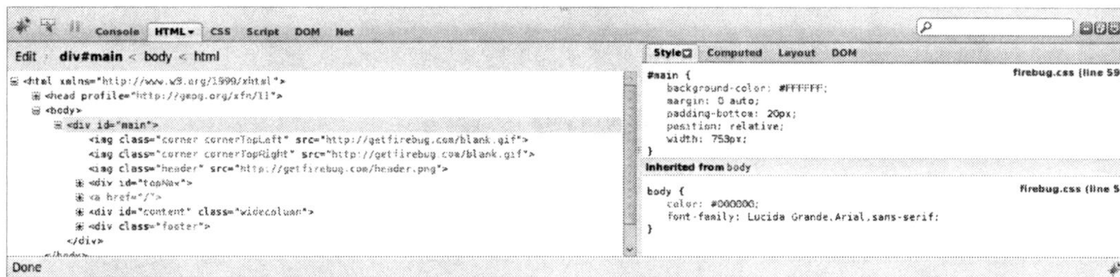

The **HTML** tab will quickly help us find how a particular web page is structured and how Firefox interprets the HTML page. In the HTML source panel, one cannot see the CSS hacks or other HTML tags that are meaningful for non-Firefox browsers. The **HTML** tab also allows us to edit HTML and tweak CSS dynamically on the fly for the live document that we are viewing.

The following is the list of things we can do with the **HTML** tab:

- **Inspect** an HTML element
- Explore the **Style** (CSS) of a particular HTML element in the document
- Explore full **HTML DOM** of the document
- **Edit** any existing HTML elements and CSS on the fly

- **Search** the internal HTML element instead of text content on the page
- Set **Break Points** on the HTML nodes, which will be triggered whenever an attribute is changed, a child element is added or removed, or the element is removed

The hierarchy of DOM nodes (the HTML source panel)

The HTML source panel is located to the left-hand side of the **HTML** tab. It shows a more advanced view of HTML than the default view source of the Firefox browser. It has many advanced features and shows us the HTML DOM in a hierarchical structure or tree-view with highlighted colors. We can always expand or collapse the HTML DOM so that it will be easy for us to understand and figure out the whole structure and hierarchy of the page.

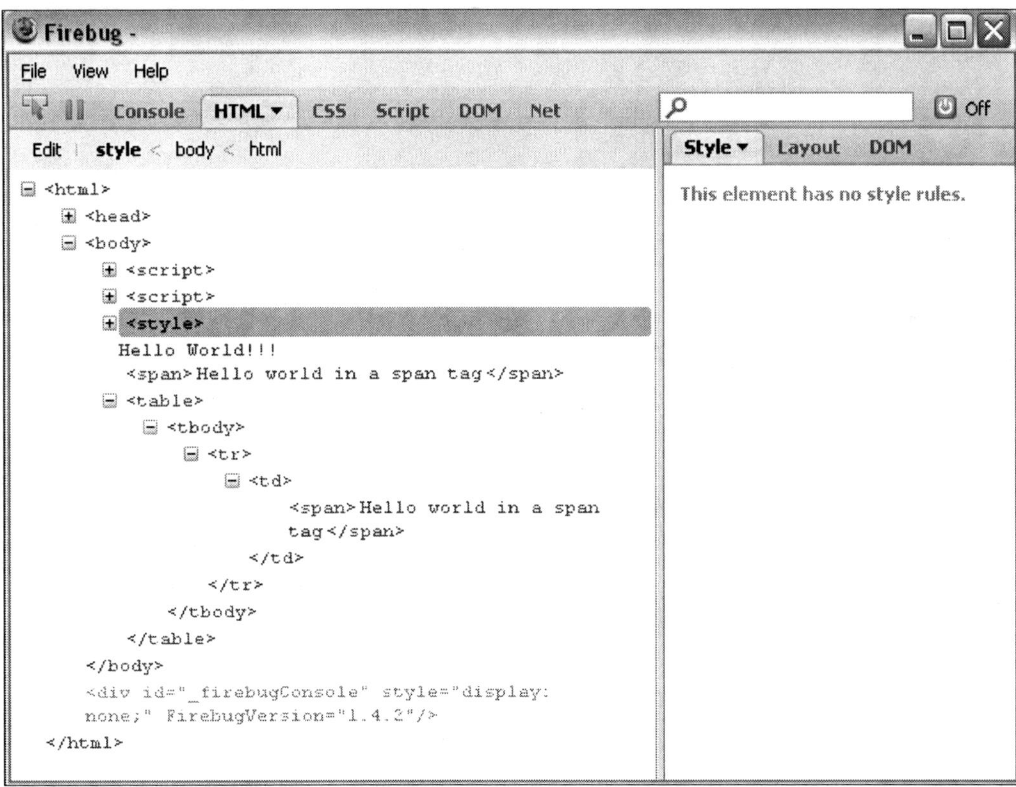

Options for HTML source panel

There are nine options in the HTML source panel. The following screenshot shows the HTML source panel:

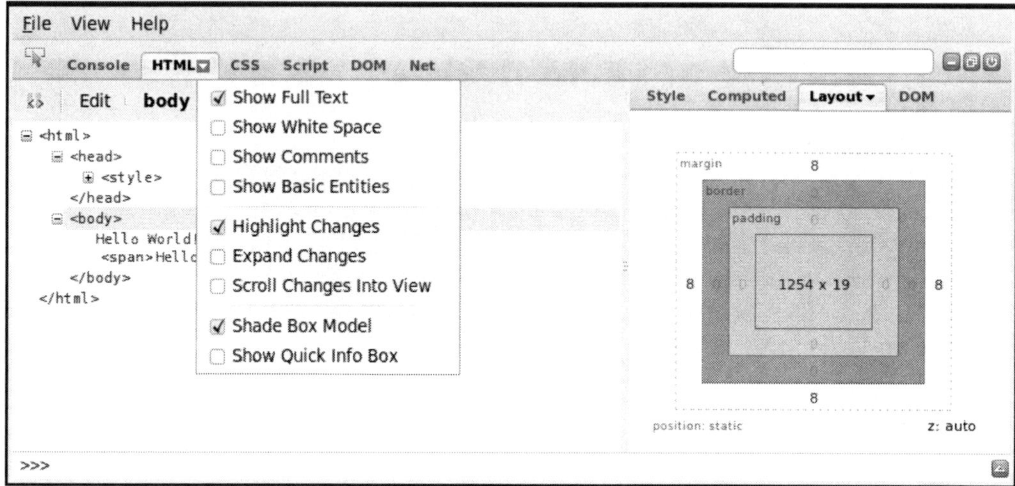

- **Show Full Text**: If the text within an element (example, `<P>` tag) is too long, then Firebug will truncate this text and will append "..." after the string.
- **Show White Space**: This shows the white spaces between each HTML element.
- **Show Comments**: Check this option if one wants to view the comments in HTML source panel, otherwise uncheck this option.
- **Show Basic Entities**: This shows the basic HTML core entities and whitespace entities in text nodes, attributes, and so on. While editing, when one types "<", ">", and "," these are converted to entities automatically. Editing with this option off, "<" and ">" are used to add elements as we type and the text is interpreted as source code.
- **Highlight Changes**: This shows, in highlighted color, any changes we make in the HTML view (that is, DOM).
- **Expand Changes**: This will expand the HTML element that has changes.
- **Scroll Changes Into View**: The scroll bar of the HTML source panel will move to the place where something on the view/document has changed.

- **Shade Box Model**: If we take our mouse pointer on any HTML tag/element within HTML tab, Shade Box Model will shade the area (in blue and purple color) covered by an HTML element on the page. Enabling this option helps to quickly find out the width and height of an HTML element.
- **Show Quick Info Box**: Enabling this option will display a small grey-colored box on the page, and we can see the CSS-related information about an element. To see it working, we need to hover the mouse on any HTML element within the HTML tab.

Editing HTML on the fly

By using this feature of Firebug, we can create or edit an HTML element and its attributes on the live document.

Editing an existing attribute of HTML element

Click on the HTML ID attribute. A textbox will be shown on the attribute to edit the content of the attribute, as shown in the following screenshot. We can just type and press *Enter* after finishing. Pressing *Esc* will cancel the editing mode.

```
<table>

    <tbody>
        <tr>
            <td>
                <span id="firstColumnId">Hello world in a span tag</span>
            </td>
        </tr>

    </tbody>
</table>
```

Editing an HTML element

To edit an HTML element, we just right-click on the HTML element we want to edit and click or select the **EDIT HTML...** from the context menu, as shown in the next screenshot. Or we can simply select an element and then click on the **Edit** button on the toolbar of the **HTML** tab. Firebug provides another easier and simpler way of editing the HTML element by double-clicking on the HTML tag. We will discuss detailed HTML source-code editing in Chapter 3, *Inspecting and Editing HTML*. Let's take an overview for now and wait for the real magic in the next chapter.

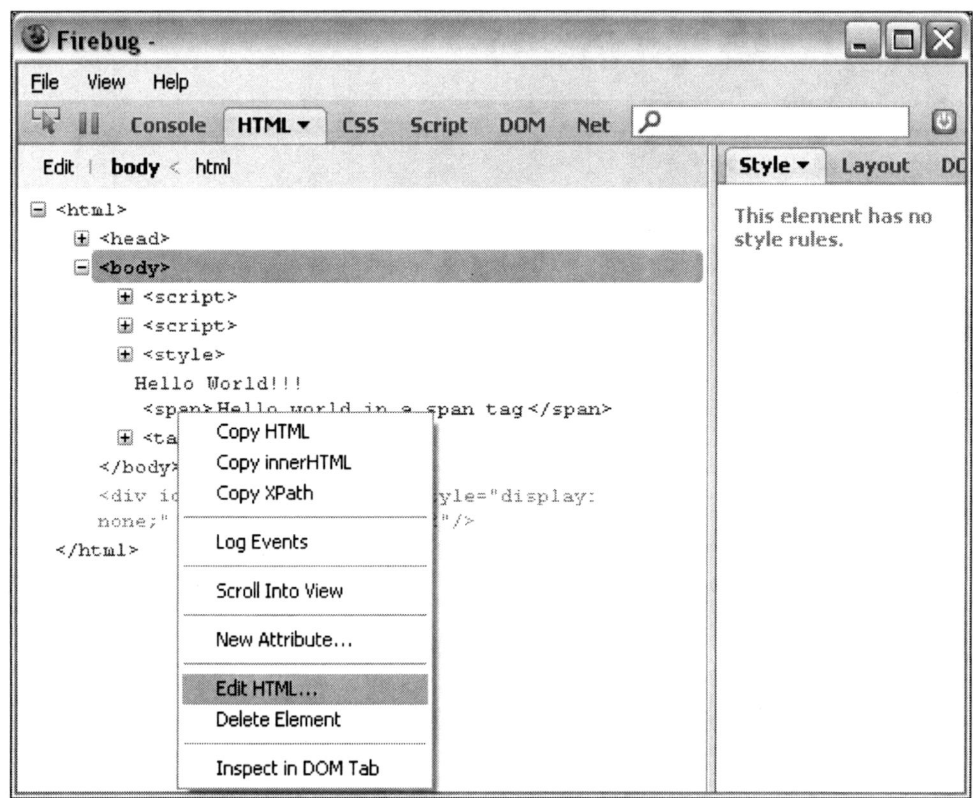

The HTML source view panel will get converted into a text-editor-type panel, as shown in the next screenshot. Now this is a playground for us, where we can easily edit the live HTML source code on the fly.

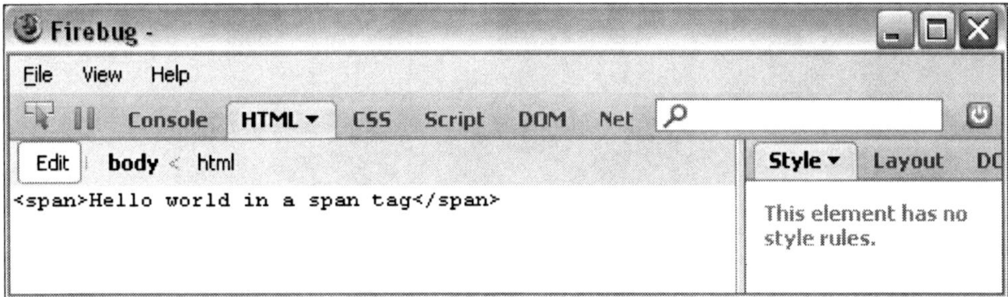

Now we can edit the existing HTML source or can add a new HTML element to it. A sample is shown in the next screenshot. Here we add a new attribute to a `<span>` tag and a new `<b>` element to show bold text on HTML. We can also change the `<span>` tag to any tag; we can change it to a `<div>` tag, or `<p>` tag, and many more.

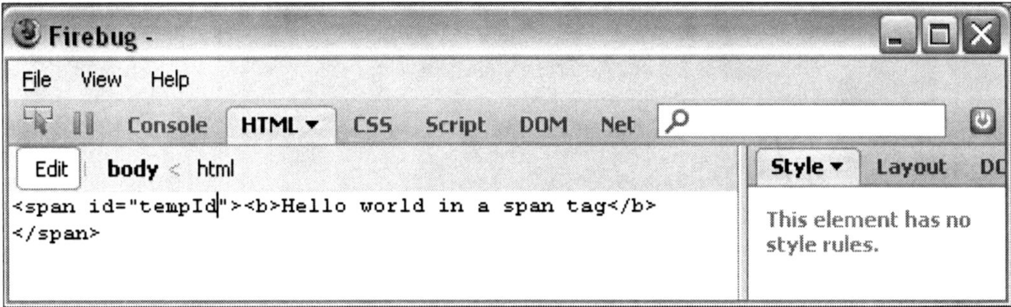

When we are done with our editing and want to view the changes on the live document, we simply click **Edit** on the toolbar of the **HTML** tab. The next screenshot shows the changes that are made on the edit HTML view panel:

Logging events

Logging an event in Firebug is very easy. In fact it is so easy that a fifth grader could use this feature for logging events. The following are the few events that are logged on an `<input type=text/>` element textbox:

- Blur
- Focus
- Mousemove
- Mouseout
- Mouseover
- Select

- Keypress
- Keyup
- Keydown

To log events for an HTML element, just right-click on the HTML element and select **Log Events,** as shown in the next screenshot:

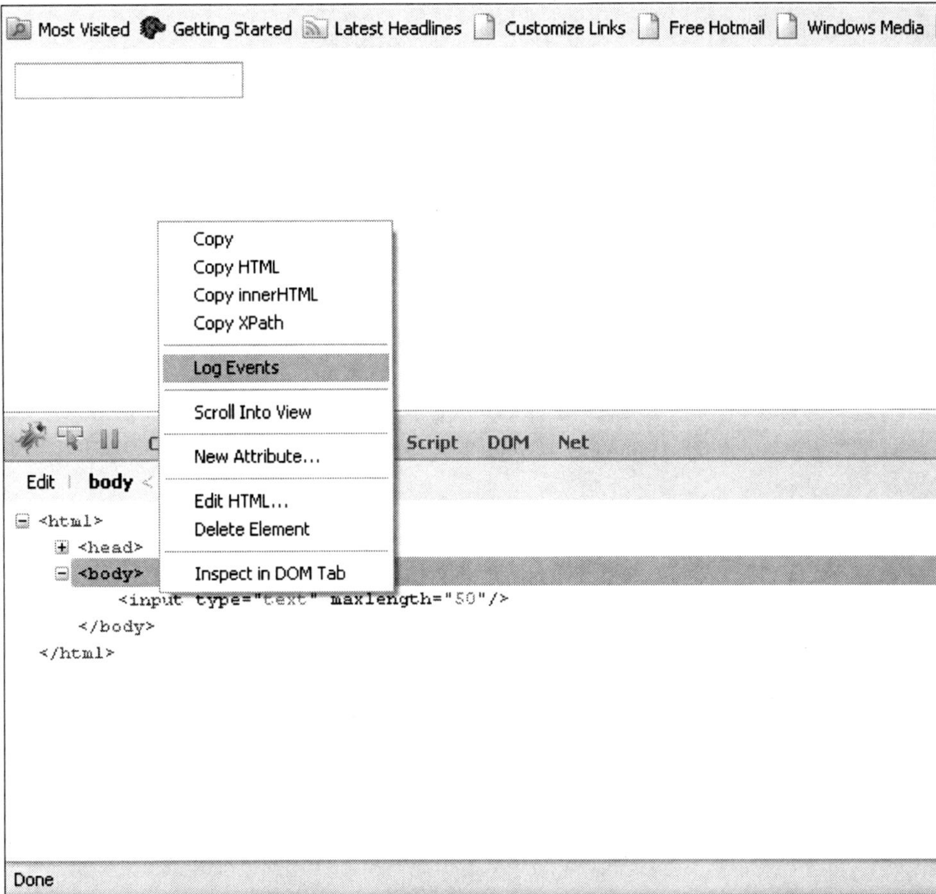

Now move on to the **Console** tab on the toolbar of Firebug. The following screenshot shows the logging of events as displayed on the **Console** tab:

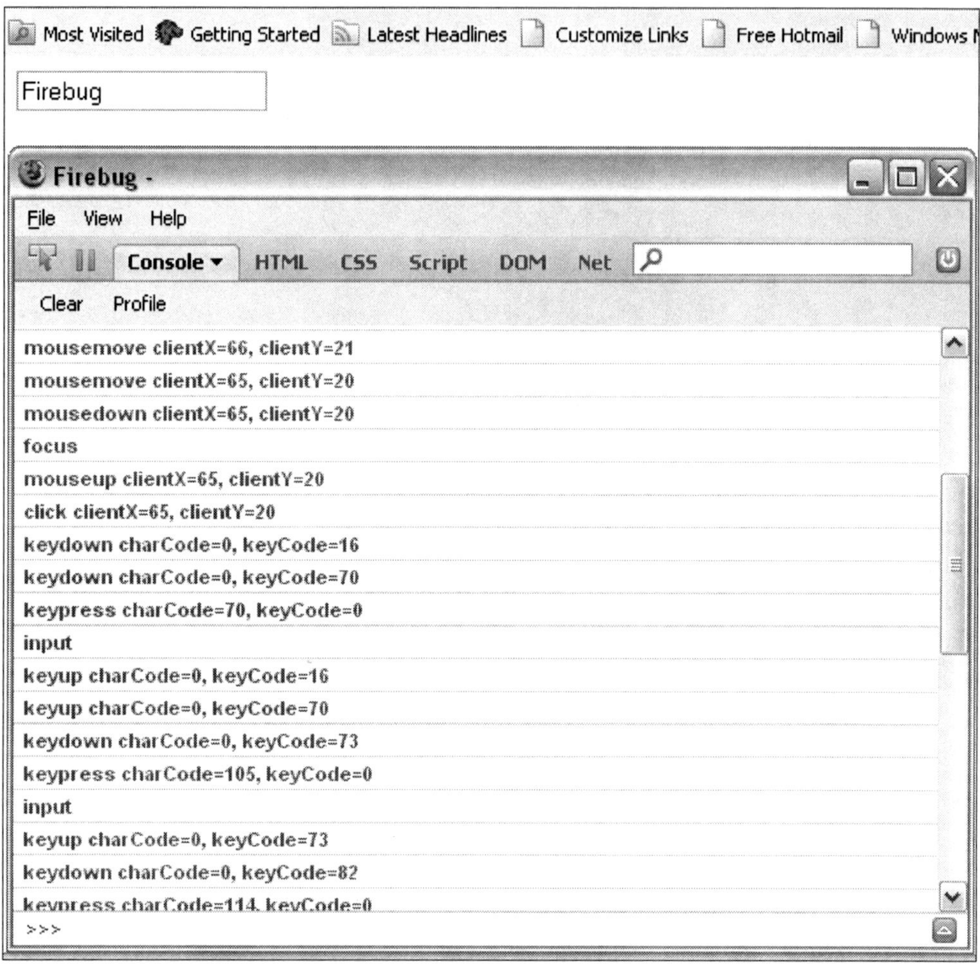

After switching to the **Console** tab, just move the mouse pointer over the textbox (the `<input>` element). Then immediately some `mousemove` and `mouseover` events start getting fired, which can be seen on the **Console** tab. Now type some text (say `Firebug`) into that textbox. We can see some `keypress`, `keydown`, and `keyup` events getting fired, which can be seen on Firebug console as shown in the previous screenshot.

CSS tab

The CSS tab allows the user to tweak the CSS stylesheet to his/her taste. We can use this tab for viewing or editing CSS stylesheets on the fly and view the results live on the current document. This tab is mostly used by the CSS developers to tweak the pixels, position, look and feel, or area of an HTML element. This tab is also useful for web developers when they want to view those elements whose CSS property `display` is set to `none` or invisible elements.

The following is the list of things that we can do under the **CSS** tab:

- Inspect the CSS styles
- View a list of loaded CSS stylesheets
- Modify CSS on the fly
- Temporarily disable CSS rules

The next screenshot shows the **CSS** tab. If there are some CSS attached with our HTML document, then they will be displayed under this tab.

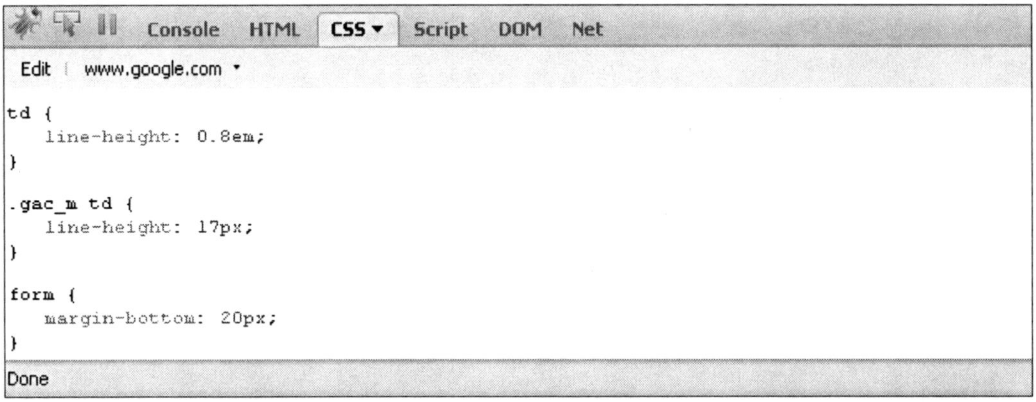

Console HTML CSS Script DOM Net

Edit | www.google.com

```
td {
   line-height: 0.8em;
}

.gac_m td {
   line-height: 17px;
}

form {
   margin-bottom: 20px;
}
```

Done

CSS inspector

Firebug behaves like an inspector as well as an editor. All the properties of CSS can be edited with a single-or double-click. As we type, the changes automatically get applied to the current document open in the browser window, and we will get immediate results.

Firebug hides those CSS rules and properties that Firefox ignores.

We will discuss more on developing and inspecting CSS in Chapter 5, *JavaScript Development*. For now let's move on viewing a list of CSS stylesheets and modifying CSS to our taste.

List of CSS files

To view all the CSS files of our page, we just go to `http://www.google.com` and activate Firebug by pressing the *F12* key.

Now go to the **CSS** tab and click the drop-down (`www.google.com` in my case) just next to the **Edit** button, as shown in the following screenshot. A drop-down menu will be shown and all CSS files will be listed. We can simply click on any CSS file that we want to view.

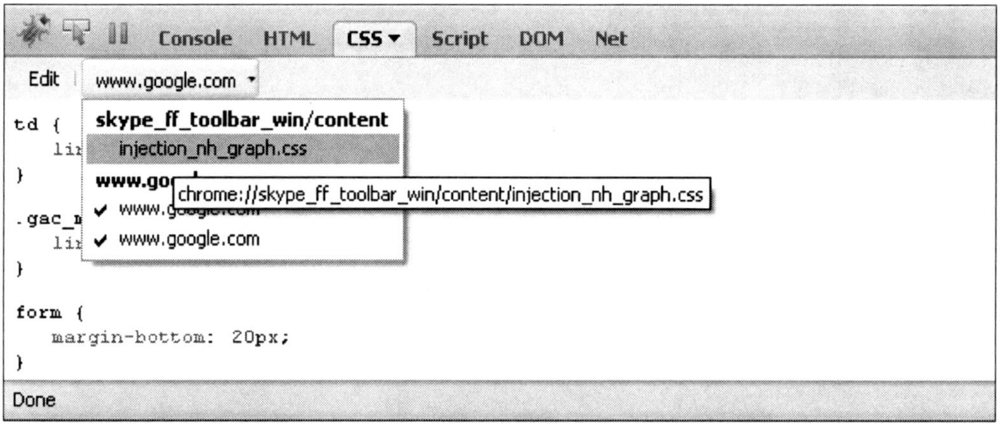

Modifying CSS

In this section we will briefly discuss how we can modify the CSS on the fly. Like the **HTML** tab, it also has an editable mode. The **CSS** tab screenshot that we have seen earlier shows the normal mode, whereas the following screenshot shows the editable mode of **CSS** tab:

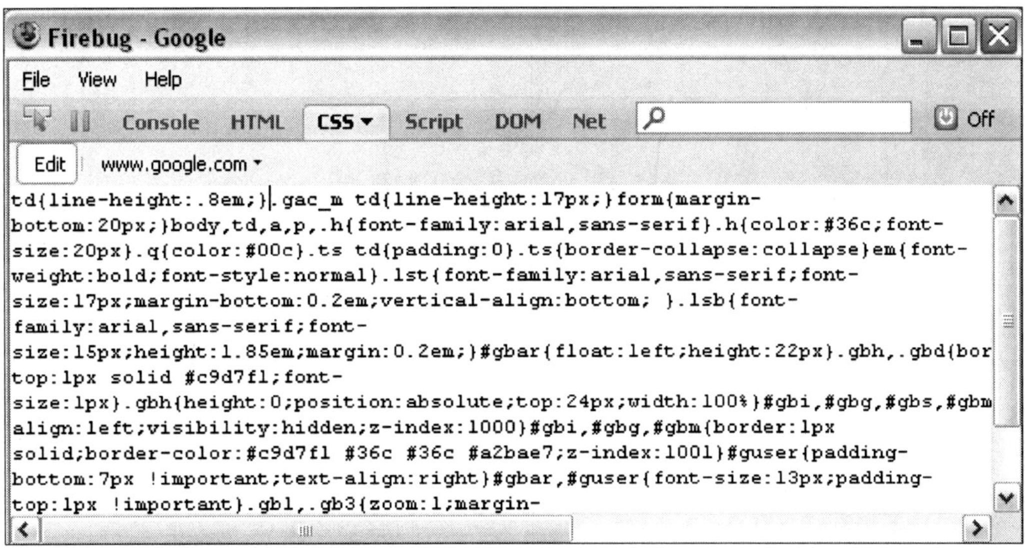

Editing and tweaking the CSS is very easy with Firebug. We only need to open Firebug on the live page and enable the edit mode of the CSS, which will take us to an editor where we can edit the CSS on the fly. Let's discuss the steps of modifying the CSS with the following example:

```
<html>
<head>
    <style>
    p{color:red;font-size:12px}
    div{color:black;font-size:20px}
    </style>
</head>
<body>
  <div>
    This is some text
    <p>
    Lorem ipsum dolor sit amet, consectetur adipisicing elit,
    sed do eiusmod tempor incididunt ut labore et dolore magna aliqua.
Ut enim ad minim veniam, quis nostrud exercitation ullamco laboris
nisi ut aliquip ex ea commodo consequat. Duis aute irure dolor in
reprehenderit in voluptate velit esse cillum dolore eu fugiat nulla
pariatur. Excepteur sint occaecat cupidatat non proident, sunt in
culpa qui officia deserunt mollit anim id est laborum
    </p>
  </div>
</body>
</html
```

Just create an HTML file on our file system and write the preceding code in it. After saving this file, open it in Firefox. Now, open Firebug by pressing the *F12* key and go to the **CSS** tab; we will see the rendered HTML output of the previously mentioned code, as shown in the following screenshot:

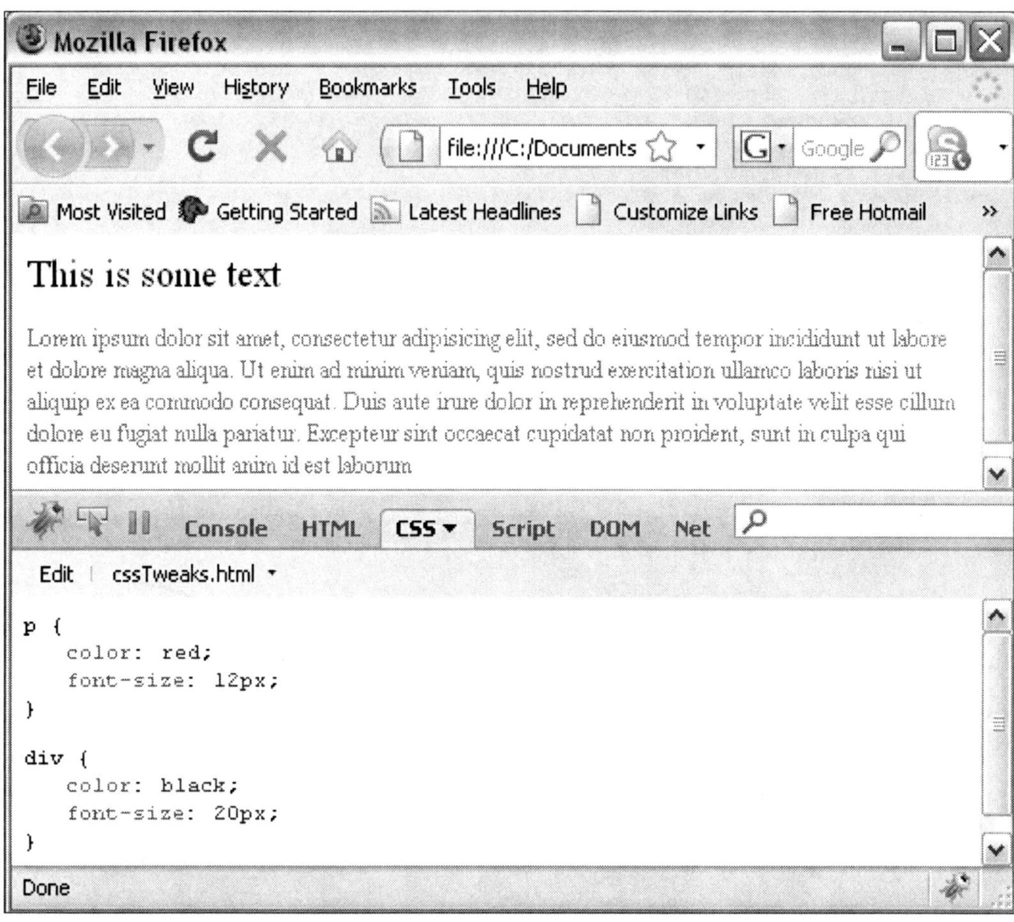

Click on the **Edit** button, which we can find in the top-left corner of the menu bar under the **CSS** tab. A notepad-type editor panel will open, as shown in the next screenshot. In this panel, the contents can be edited as discussed earlier.

In this panel we can edit, add, and remove the CSS rules and properties. The next screenshot shows some of the CSS properties that are changed and added, and the styles that are edited.

Please note the difference between the old and new CSS styles in the previous and next screenshot. The `color` property of `<p>` tag is changed from `red` to `blue`. Similarly, the `color` property of `<div>` tag is changed from `black` to `red`.

One more thing that we should notice when we try the previous example is that while editing the CSS styles, we don't need to wait for styles to get applied and see a preview; we get the result instantly on the browser's window. This editing of CSS on the fly and getting results in real time on our live document makes CSS development so easy and powerful that even a beginner, who wants to learn CSS, can easily and quickly learn and understand the CSS rules and its properties.

Please don't forget to refresh the web page if something goes wrong with Firebug while editing or debugging. Firebug is a very powerful tool for inspecting, editing, and debugging; however, there are some issues and limitations of Firebug. If we find any bug, then we can report it on `http://code.google.com/p/fbug/issues/entry` or we can find an existing issue on `http://code.google.com/p/fbug/issues/list`.

Script tab

The Script tab is the next gem that Firebug provides us with. This tab allows us to debug JavaScript code on the browser. We'll not go into the details of debugging JavaScript under this tab because in Chapter 5 we will cover all the details and ways of debugging JavaScript. For now we take an overview of this tab and briefly discuss the features of this tab.

The following can be performed under the **Script** tab:

- Viewing the list of JavaScript files that are loaded with our document
- Debugging the JavaScripts
- Inserting and removing breakpoints
- Inserting and removing conditional breakpoints
- Viewing the stack trace
- Viewing a list of breakpoints
- Adding new watch expressions
- Keeping an eye on the watches for viewing the values of variables
- Debugging an AJAX call

The next screenshot shows the layout of the **Script** tab. On the left panel, there is a **JavaScript** editor for debugging the JavaScript. With the JavaScript editor, we can debug the JavaScript code. In Firebug 1.4.x, an option called "Break on All Errors" can be found under this editor. If we check this option, the script execution will be paused if the error occurs in our JavaScript code.

In Firebug 1.5.x, the "Break on errors" option has been completely redesigned and this option is no longer available under the **Script** tab. We can still get this behavior by clicking the pause **| |** button next to the **Console** tab. This pause button acts differently on the **Script** tab; it breaks on the next executed line of JavaScript. On the **HTML** tab, it "Breaks on Mutate", that is, the execution will be paused when the HTML's DOM structure gets changed.

On the right-hand side panel, there are three more subtabs—**Watch**, **Stack**, and **Breakpoints**.

- **Watch**: This panel displays the value of variables as a list in this panel. It shows values of those variables that are in current scope.

- **Breakpoints**: This panel displays the list of all the breakpoints that we have attached with our code using Firebug or Firebug's API.
- **Stack**: This panel shows the stack of the function calls of the current function.

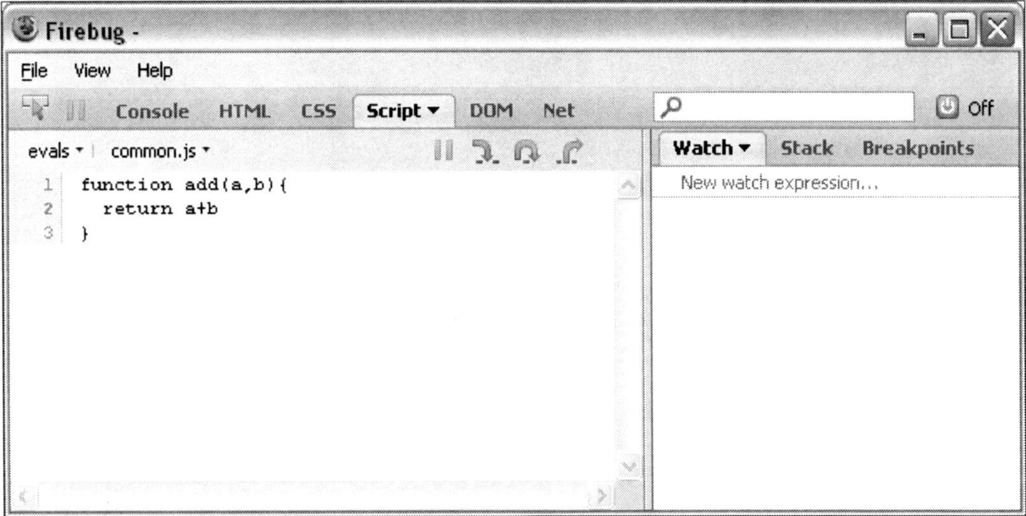

If we want to view the list of JavaScripts attached with the document then:

1. Open Firebug using the *F12* key.
2. Go to the **Script** tab.
3. Click on the drop-down (in this case `ajax.js`) just next to the **evals** button.

The next screenshot shows the list of JavaScript files that are attached with the document. To debug the JavaScript using Firebug, select any one of them from the list and the JavaScript written in that file will get displayed on the left-hand side of Firebug.

If Firebug doesn't display the list, then refresh the document without closing Firebug.

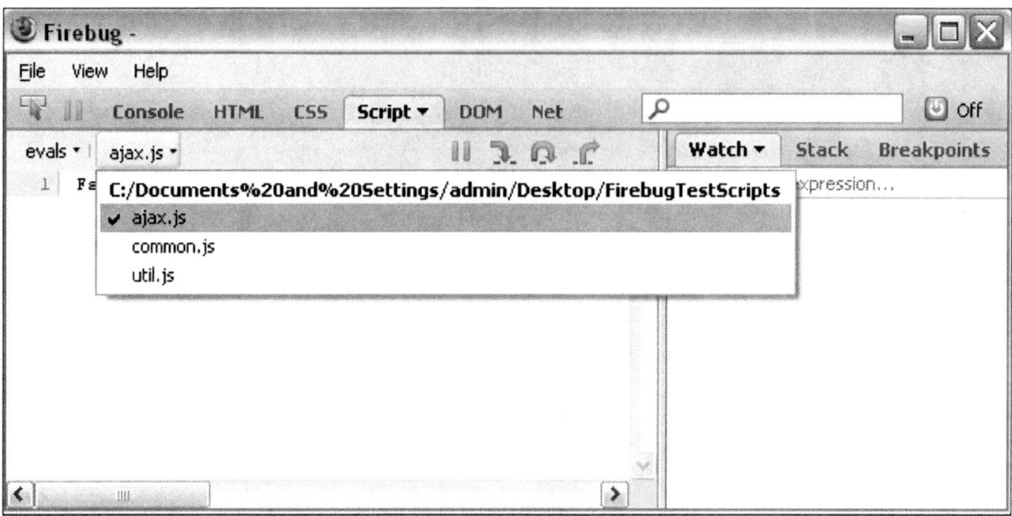

DOM tab

HTML elements are also known as DOM elements. **DOM**, that is, **Document Object Model,** represents the hierarchy of the HTML elements and functions. One can traverse in any direction within the DOM using JavaScript. The DOM elements have parent, child, and sibling relationships between them.

The **DOM** tab in Firebug shows default values for the following:

- DOM properties
- DOM functions
- DOM constants
- User-defined properties
- User-defined functions

If we want to find out how many functions or properties included our scripts, then we can easily find out by using this tab. This DOM tab is very useful for those who know JavaScript but don't know the default methods and constants they can use.

The following is a sample HTML code to illustrate the DOM tab:

```
<HTML>
<head>
   <script>
         function listOfStates(country){
         }
   function country(){
         }
   </script>
</head>
<body>
</body>
</HTML>
```

To see the working of the **DOM** tab against the preceding code, just follow these steps:

1. Write the preceding code in a file and save it with `.html` extension.
2. Open the saved file in Firefox and press the *F12* key to open Firebug.
3. Go to **DOM** tab and choose **Show User-defined Functions** from the drop-down menu.

Now we can see that the two functions—`country()` and `listOfStates(country)`—that we have written in <script> tag are in the list, as shown in following screenshot:

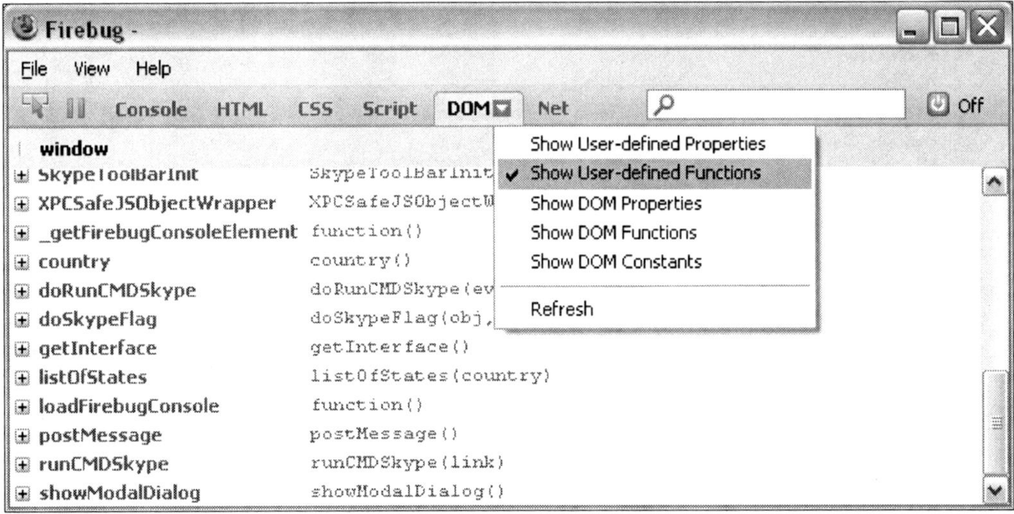

Net tab

The **Net** tab allows us to monitor the network for our page. This tab measures the performance of our web page and very quickly shows useful information such as:

- The time taken to load the page
- The size of each file
- The loading time of each file
- The number of requests the browser sends to load the page

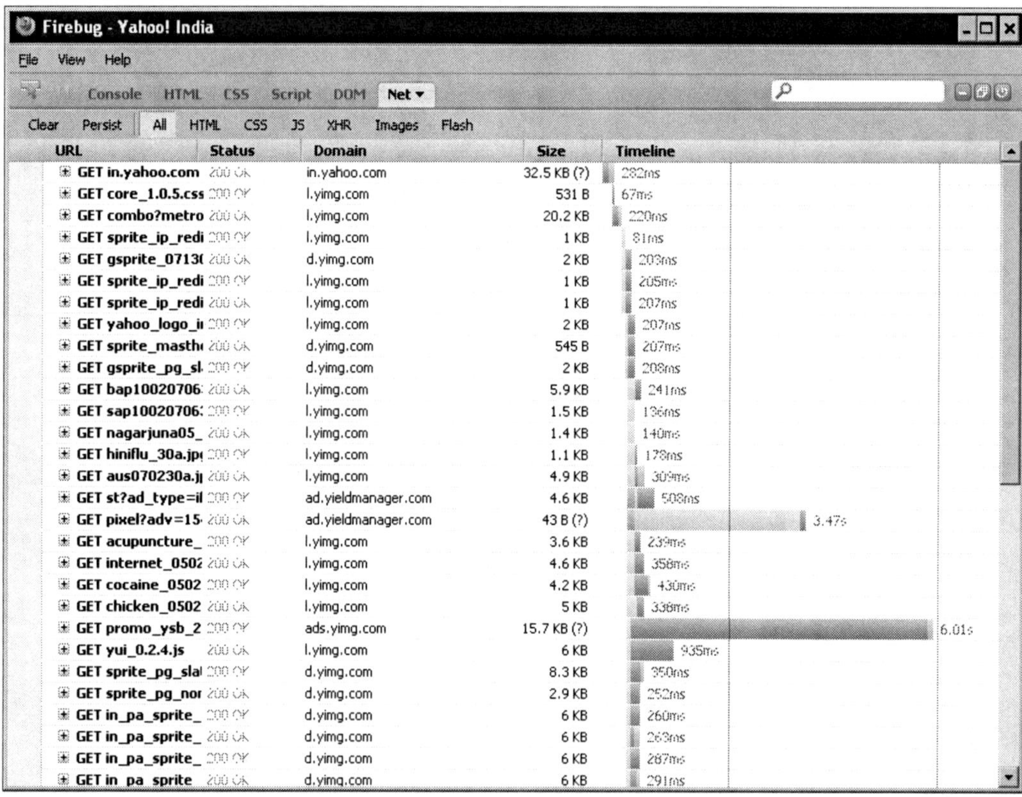

The **Net** tab also shows whether the file that was requested by the browser is loaded from cache or it has been fetched from the server. In the latest version of Firebug (1.5), there are five columns in the **Net** tab to display the statistics. They are as follows:

- **URL**: This first column shows the name of each file that is included in our web page. This column also shows which type of request (GET or POST) is made to the server. When we hover the mouse over URL, we can see the full URL of the file.

- **Status**: This is the second column and shows the HTTP status code and the message returned from the server.
- **Domain**: The third column shows the domain or base URL of each file. If we are using some files from external servers (for example, image links from another site, Google ads, or scripts), then the different URL(s) will be shown in this column.
- **Size**: This is the fourth column and shows the size of each file.
- **Timeline**: This last column shows the loading time of each file and whether or not those files are loaded from cache. It also shows the status of each file in different colors:
    - Light Blue: DNS (Domain Name Server) lookup.
    - Green: Connecting to server.
    - Cream Pink: Represents queuing time.
    - Purple: Represents the waiting time.
    - Dark Grey: Request sent to server now receiving data from server
    - Light Grey: Request sent to server, "Not Modified" received, received data from the cache.
    - No bar for the file: No request sent to server, file loaded from cache.

0ms : DNS Lookup	0ms : DNS Lookup
0ms : Connecting	103ms : Connecting
195ms : Queuing	0ms : Queuing
116ms : Waiting For Response	195ms : Waiting For Response
0ms : Receiving Data	88ms : Receiving Data
+1.59s : 'DOMContentLoaded' (event)	+1.61s : 'DOMContentLoaded' (event)
+3.92s : 'load' (event)	+3.93s : 'load' (event)

We can see the actual colored image in Firebug's **Net** panel.

Apart from loading time bars, we can also see two vertical lines—one in red and another in blue. The vertical blue line represents that the DOM content is loaded and the red vertical line represents that all the elements and events of the DOM are loaded. We can assume that these two vertical lines are the milestones that a web page has to achieve as quickly as possible to show the best results such as speed.

Summary

In this chapter, we discussed the overview of Firebug's tabs and for what purposes they are used. We discussed some key features of each tab that Firebug offers. Each tab in the Firebug is like a tool that the web developer can use to fight any client-side-related bugs.

Editing HTML and CSS on the fly becomes very easy by using Firebug. In next chapters, we'll discuss each feature of the Firebug individually. We will discuss how easy it can be to debug a JavaScript code, and how easy it is to change the look and feel of the live current page.

3

Inspecting and Editing HTML

This chapter provides an understanding of using Firebug to inspect, edit, search, and play with the HTML source of the document.

The chapter will cover how to:

- View source live
- See changes highlighted
- Modify the source on the fly
- Inspect page components, edit, and reload
- Search within an HTML document
- Find an HTML element on the page
- Set breakpoints on an HTML element

Viewing source live

Firefox and most other browsers have a feature for viewing the "source" of the HTML document sent by the server. However, it is possible to modify or transform (add elements, modify CSS styles, remove or hide elements, and so on) using JavaScript on the browser after the HTML document has been served. The "view source" feature of the browser does not show the modified or transformed version of the HTML source.

Firebug's **HTML** tab shows us what the HTML looks like right now. In addition to the **HTML** tab, there are three tabs on the right that let us view and modify the properties of an individual element, including the CSS rules that are being applied to the element, the layout of the element in the document, and its DOM properties.

Firebug's HTML view has more advanced features than the default source view of the Firefox browser. It shows the HTML DOM in a hierarchical structure or tree view with some highlighted color. It allows us to expand or collapse the HTML DOM for easy navigation and visualization of the HTML page. It is a viewer as well as an editor—it allows us to edit or delete the HTML elements or attributes on the fly, and the changes are immediately applied to the page being currently viewed and rendered by the browser.

The following screenshot displays the view of the **HTML** tab after the document has been loaded by the browser, but before any modifications have been made to the HTML document by JavaScript:

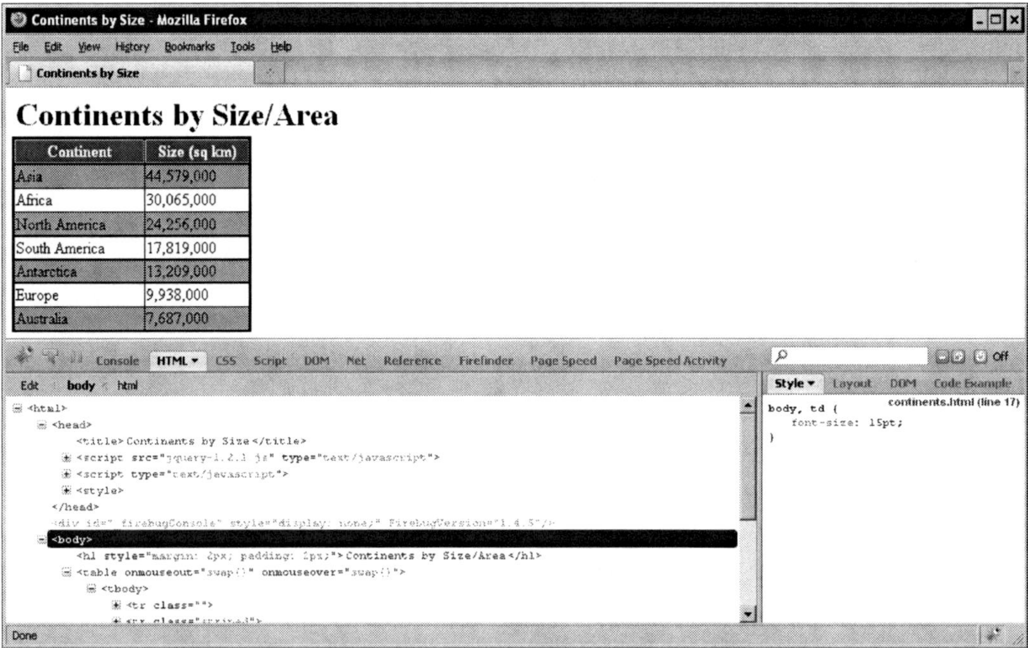

Executing the following JavaScript code would add an element to the HTML DOM:

```
jQuery('#lastRow').after('<tr><td>Total</td><td>147,553,000
                                                   </td></tr>')
```

The following screenshot displays the view of the **HTML** tab after the document has been loaded by the browser and any required modifications have been made to the HTML document by JavaScript:

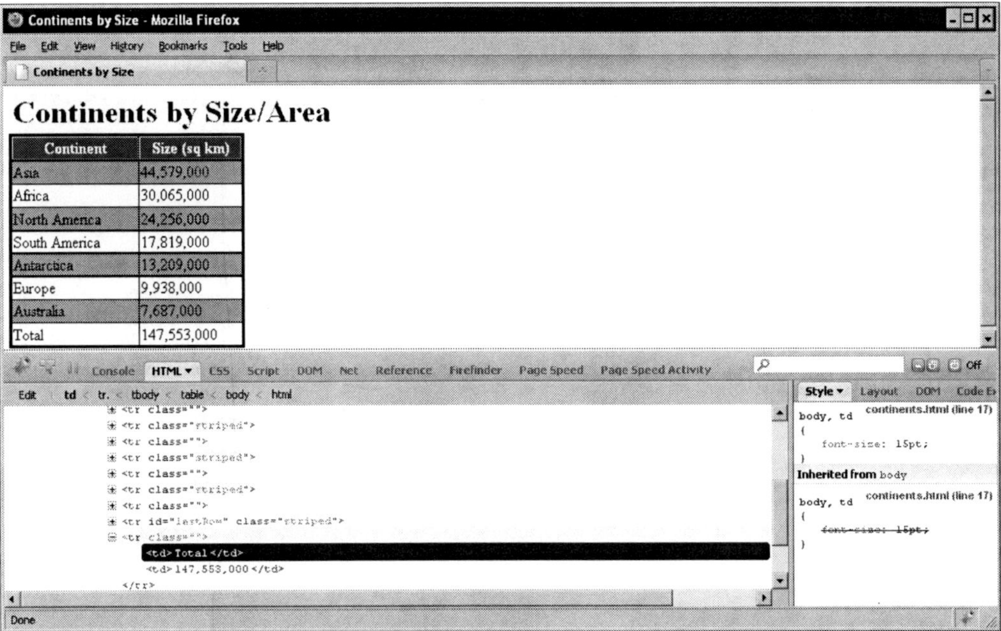

Please note that the Firebug's **HTML** tab is showing the modified HTML document. However, the browser view source window will continue to display the original source.

Seeing changes highlighted

Real life web pages are complex and may require complex changes in the HTML document in many ways. Sometimes, we have to understand JavaScript code not written by ourselves and more importantly, understand the changes JavaScript code makes to the HTML document. Sounds hard! Not really with Firebug's support for *highlighting the changes*.

Expanding further the example used earlier in the chapter, the page has been implemented such that when the mouse cursor goes over the table, the background color of the rows in the table interchange. In order to understand what changes have been made to the HTML DOM, let's quickly turn on the **Highlight changes** feature and take a look at the **HTML** tab.

The following screenshot displays the view of the **HTML** tab when the mouse is hovered over the table:

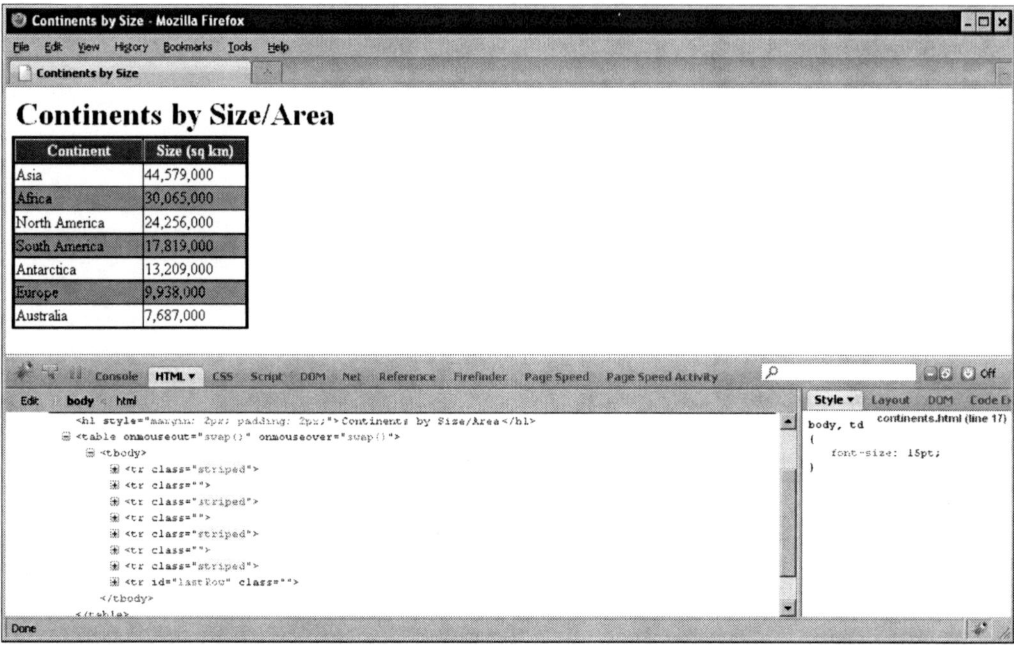

As we can see, the changes made to the HTML document have been highlighted in the **HTML** tab.

Modifying the source on the fly

Firebug makes it really easy to make experimental HTML changes and see them implement instantly. We can create, delete, modify HTML attributes, or create new HTML elements, or completely modify the source of the document.

This feature is most useful for scenarios where we have to make minor tweaks to any of the HTML attributes on the server side and then keep refreshing the browser page to see how the changes look. Firebug allows us to tweak and fine tune our HTML attributes very easily; the changes are applied immediately as we type.

How to modify the value of an HTML attribute

In order to modify the value of an HTML attribute on a page, let's do the following steps:

1. Open Firebug.
2. Click on the **HTML** tab. This will show the source of the document.
3. Locate the element that we want to modify in the source tree. (We might have to expand nodes in order to reach the element that we are trying to modify.)
4. Simply click on the attribute value that we want to modify. On clicking, the attribute value turns into an editable textbox. We can modify the value and see it taking effect instantly.

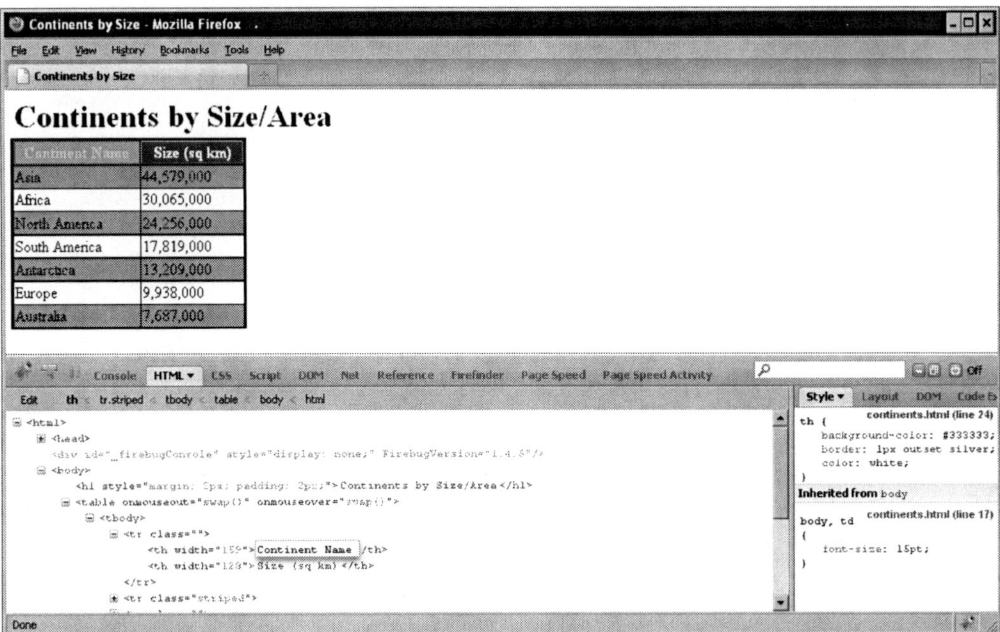

Using the up and down arrow keys to modify attribute values

For HTML attributes that take a numeric value, it is possible to easily increase and decrease the values by pressing the up and down arrow keys. For example, if we are trying to set the width of a table column to a certain size, then it is very easy to keep pressing the up or down arrow keys and see the corresponding change in Firefox window.

Using tab to navigate between elements

If we find ourself navigating to many attributes by clicking on the attribute names and values, then Firebug provides an easy way to do that. We can use the *Tab* key to navigate forward and *Shift* + *Tab* keys to navigate backward between different attributes.

How to add a new attribute to an existing HTML element

In order to add a new HTML attribute to an element, let's do the following steps:

1. Open Firebug and locate the element (in the **HTML** tab) that we want to modify.
2. Right-click on the element and choose the **New Attribute...** option.
3. Enter the name of the attribute, press the *Tab* key, and then enter the value for the attribute. The new attribute gets applied as we type, without us having to click outside the textbox or doing anything else.

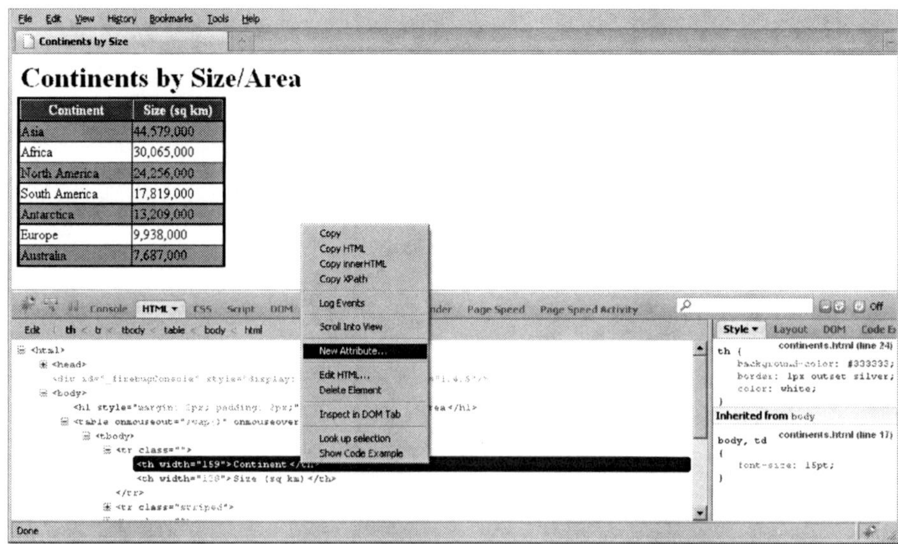

How to delete an HTML element

In order to delete an existing node in the HTML source tree, do the following steps:

1. Open Firebug and locate the element (in the **HTML** tab) that we want to delete.
2. Right-click on the node that we want to delete and choose **Delete Element**.

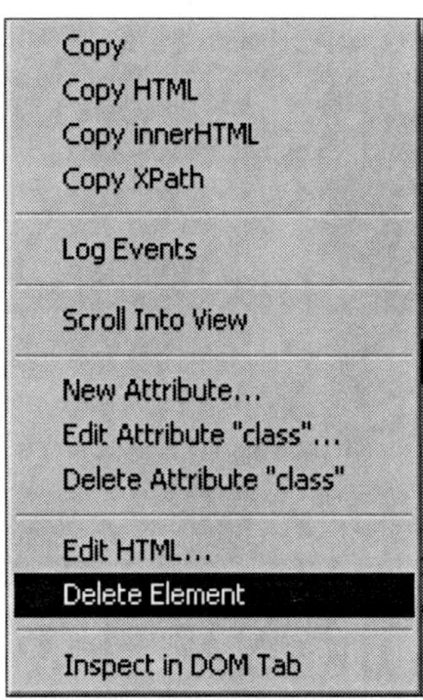

How to modify the source for an HTML element

If we're looking to do more than just make minor tweaks, Firebug allows us to edit the entire HTML source of any element. In order to modify the source for an HTML element, let's do the following steps:

1. Open Firebug and locate the element (in the **HTML** tab) that we want to modify.
2. Right-click on the element and choose the **Edit HTML...** option from the menu. This will open the HTML code for the element in a separate tab, which allows us to edit the source just as we do in a text editor. The changes that we made take effect as we type them. (We can also enter the **Edit** mode for an HTML node by double-clicking on the node).

3. Click on the **Edit** button again to go back to the **HTML** tab view to see the complete document source tree.

```
<tr class="">
        <th width="159">Continent</th>
        <th width="128">Size (sq km)</th>
    </tr>
```

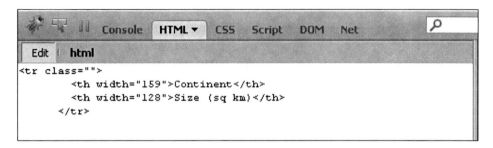

Inspecting page components, editing, and reloading

Something on our page doesn't look quite right and we want to know why. We are looking at a page, and we want to understand how a particular section of the page has been constructed. Firebug's "Inspect" functionality allows us to do that in the fastest possible manner, using minimum clicks or mouse strokes. As we move around the page, Firebug creates visual frames around various page components or sections, and shows the HTML and CSS behind the page section.

The inspect button icon (shown in the next screenshot) to the left-hand side of HTML toolbar allows us to inspect the HTML element of the web page we are looking at. In order to inspect elements on a page, just click the inspect button icon and move the mouse around the web page. The HTML element under the mouse cursor will be highlighted and the related elements will be selected in the **HTML** tab of Firebug, showing the HTML and CSS controlling the look and feel of the HTML element.

This feature is very useful for web developers and designers as it allows them to understand very easily why a certain component on the web page looks the way it does.

In order to inspect an element on a web page, let's do the following steps:

1. Click the inspect button icon on the Firebug console toolbar.
2. Move the mouse cursor on to the page component or section that we want to inspect.

3. Click on the page component or section to select the element in the HTML panel.

In our experience, this is one of the most frequently used features while tweaking the look and feel of our web application. Inspecting page elements and doing tweaks (editing HTML attributes, CSS rules, and so on) are real time savers during fine tuning of a web application's look and feel.

When we inspect an element, a visual frame is created around the element and the HTML source of the element is shown highlighted in the Firebug window.

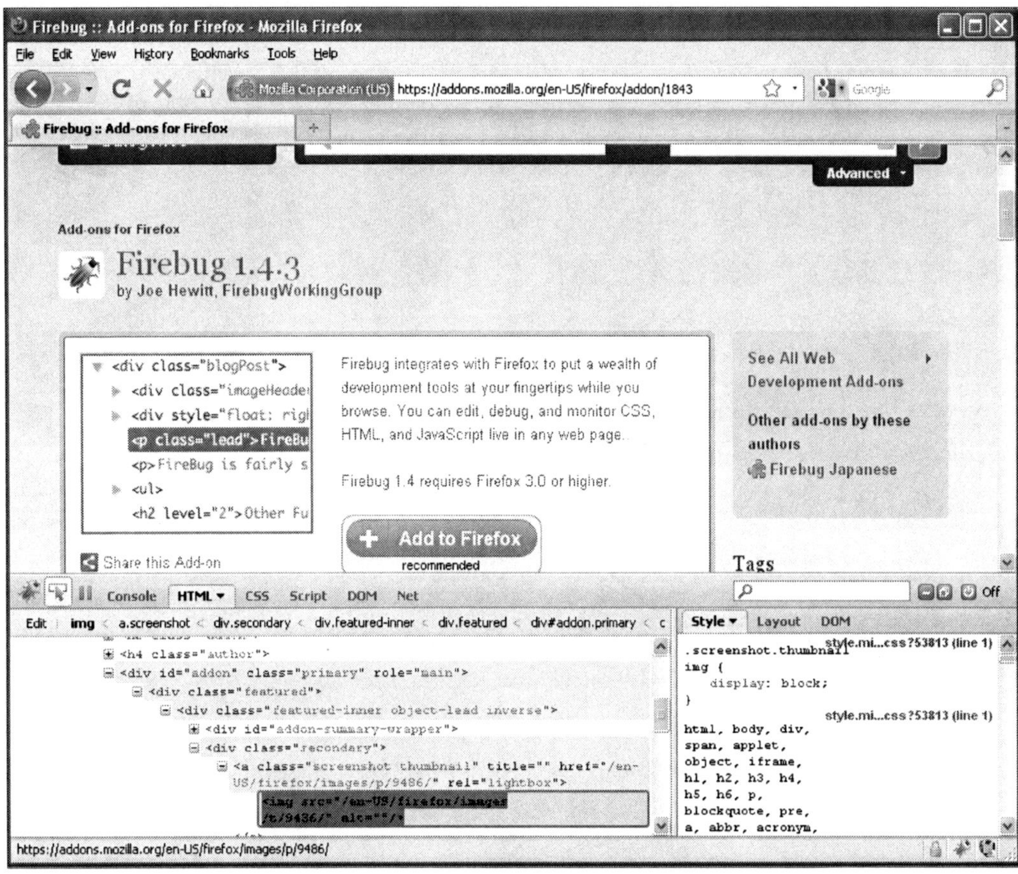

Using right-click to inspect

We can even inspect an element by right-clicking on the element in the browser window and selecting the **Inspect Element** option from the menu. This allows us to inspect an element without opening the Firebug window, and with minimum mouse-clicks.

The inspection feature also acts as a great learning tool when we are looking at web pages developed by others. Firebug tells us exactly which code is used to make a particular object on a web page.

When we inspect an element in the **HTML** tab, we can reload the page and Firebug will continue to show that same element (if it still exists) after the reload. This makes it easy to test when we make a change in an external editor (or on the server-side code) and reload the page in Firefox to see how it looks.

Searching within an HTML document

Firefox has a search feature that allows us to search for the text on a web page. Firefox's search feature is good for viewers of the web page who are searching for some content on the page. But if we need to perform a search in the source code of the HTML, then we have to view the source and search in the source window. There are two main issues with using Firefox's default search feature:

- The HTML source appears as a flat file (without any structure)
- There is no linkage between the source window and the page

Firebug comes to the rescue here as well. Firebug provides a "search box" on the right-hand side of the console toolbar. Using the quick search box in Firebug's toolbar, we can search the HTML source and see the results highlighted as we type.

In order to search for something in the source of the web page that we are looking at, simply open the Firebug console and type something in the search box.

Finding an HTML element on the page

While looking into the code of an HTML document in the **HTML** tab of Firebug, if we want to check where the element is displayed on the page, it is very easy to do so using the **Scroll Into View** feature. In order to find where in the page the HTML element is rendered, simply right-click on the HTML element and choose the **Scroll Into View** option from the menu.

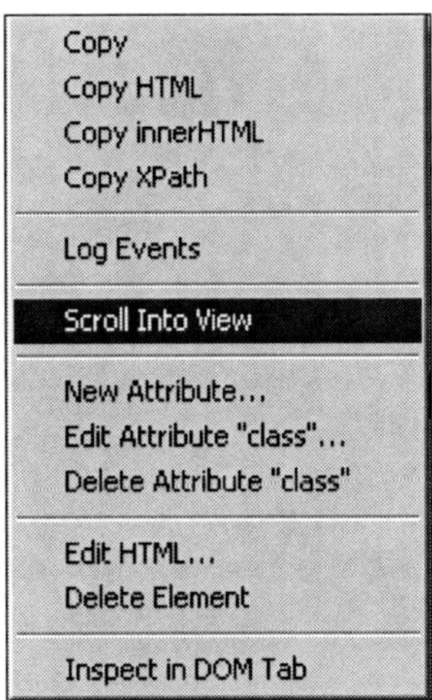

This is the exact reverse of inspecting an element on the page when Firebug finds the component on the page in the HTML source tree. Here we are finding an element in the HTML source tree on the page.

Copying HTML source for an HTML element

In order to copy the source of an HTML element, right-click on the element and choose either the **Copy HTML** or the **Copy innerHTML** option from the menu.

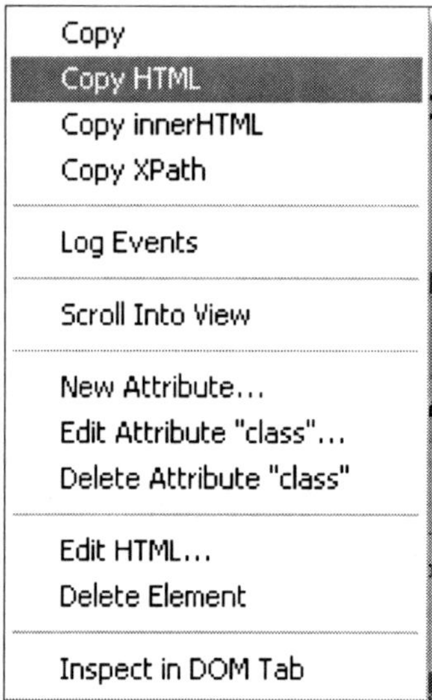

Setting breakpoints on HTML element

We have already discussed this topic in Chapter 2, *Firebug Window Overview*, but here we'll discuss it in detail.

In Firebug 1.5, there is an option for setting up the breakpoints on an HTML node too. These breakpoints are triggered whenever an attribute is changed, a child element is added or removed, or the element is removed. The following are the steps to set up breakpoints on an HTML node:

1. Inspect the element on which we want breakpoint to be inserted. Within the **HTML** tab, right-click on the element.

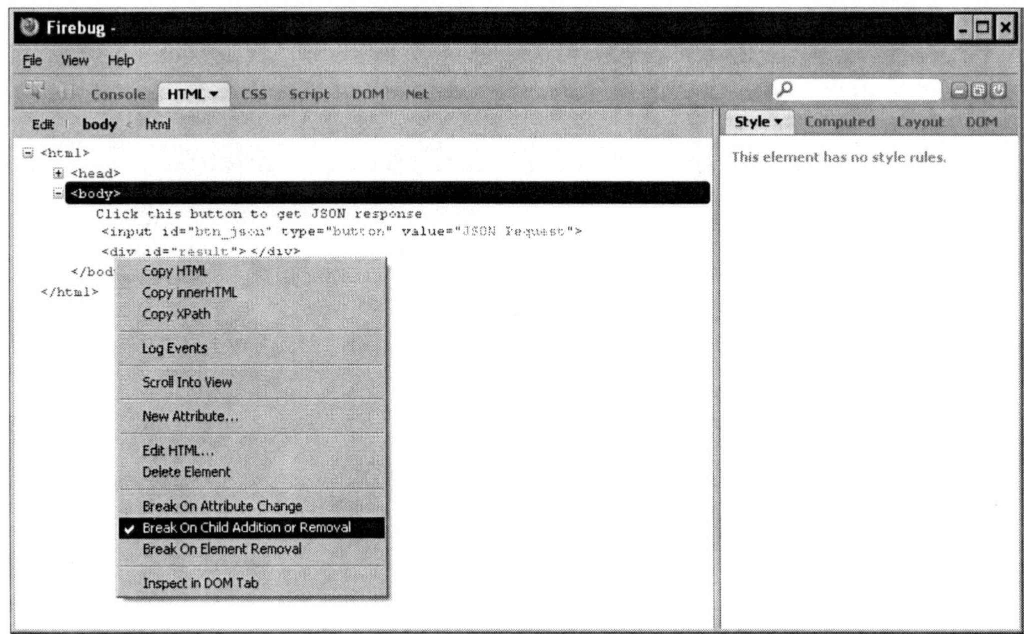

2. Select an option (**Break On Attribute Change, Break On Child Addition or Removal**, or **Break On Element Removal**) from the context menu. On selecting one, Firebug will keep an eye on the node.

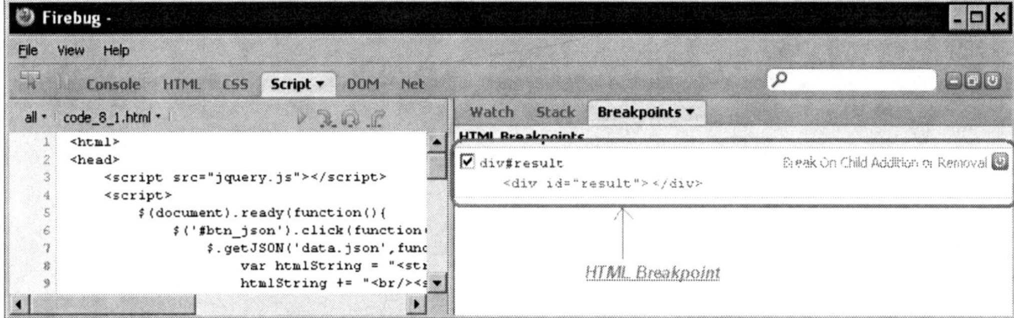

3. Now, whenever the HTML within the marked node changes, Firebug will trigger the breakpoint and take us to the line in the JavaScript code whose execution is changing the DOM/HTML of the marked element.

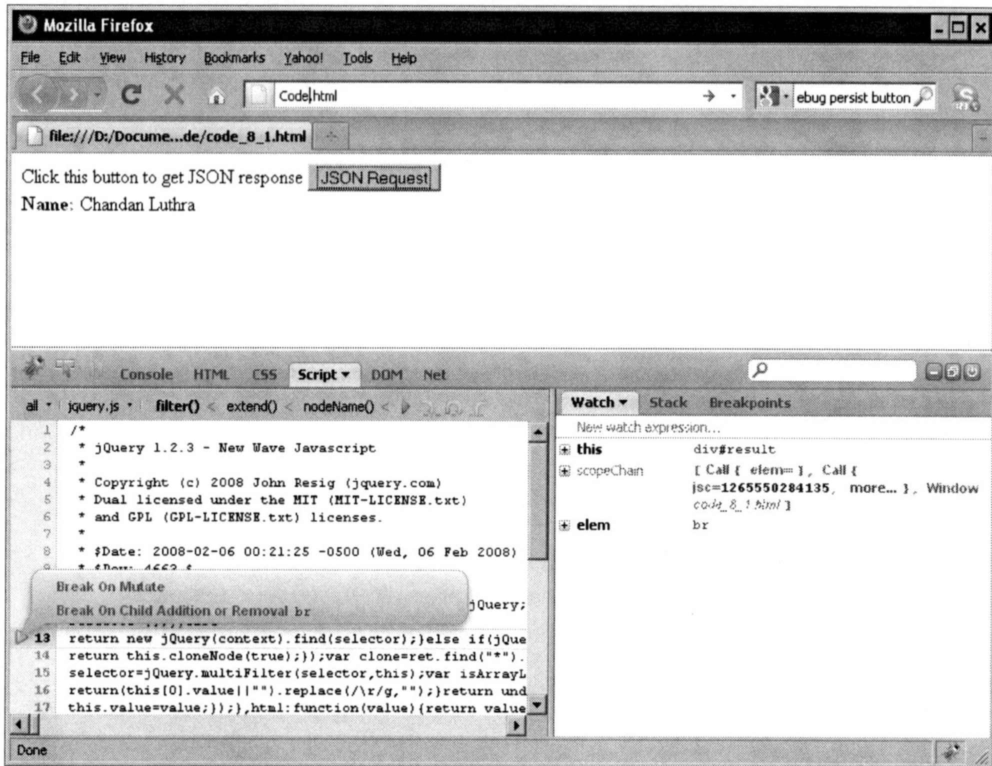

4. By pressing *F10* (**Step Over**) or *F11* (**Step Into**), we can debug the JavaScript in the **Script** tab.

Summary

In this chapter, we looked at various ways to analyze and study the HTML source of the page we are looking at, using various tools and utilities provided by Firebug. Firebug makes it extremely easy to understand the HTML source of a page. It allows easy editing of the HTML document and viewing of the changes to the rendered page. In the following chapter, we will learn how to control and enhance the look and feel of web pages by changing the CSS of the page with the help of Firebug.

4
CSS Development

This chapter aims to help the reader to understand the useful tools and utilities provided by Firebug for CSS development. Firebug is a great tool to increase one's learning of CSS rules and how they will impact a document, whether an individual is a beginner or has intermediate skills of CSS.

In this chapter, we'll learn step-by-step how CSS development can be done using Firebug.

Throughout this chapter, we'll use `http://www.csszengarden.com` as a sample to explain CSS development. This site demonstrates what can be accomplished visually through CSS-based design.

Inspecting cascading rules

With non-Firefox browsers, one is left banging his/her head against a wall when the color of a paragraph comes out red instead of blue. But thanks to Firebug we can easily inspect the problematic HTML element, and find the CSS rule that is causing the problem, before you can blink.

Inspecting a CSS element is very simple. It is similar to inspecting an HTML element as described in the previous chapter. To inspect a CSS element, we just need to open Firebug in inspect mode.

We can open Firebug in inspect mode in the following two ways:

- Directly in inspect mode by pressing *Ctrl* + *Shift* + *C*
- By pressing *F12* and then clicking icon just next to the bug icon on the top-left corner of the Firebug window

The following screenshot depicts the inspection of CSS for an HTML element (observe the rectangular box around **Zen Garden**):

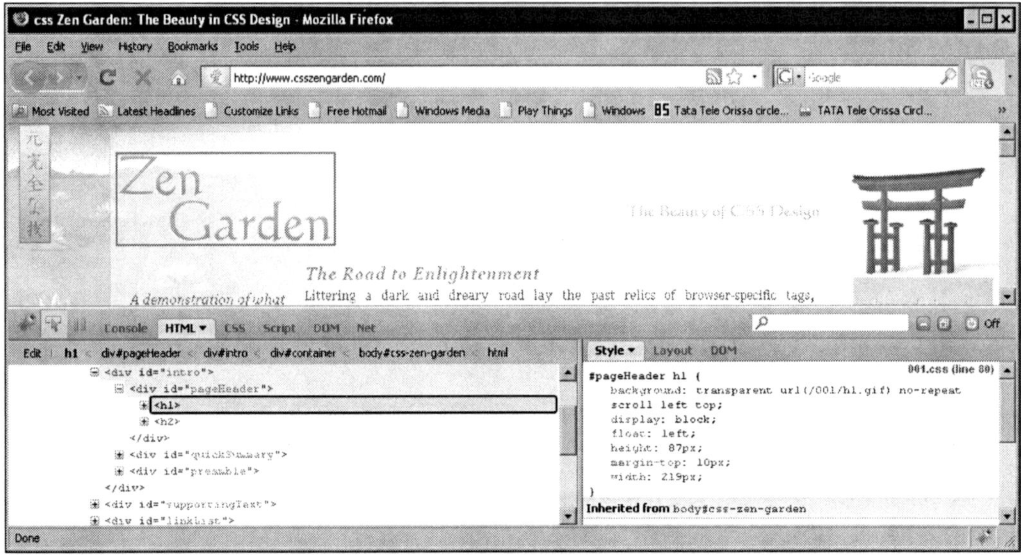

The following are the steps to find and inspect the CSS of an HTML element with the mouse:

1. Open any site (in our case its `http://www.csszengarden.com`) and press *Ctrl* + *Shift* + *C* (default shortcut) to open Firebug in inspect mode.
2. Move the mouse pointer on the HTML element on the page that we want to inspect, as shown in the next screenshot (in our case it is the image on which "Zen Garden" is engraved). With the movement of the pointer of the mouse we can see a blue box beneath the pointer. Whatever is wrapped in that box will be instantly revealed within Firebug, which shows HTML on the left panel and CSS on the right panel.
3. When we reach the problematic HTML element, click on it. As soon as we do that, the box will vanish, and the HTML and CSS rules of that element will be shown.

Firebug also shows the link, with the line number indicated, to the CSS file that the CSS property is getting applied to. When we click on the link, Firebug will switch to the **CSS** tab and take us to that file, and specifically to the line number indicated in the link. This property helps the web developer and web designer to easily find the exact CSS file and line number that he or she wants to tweak.

Preview colors and images

To verify whether we have selected the right element, move the mouse pointer over the URL value of the background in the CSS rule, as shown in the following screenshot, which illustrates the preview of the image within Firebug. As soon as we move over that value, Firebug will show a handy tool tip that previews the "Zen Garden" image with its width and height.

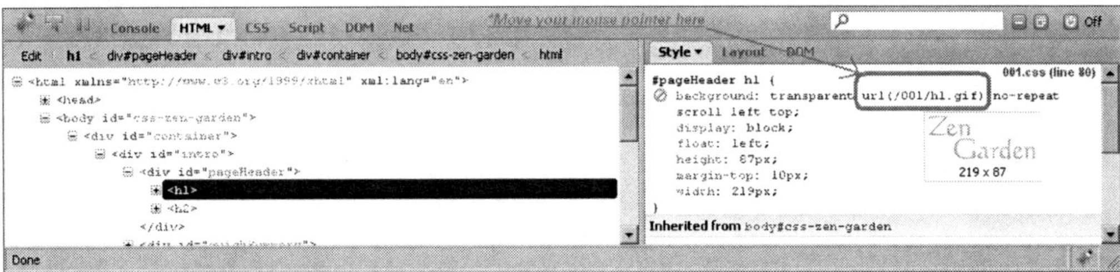

Similarly, we can also preview colors within Firebug. For example, we'll inspect the `<h3>` element, **The Road to Enlightment**, as shown in the following screenshot:

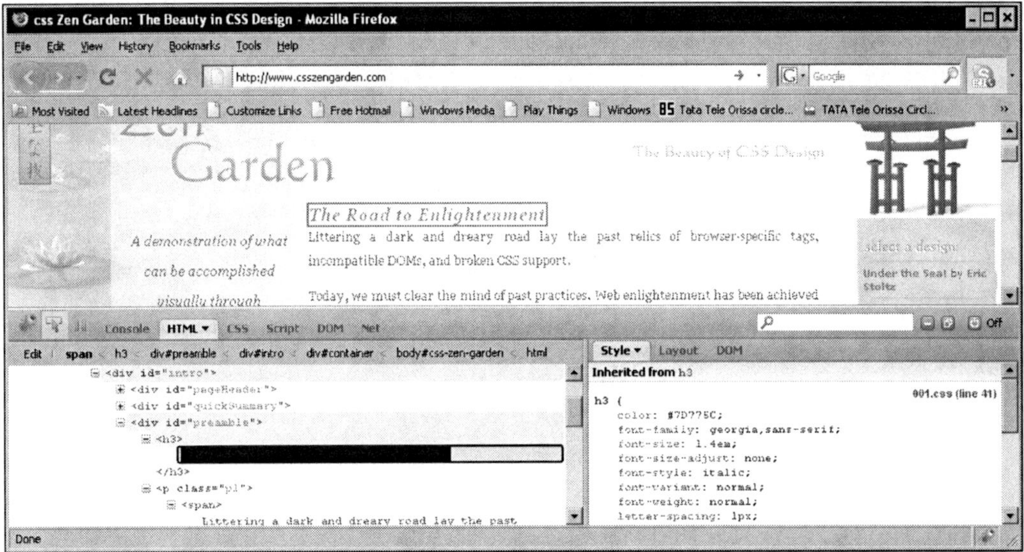

To inspect the text or any other HTML element, follow the steps explained under section *Inspecting cascading rules* of this chapter.

Now, we move our mouse pointer over the value of the CSS property—color (in our case its **#7D775C**) as shown in the following screenshot:

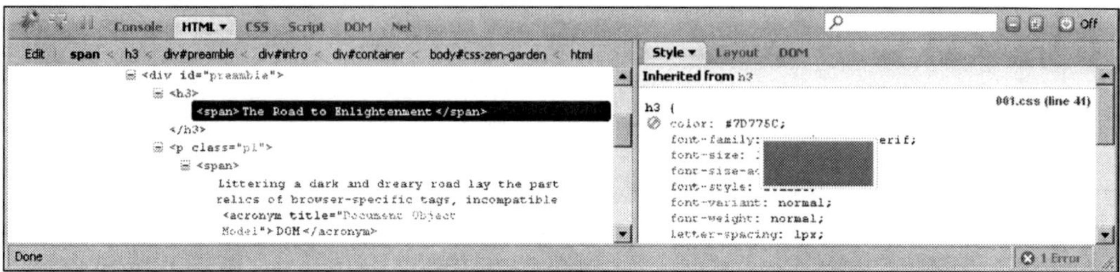

Tweaking CSS on the fly

Gone are the days when one had to edit the CSS rules and properties, in the CSS file associated with the document and reload the page to view changes. This is a new generation folks; with Firebug one can edit the CSS rules, tweak the CSS properties on the fly, and view the live changes on the page instantly in real time. We don't have to reload the page every time some changes are made to CSS files. This feature of Firebug not only saves our development time and cost but also helps us to get rid of CSS errors and issues.

Firebug shows all the CSS rules that are impacting the selected HTML element and the CSS rules that an element inherits from its ancestor elements. If some CSS property or style is overridden, that rule and property is also shown by Firebug in strike (for example, ~~color : red~~) fashion.

While editing the CSS properties, one can press the *ESC* key to cancel the editing.

Let's discuss tweaking CSS with our previous example, "The Road to Enlightment", which we saw in the previous screenshots. Now, recall the color property on the `<h3>` element or we can refer to the following CSS style:

```
h3 {
    color:#7D775C;
    font-family:georgia,sans-serif;
    font-size:1.4em;
```

```
    font-size-adjust:none;
    font-style:italic;
    font-variant:normal;
    font-weight:normal;
    letter-spacing:1px;
    line-height:normal;
}
```

To edit the CSS rule from Firebug, just follow these steps:

1. Open Firebug and inspect the problematic HTML element whose CSS rule is to be edited.
2. Click on the *value* of the CSS property under the **Style** panel of the **HTML** tab (in our case click on the value **#7D775C** of the CSS property `color`). As soon as we click, a little text editor will appear as shown in the following screenshot:

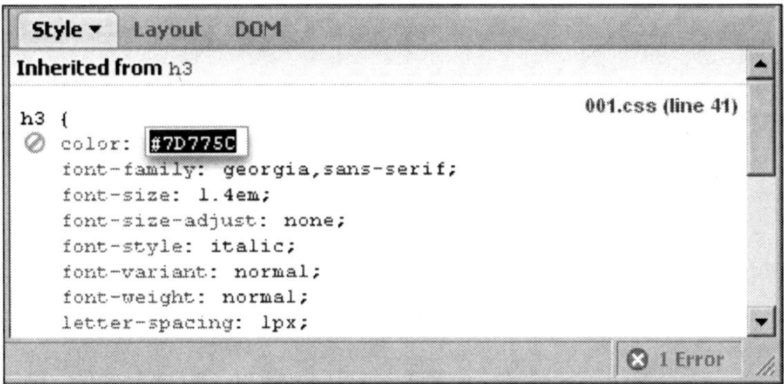

3. Now, type *red* in place of #7D775C. The result can be seen instantly on the page; the color of the selected element's text turns to red without having to reload the page.

> When the CSS property is in editable mode, one can navigate between the CSS properties and their values, to and fro, by pressing the *Tab* key (to navigate in forward direction) and *Shift* + *Tab* keys (to navigate in backward direction).

There is another easy way of editing the CSS stylesheet. Just click on the **Edit** button under the **CSS** tab and Firebug will convert the CSS panel into a text editor. When we are done with editing, click on the **Edit** button again. Clicking on this button will save our changes and toggle the panel from the text editor to the normal CSS panel.

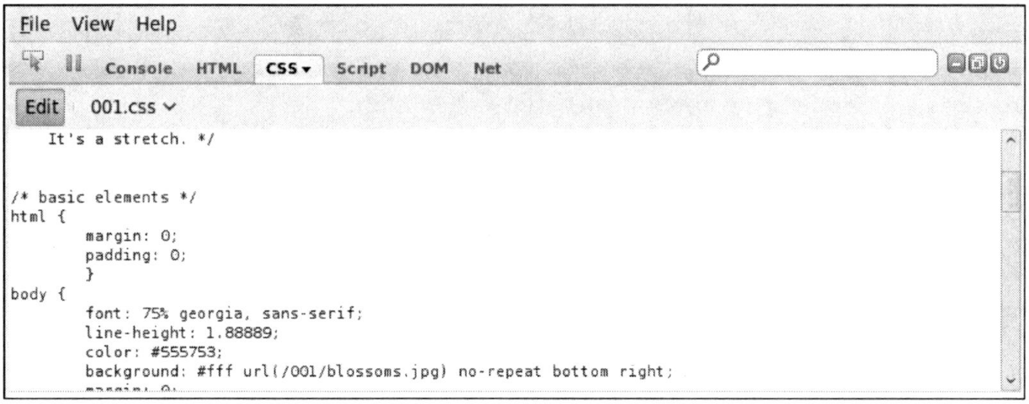

File View Help

Console HTML CSS Script DOM Net

Edit 001.css

```
   It's a stretch. */


/* basic elements */
html {
        margin: 0;
        padding: 0;
        }
body {
        font: 75% georgia, sans-serif;
        line-height: 1.88889;
        color: #555753;
        background: #fff url(/001/blossoms.jpg) no-repeat bottom right;
```

Enabling and disabling specific CSS rules

Firebug allows us to turn off styles impacting an element within the CSS. When we turn off an attribute, and if that attribute value was overriding a different value in the cascade, then the formerly crossed out value will become active and we can test the page with the attribute value removed. In order to *turn off* an attribute, click to the left of the attribute in the **Style** panel where a red *do not* icon will appear; the attribute will be grayed out or disappear. The strike-through of the new attribute value affecting the element from the cascade will be removed. We can toggle the attribute's value back to "*on*" by clicking on the *do not* icon again. However, if the attribute has *disappeared* as it has been overwritten, we will have to re-inspect the element to see the missing attribute and then turn it on.

The next two screenshots illustrate enabling and disabling the CSS properties:

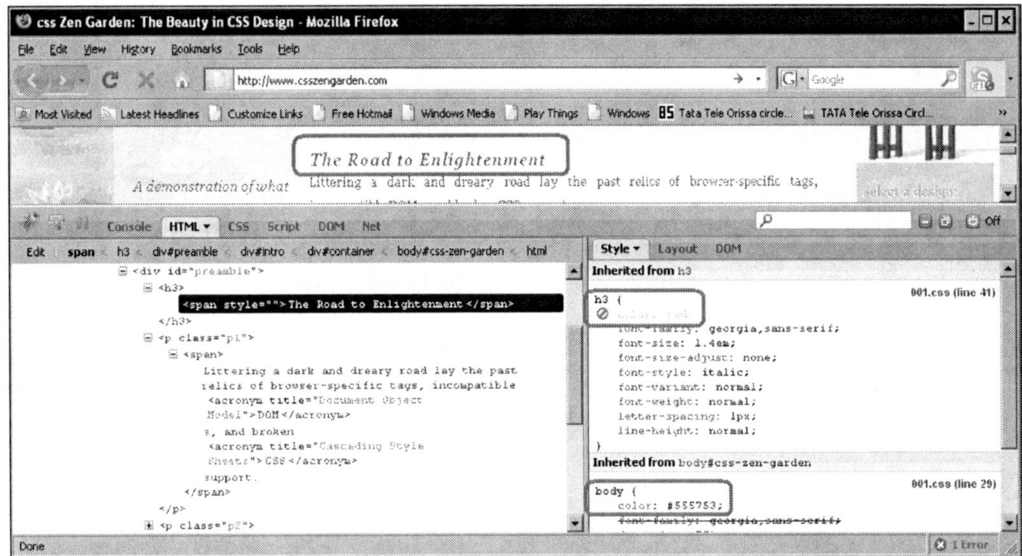

When we disable the `color` property of CSS from rule *h3* the following changes appear:

1. The color of the `<h3>` element, "The Road to Enlightment", is changed.
2. The property that we disable is grayed out.
3. The strike-through of the `color` attribute value affecting the element from the body rule is removed.

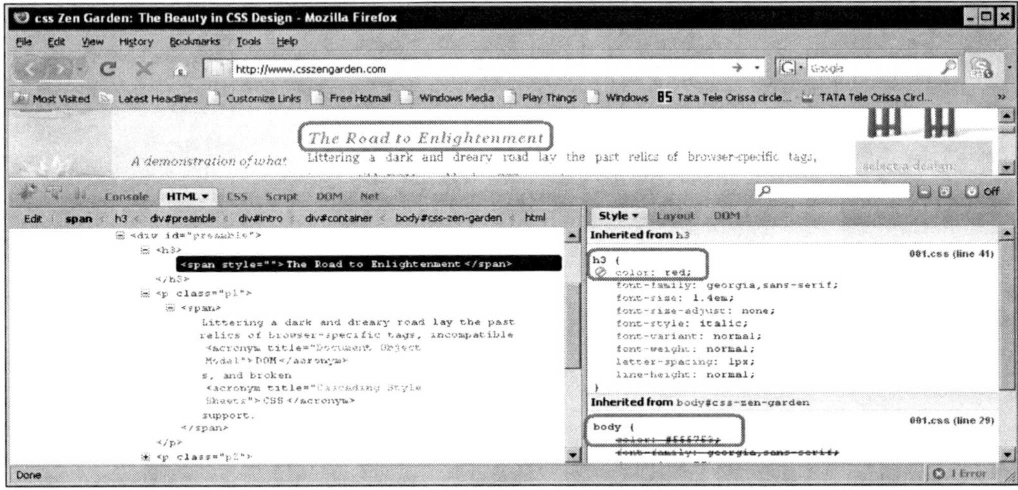

The effects after enabling the CSS property are highlighted in the preceding screenshot. The color of the text changes to red again, the *CSS* attribute color of the body rules gets overridden and struck-through.

Inspecting our stylesheet

Firebug's **HTML** tab only lets us inspect the CSS of a single element, whereas the main **CSS** tab allows us to view entire stylesheets imported in the page. To inspect the stylesheets imported in the current HTML page, we need to go to **CSS** tab. The following screenshot shows how to select the stylesheet from dropdown to inspect it:

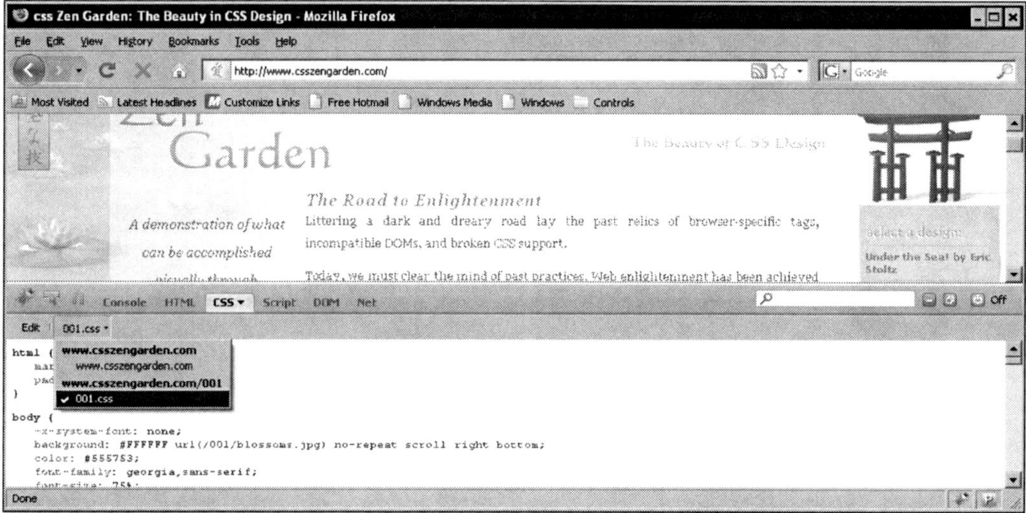

In the **CSS** tab, we will find a drop-down in the top-left corner next to the **Edit** button. On clicking the drop-down, it shows the list of the stylesheets that are imported on the page. Now we can easily select any stylesheet for inspection in the **CSS** tab.

As soon as we select a cascade stylesheet from the list, it will open in the **CSS** tab for inspection.

Modifying CSS from Firebug's UI

When we right-click on the CSS property within Firebug, a context menu will appear with few options related to CSS as shown in the following screenshot. The context menu is dynamic and shows the edit, delete, disable options with respect to the CSS property on which we have right-clicked:

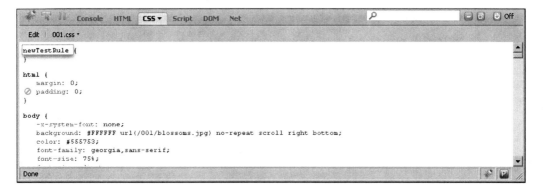

Let's now learn the various options of the context menu:

- **New Rule**:

  When we click on the **New Rule...** option, a mini-editor will pop up in the Firebug window. Here we can define a new CSS selector, that is, a CSS class or an ID. Press the *Tab* key to commit the change.

- **New Property**:

  When we click on the **New Property** option, Firebug will open a mini-editor within the CSS rule to define new CSS properties of the rule on which we have right-clicked. We can type any CSS property (such as margin, padding, background, color, and so on) in this area.

  To give the value to the new property, we press *Tab* key and type the value that we want.

We can also define a new property by double-clicking in front of any CSS rule.

The following screenshot shows the **New Property** option of the context menu:

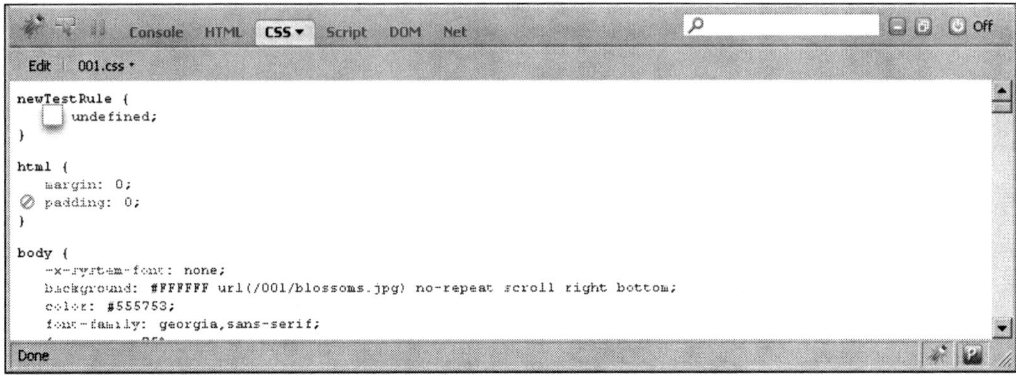

- **Edit "<property>":**

  By selecting this option, Firebug allows us to edit the CSS property that is shown in the option of the context menu.

We can also edit any CSS property simply by clicking on that property. As soon as we click on the CSS property, Firebug makes it editable. If we want to cancel the editing, we press the *Esc* key.

- **Delete "<property>":**

  This option will remove the property from the CSS. If we want the removed CSS property back then we refresh our page.

- **Disable "<property>":**

  This option of context menu will disable the CSS property. Disabling the property doesn't remove it from the document, we can always enable it by clicking the red *do not* icon.

Inspecting and tweaking the box model

The box model gives us the way to evaluate the height, width, padding, border, and margin of a selected HTML element. While inspecting an element, the left panel shows the HTML and the right panel displays the CSS. At the top of the right panel, under the **HTML** tab, is a **Layout** tab. In order to evaluate the height or width of any element on the page, click the inspect icon or press *Ctrl* + *Shift* + *C* while this window is open and hover our mouse over the inline or block level element we wish to inspect.

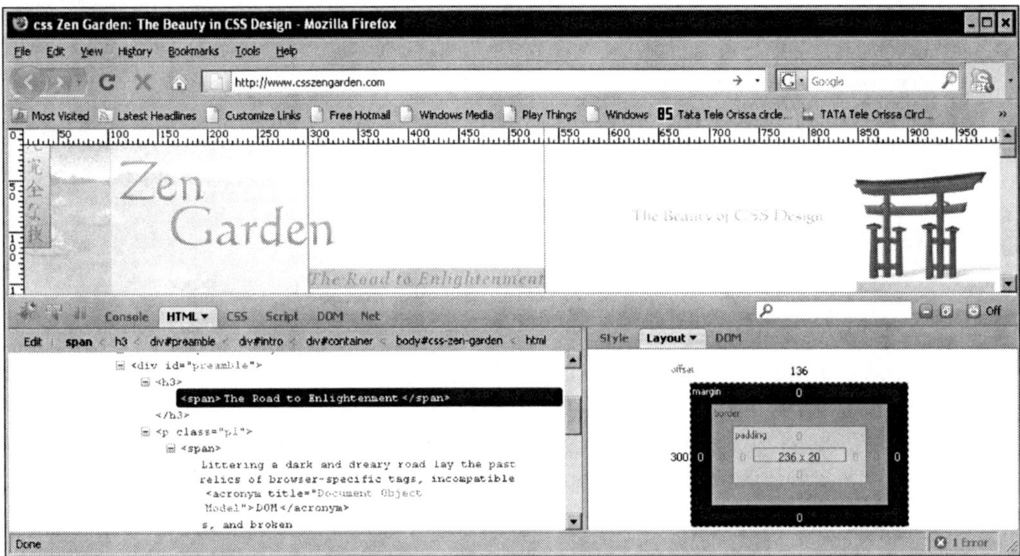

Searching under the CSS tab

To search within the **CSS** tab all we need to do is use Firebug's search box and write the search string within that box. On the **CSS** tab, the search box behavior changes and search space becomes the current CSS file.

To be more specific with upper/lower case string while searching, we can choose the **Force Case Sensitive** option from the menu that appears when we focus on the search box.

We can also choose the **Multiple Files** option from the menu. Selecting this option increases the search space and Firebug will search the inputted string within all the CSS files.

The **Previous** and **Next** buttons are used to navigate between the results.

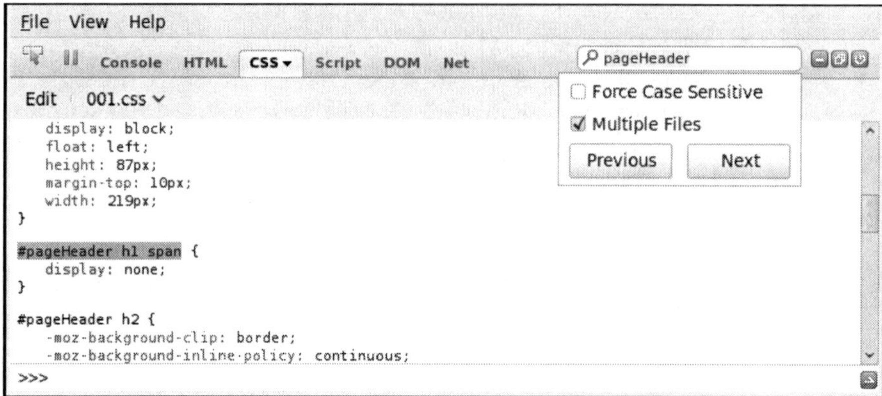

Summary

In this chapter, we discussed how easily and quickly we can tweak the CSS styles on the fly using Firebug. We can see live changes instantly on the page that we are editing.

We learned how to inspect an element that is causing problems within the DOM and tweak its styles/CSS rules. If an element has a *color* or *background* (image) CSS attribute, then we can preview the colors and images within the tool tip pop up of Firebug.

If we want to remove some CSS attributes from an element then we can enable/disable those attributes by clicking on the *do not* icon.

5

JavaScript Development

In this chapter, we'll discuss the various tools/utilities provided by Firebug to aid JavaScript development, debugging, profiling, and testing. Here, we take typical use-cases with JavaScript and explain how they can be achieved using Firebug.

In this chapter we'll discuss the following topics:

- The command line API and its functions
- The console API
- Step-by-step JavaScript debugging
- Inserting conditional and non-conditional breakpoints

The command line API

As we have already seen the use of the command line in Chapter 2, *Firebug Window Overview* here we'll discuss some methods provided by the command line API. These methods help us in debugging JavaScript. The following are the methods with their description and usage:

$(id)

This method is similar to `document.getElementById()` in JavaScript. It returns the single element with the given ID.

Cannot be used with jQuery loaded. Is a conflict!

The following is the HTML code snippet that we will use to explain the `$(id)` method. Write the code in an HTML file and open it in Firefox.

```
<html>
   <body>
      <input name="myText" id="test_id" type="text">
   </body>
</html>
```

Now, considering that we are executing the following code line in Firebug's command line, we will see the following output window:

```
$("test_id")
```

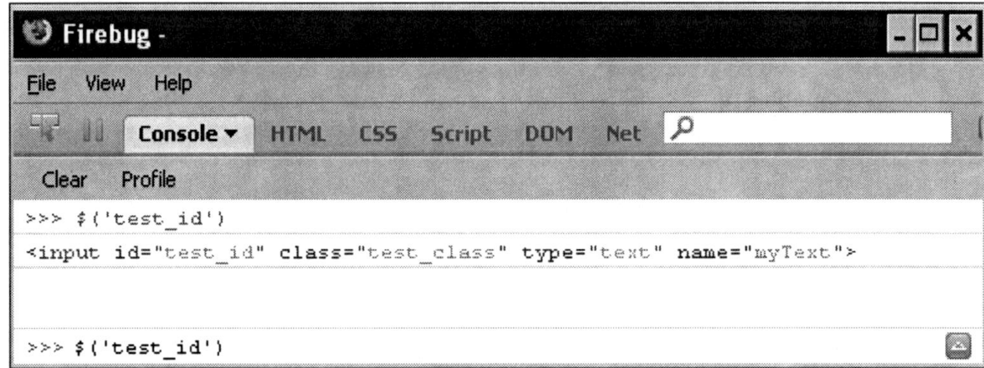

$$$(selector)

This method returns an array of elements that matches the given CSS selector.

For more information on CSS selector, refer to this link `http://www.w3.org/TR/css3-selectors`.

The following HTML code snippet has four `<input>` HTML elements in its DOM and we'll select all four of them using the `$$(selector)` method:

```
<html>
   <body>
      <input name="myText1" type="text" class="test_class" >
      <input name="myText2" type="text" class="test_class" >
      <input name="myText3" type="text" class="test_class" >
      <input name="myText4" type="text" class="test_class" >
   </body>
</html>
```

The following screenshot shows the output that we get after executing the `$$('input')` method on the command line of Firebug:

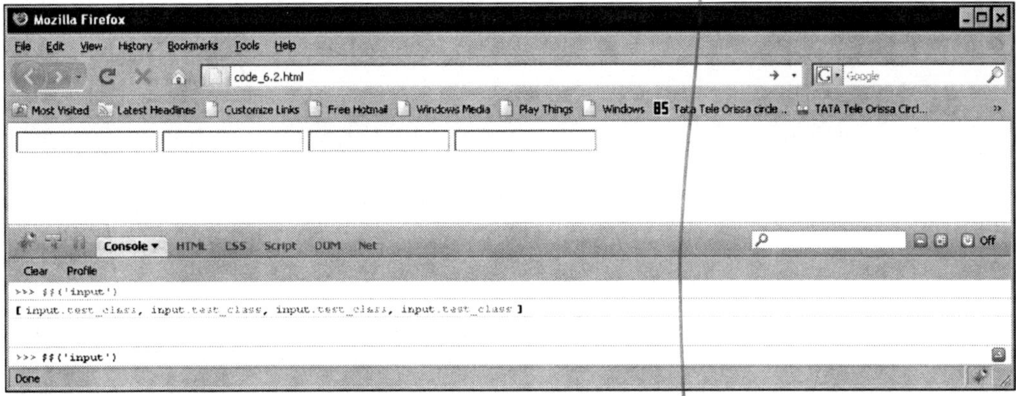

[To execute the code in Firebug's single line command line, make sure we uncheck the **Larger Command Line** option in the drop-down list for **Console** tab.]

$x(xpath)

This method returns an array of elements that match the given XPath expression.

[For information on **XPath** refer to `http://www.w3schools.com/xpath`]

For explaining this method we'll take the previous HTML file. Now, when we execute the following code in the multiline command line of Firebug, we will see the output in Firebug's **Console** tab:

```
var objs = $x('html/body/input')
console.log(objs[0].name)
console.log(objs[1].name)
console.log(objs[3].name)
console.log(objs[3].name)
```

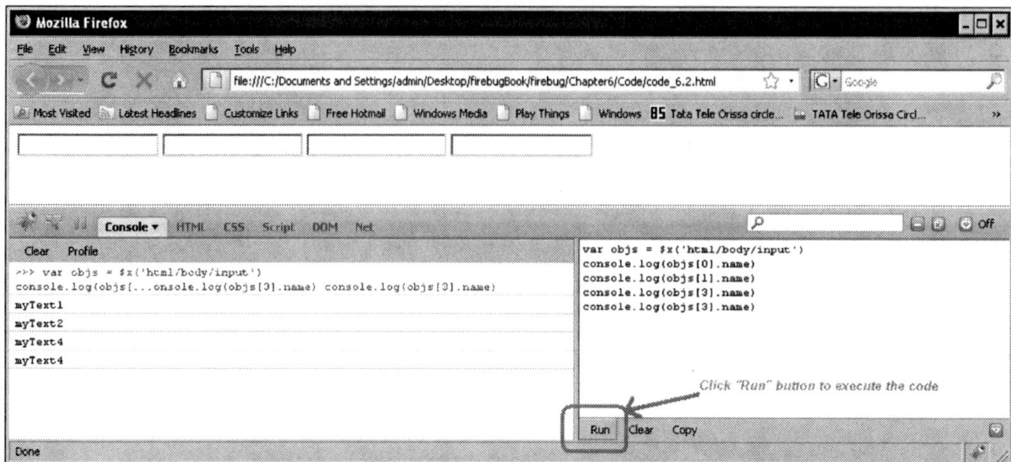

Multiline command line: For our convenience, Firebug provides a multiline command line editor. This is a mini text editor where we can type multiple lines of JavaScript or even a full JavaScript program, and can execute those lines on the fly. We can open the multiline command line editor by clicking on a red color icon on the bottom-right-hand side in the **Console** tab.

dir(object)

This method prints an interactive listing of all the properties of the object. This looks identical to the view that we would see in the **DOM** tab.

Let's consider the same HTML code snippet that we used for the `$$(selector)` method. If we execute the following code on the command line of Firebug, then we'll get the output shown in next screenshot:

```
var objs = $x('html/body/input')
dir(objs)
```

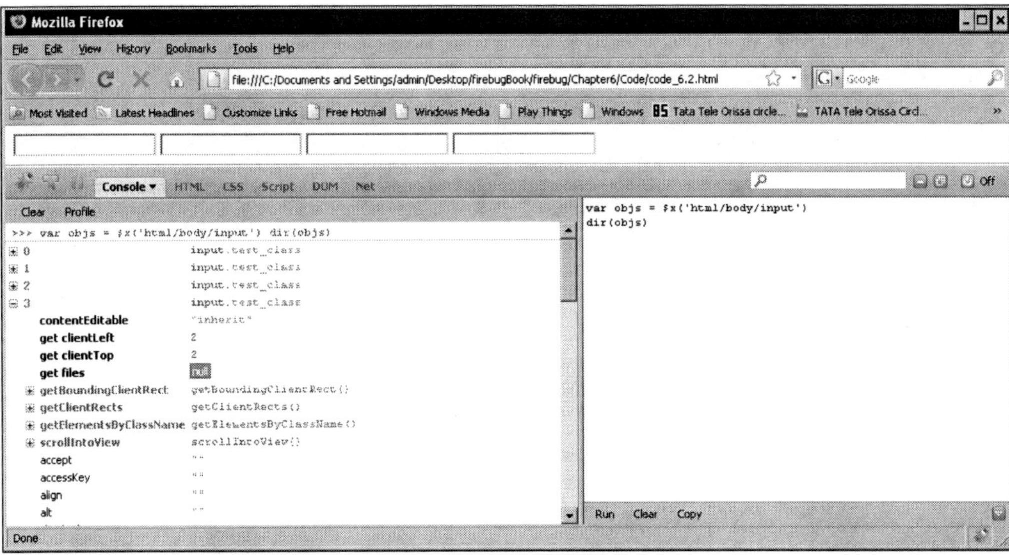

dirxml(node)

This method prints the XML source tree of an HTML or XML element. This looks identical to the view that we would see in the **HTML** tab. We can click on any node to inspect it in the **HTML** tab.

Consider the same HTML file and execute the following code in Firebug's command line to get the XML source tree. The next screenshot shows the output in the **Console** tab.

```
var obj = $$('body')[0]
dirxml(obj)
```

We can pass any node to this method by selecting it using the **$(id)** method, or any other method similar to this which returns a single node.

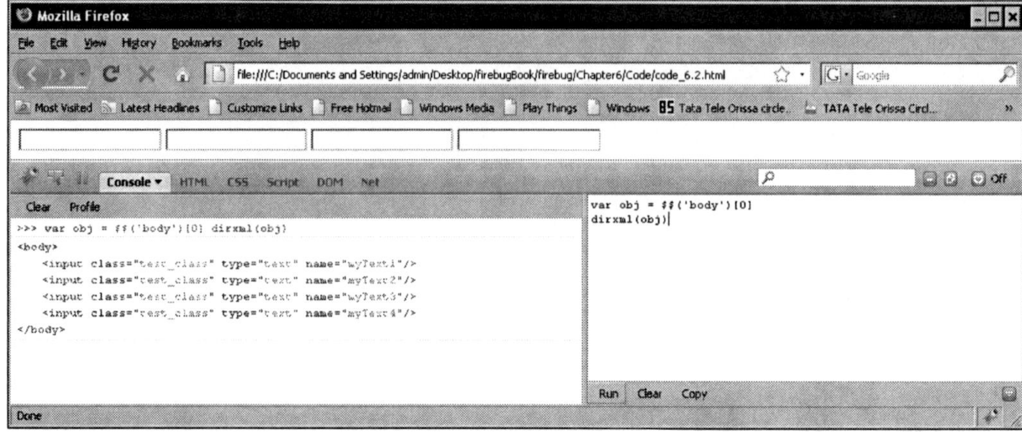

By default, command line expressions are relative to the top-level window of the page. `cd()` method, which allows us to use the window of a frame in the page instead.

clear()

This method clears the console. The functionality provided by the `clear()` method can also be achieved by clicking on the **Clear** button, which can be found in the top-left corner under the **Console** tab.

inspect(object[, tabName])

This method allows us to inspect an object in the most suitable tab, or the tab identified by the optional argument `tabName`.

The available tab names are HTML, CSS, SCRIPT, and DOM.

Now, type the following code in the command line of Firebug against the opened HTML document that we are using. The output will be seen in the **HTML** tab, as shown in the next screenshot.

```
inspect($$('input')[0],'html')
```

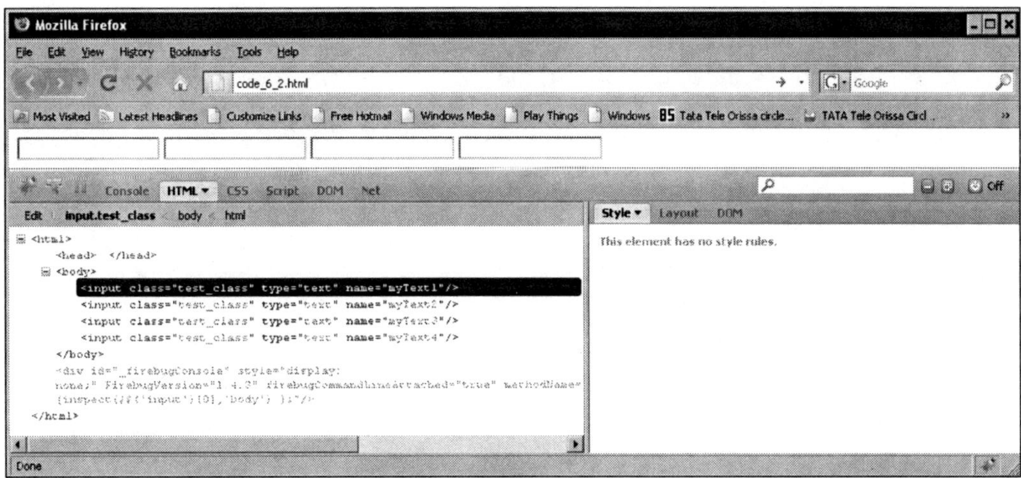

keys(object)

This method returns an array containing the names of all the properties of the object.

Executing the following code in the same HTML file that we are using shows all the attributes, properties, functions, and constant of first input tag:

```
keys($$('input')[0])
```

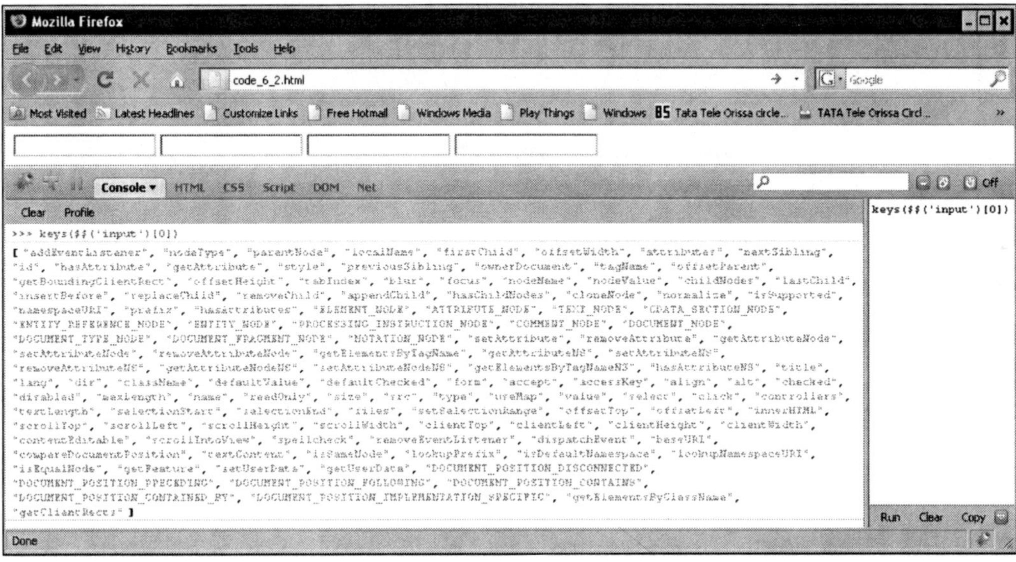

values(object)

This method returns an array containing the values of all properties of the object.

Executing the following code would show the values of properties for first input tag in DOM:

```
values($$('input')[0])
```

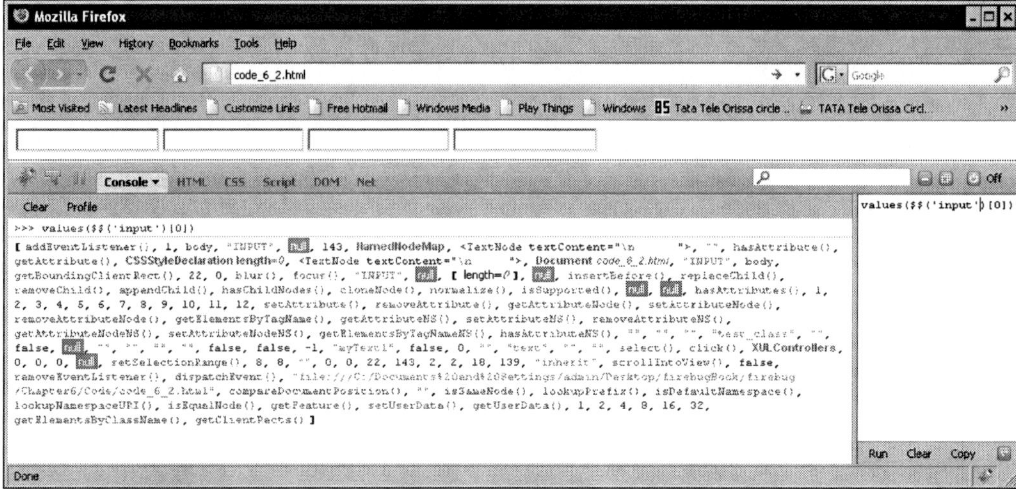

debug(fn) and undebug(fn)

These methods add or remove a breakpoint on the first line of a function.

We will learn these methods in the coming section and in detail in Chapter 8, *AJAX Development*.

monitor(functionName) and unmonitor(functionName)

These methods are used to turn on/off logging for all calls to a function.

Normally, to find whether a function in a JavaScript is invoked, we put an `alert()` or `console.log()` method inside that method. This is a very cumbersome process. First we have to find the method in a large JavaScript file, then we need to put alert or log methods. Next, when we find that everything is fine, we need to remove all the log statements from the code.

Firebug does this monitoring in style. To determine whether a function is invoked, we only need to know the function name. By using the `monitor()` method, we can trace how many times that function is invoked. We will get the notifications in the console, telling us whether the function that we monitored is invoked. Also, it will give us a link that is pointing the function in script.

Let's discuss this by creating an HTML file with the following code and open it in the Firefox browser:

```
<html>
   <script>
      function function1(){
         return true;
         //some statement
      }
      function function2(){
         return true;
         //some statement
      }
      function function3(){
         return true;
         //some statement
      }
   </script>

   <body>

       This is the body

      <input id="button1" type="button" value="Invoke function1()"
                                     onclick="function1();"/>
      <input id="button2" type="button" value="Invoke function2()"
                                     onclick="function2();"/>
      <input id="button3" type="button" value="Invoke function3()"
                                     onclick="function3();"/>
   </body>
</html>
```

Now, on the command line, type the following code and execute it:

```
monitor(function1);
```

Click the button **Invoke function1()** of the document. We will see that whenever a call is made to `function1()`, Firebug shows its log on the **Console** tab. If we click on the link to `function1()` on the **Console** tab, then it will take us to the exact line number where the code for `function1()` is written.

The following code will *unmonitor* the `function1()`:

```
unmonitor(function1)
```

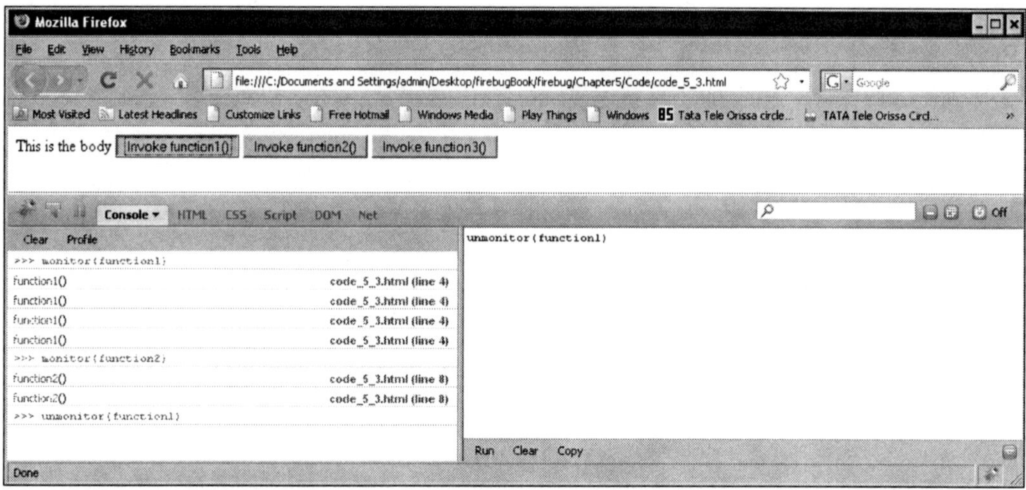

monitorEvents(object[, types])

This method turns on logging for all events dispatched to an object. The optional argument types may specify a specific family of events to log. The most commonly used values for types are mouse and key.

The full list of available types include—composition, context menu, drag, focus, form, key, load, mouse, mutation, paint, scroll, text, ui, and xul.

unmonitorEvents(object[, types])

This turns off logging for all events dispatched to an object.

Monitoring and unmonitoring events is the same as logging events, which we have already discussed in previous chapters.

Let's consider the previous HTML file that we used for monitoring and unmonitoring methods. Execute the following code in the command line and click on the first button:

```
monitorEvents($("button1"))
```

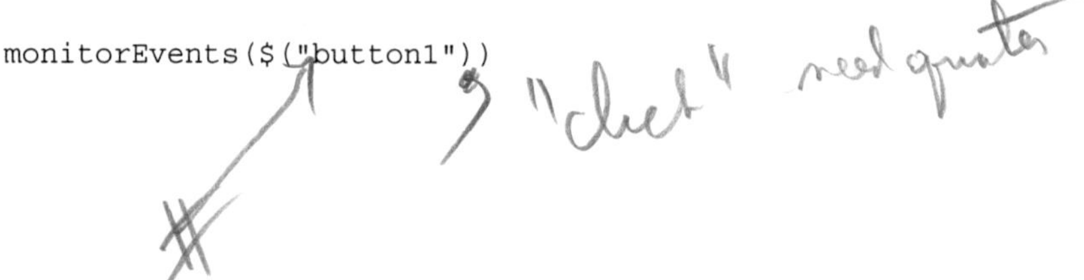

The following screenshot shows the monitoring of events:

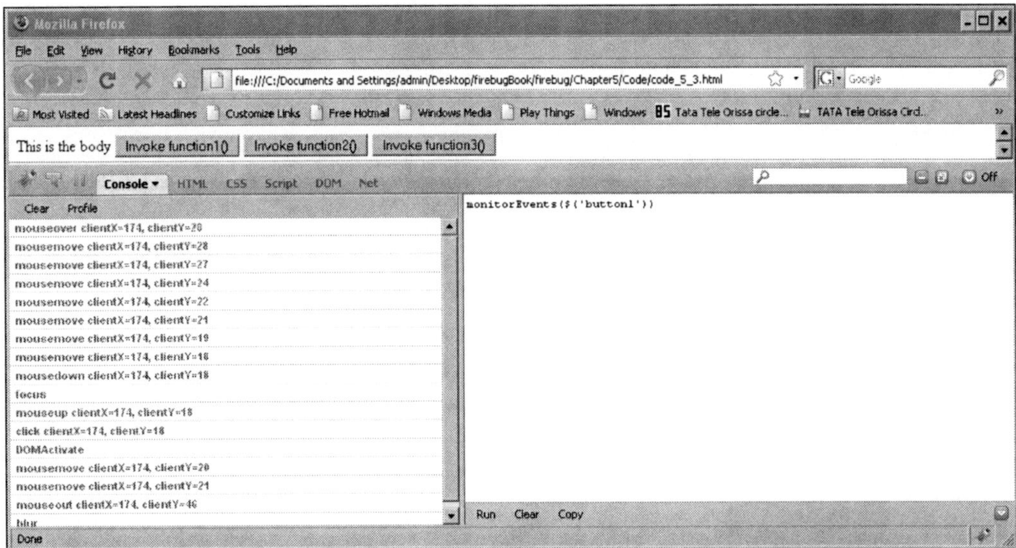

profile([title]) and profileEnd()

This turns on/off the JavaScript profiler. The optional argument `title` would contain the text to be printed in the header of the profile report.

Here are three ways to start the JavaScript profiler in Firebug:

- By clicking the **Profile** button under the **Console** tab
- By using `console.profile("Profiler Title")` from JavaScript code
- By using `profile("Profiler Title")` from the command line

To view statistics generated by the profiler, type the following HTML code, save it as an HTML file, and open it in the browser. Press *F12* to open Firebug and click on the **Start** button.

```
<html>
<head>
<title>Firebug</title>
<script>
function bar(){
    console.profile('Measuring time');
    foo();
    console.profileEnd();
}
```

```
function foo(){
    loop(1000);
    loop(100000);
    loop(10000);
}
function loop(count){
    for(var i=0;i<count;i++){}
}
</script>
</head>
<body>
    Click this button to profile JavaScript
    <input type="button" value="Start" onclick="bar();"/>
</body>
</html>
```

The following screenshot shows the statistics generated by the profiler:

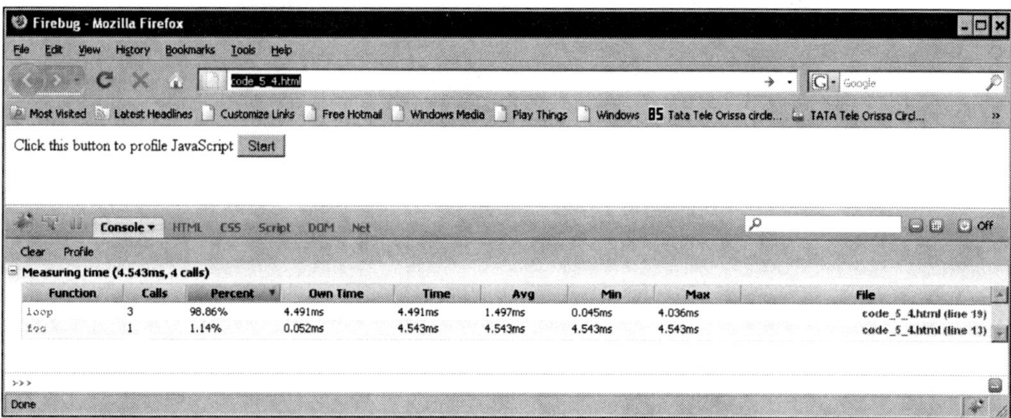

Columns and description of the profiler

- **Function**: This column shows the name of each function.
- **Call**: This shows the count of how many times a particular function has been invoked. (**3** times for `loop()` in our case.)
- **Percent**: This shows the time consumption of each function as a percentage.
- **Own Time**: This shows the duration of own script in a particular function. For example, `foo()` has none of its own code. Instead, it is just calling other functions. So, its own execution time will be approximately ~0ms. If we want to see some values for that column, we add some looping in this function.

- **Time**: This shows the duration of execution from the start point of a function to the end point of a function. For example, `foo()` has no code. So, its own execution time is approx ~0ms, but we call other functions in that function. So, the total execution time of other functions is **4.491ms**. So, it shows **4.54ms** in that column, which is equal to own time taken by three `loop()` functions plus the own time of `foo()`.
- **Avg**: This shows the average execution time of a particular function. If we are calling a function only once, we won't see the difference. But if the function is called more than once, the difference can be seen. The formula for calculating the average is:

  Avg = Own time / Calls
- **Min and Max columns**: This shows the minimum execution time of a particular function. In our example, we call `loop()` three times. When we passed `1000` as a parameter, it probably took only a few millisecond (let's say **0.045ms**) and when, we passed `100000` to that function, it took much longer than the first time (say **4.036ms**). So, in that case, **0.045ms** will be shown in **Min** column and **4.036ms** will be shown in **Max** column.
- **File**: This shows the filename of the file with the line number where the function is located.

The console API

Firebug adds a global variable named "console" to all web pages loaded in Firefox. This object contains many methods that allow us to write to the Firebug console to expose information that is flowing through our scripts.

console.log(object[, object, ...])

This method writes a message to the console. We may pass as many arguments as we like, and they will all be joined together in a space-delimited line.

The first argument to log may be a string containing `printf`-like string substitution patterns. For example:

```
console.log("The %s jumped over %d tall buildings", animal, count);
```

The previous example can be re-written without string substitution to achieve the same result:

```
console.log("The", animal, "jumped over", count, "tall buildings");
```

These two techniques can be combined. If we use string substitution but provide more arguments than there are in the substitution patterns, the remaining arguments will be appended in a space-delimited line, as shown in the following code:

```
console.log("I am %s and I have:", myName, thing1, thing2, thing3);
```

If objects are logged, they will be written not as static text, but as interactive hyperlinks that can be clicked to inspect the object in Firebug's HTML, CSS, Script, or DOM tabs. We may also use the `%o` pattern to substitute a hyperlink in a string.

Here is the complete set of patterns that we may use for string substitution:

String	Substitution patterns
%s	String
%d, %i	Integer (numeric formatting is not yet supported)
%f	Floating point number (numeric formatting is not yet supported)
%o	Object hyperlink

console.debug(object[, object, ...])

This method writes a message to the console, including a hyperlink to the line where it is called.

console.info(object[, object, ...])

This method writes a message to the console with the visual *info* icon, color coding, and a hyperlink to the line where it is called.

console.warn(object[, object, ...])

This method writes a message to the console with the visual *warning* icon, color coding, and a hyperlink to the line where it is called.

console.error(object[, object, ...])

This method writes a message to the console, with the visual *error* icon, color coding, along with a hyperlink to the line where it was called.

console.assert(expression[, object, ...])

This method tests whether an expression is true. If not, it will write a message to the console and throw an exception.

console.dir(object)

This method prints an interactive listing of all the properties of the object. This looks identical to the view that we would see in the **DOM** tab.

console.dirxml(node)

This method prints the XML source tree of an HTML or XML element. This looks identical to the view that we would see in the **HTML** tab. We can click on any node to inspect it in the **HTML** tab.

console.trace()

This method prints an interactive stack trace of JavaScript execution at the point where it is called.

The stack trace details the functions on the stack, as well as the values that were passed as arguments to each function. We can click each function to take us to its source in the **Script** tab, and click each argument value to inspect it in the **DOM** or **HTML** tab.

console.group(object[, object, ...])

This method writes a message to the console and opens a nested block to indent all future messages sent to the console. Call `console.groupEnd()` to close the block.

console.groupCollapsed(object[, object, ...])

This method works just like `console.group()`, but the block is initially collapsed.

console.groupEnd()

This method closes the most recently opened block created by a call to `console.group()` or `console.groupEnd()`.

console.time(name)

This method creates a new timer under the given name. Call `console.timeEnd(name)` with the same name to stop the timer and print the time elapsed.

console.timeEnd(name)

This method stops a timer created by a call to `console.time(name)` and writes the time elapsed.

console.profile([title])

This method turns on the JavaScript profiler. The optional argument title would contain the text to be printed in the header of the profile report.

console.profileEnd()

This method turns off the JavaScript profiler and prints its report.

console.count([title])

This method returns the number of times that the line of code is executed where count is called. The optional argument title will print a message in addition to the number of the count.

> The console is an object attached to the window object in the web page. In Firebug for Firefox the object is attached only if the console panel is enabled. In Firebug Lite, the console is attached if Lite is installed in the page.

JavaScript debugging

This section explains how to debug the JavaScript(s), internal or external, using Firebug. Before starting this section, just recall the following things from the previous chapters and sections:

- Script tab
- Command line API
- Console API

Debugging JavaScript is a very straightforward process with Mozilla Firefox and Firebug. If we are Visual Studio developers, we won't see any difference when debugging the JavaScript code with Firebug, except that the debugger runs as part of browser.

Steps to debug JavaScript code with Firebug

Type the following code in some text editor, save the file as `.html`, and open it in Firefox:

```
<html>
<head>
<title>Javascript Debugging</title>
<script>
   function populateDiv(){
   var divElement = document.getElementById('messageLabel');
   divElement.innerHTML = "Lorem ipsum dollor";
   }
</script>
</head>
<body>
   <div id="messageLabel"></div>
   <input type="button" value="Click Me!" onclick="populateDiv();" />
</body>
</html>
```

Now, open/activate Firebug on the browser by pressing the *F12* key. Click on the **Script** tab and insert a break point on line number **6**, as shown in the following screenshot:

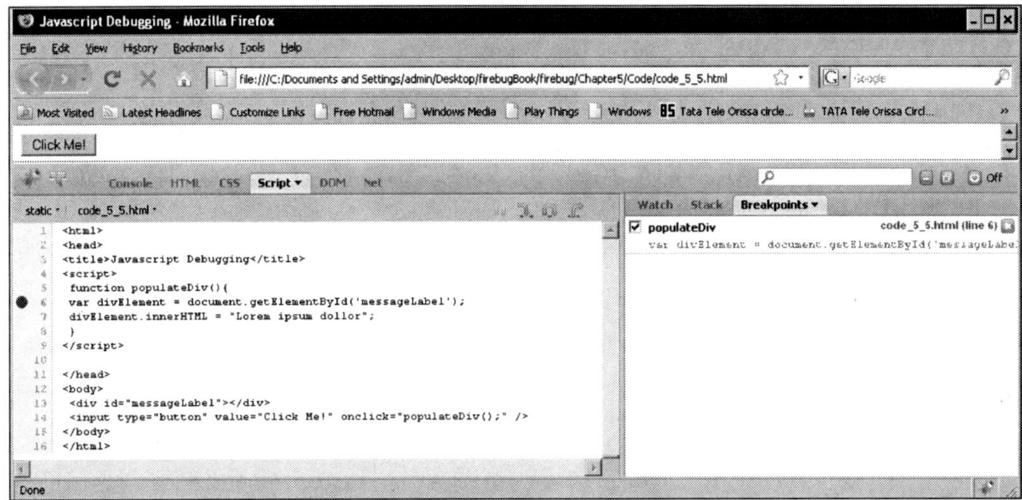

To verify that we have inserted a break point, we can see the list of breakpoints in the **Breakpoints** panel on the right-hand side of the **Script** tab.

A big red dot on line **6** shows that a breakpoint is inserted. Now, click on the **Click Me!** button to start the execution of JavaScript.

As soon as we click, the JavaScript execution will stop at the breakpoint that we set on line **6**.

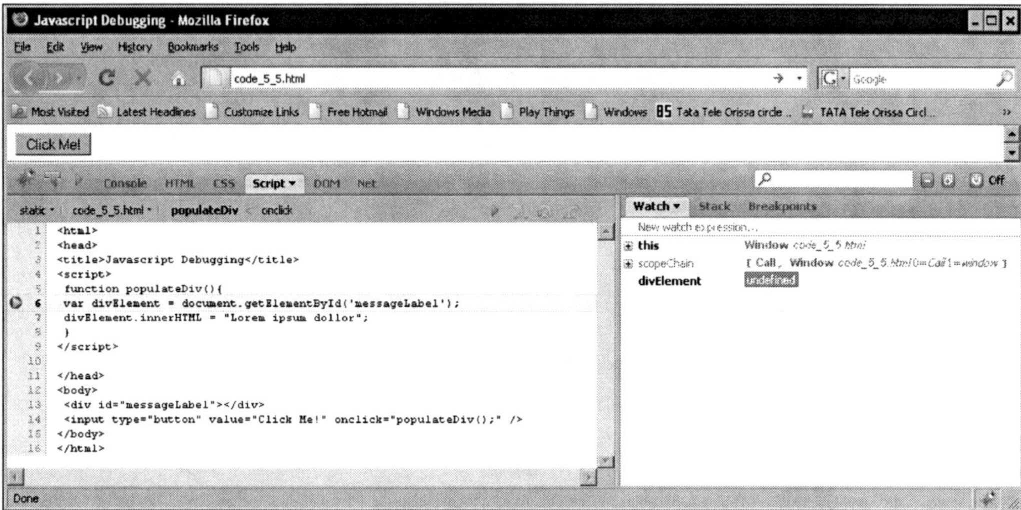

We can now step debug the JavaScript by pressing one of these buttons(**Continue**, **Step Into**, **Step Over**, and **Step Out**) under the **Script** tab.

- **Continue (F8)**: Allows us to resume the script execution once it has been stopped via another breakpoint
- **Step Into (F11)**: Allows us to step into the body of another function
- **Step Over (F10)**: Allows us to step over the function call
- **Step Out**: Allows us to resume the script execution and will stop at the next breakpoint

Now, let's click on **Step Over** or press the *F10* key to execute the line 6 and move on to line 7. Notice the value of `divElement` in the **Watch** panel on the right-hand side. Before the execution of line 6 the value for the variable **divElement** was undefined, and after the execution of line 6 it is populated with an HTML `div` element. Let's look at the following screenshot:

If we want to see the stack of call and execution flow, then just click on the **Stack** tab on the right panel of **Script** tab.

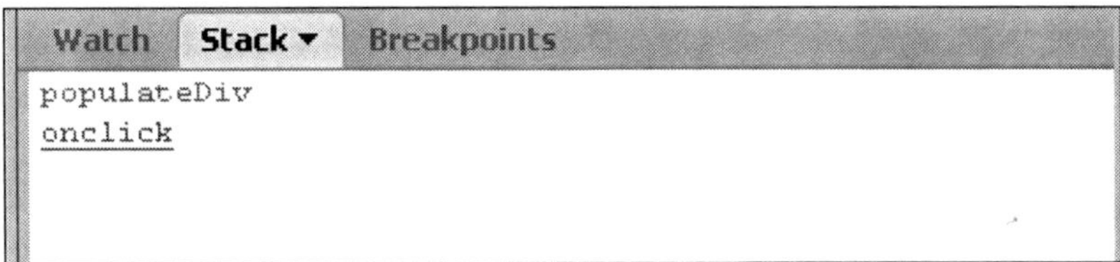

The stack for our example is:

```
populateDiv
onclick
```

The stack (in our case) shows that first we fired an `onclick` event and then the function `populateDiv` was invoked.

Now, again press *F10* or click the **Step Over** icon to take the execution on to the next line. As there is no other line in our example, the execution would stop.

> If we want to debug external JavaScripts files, then we can select that file from the drop-down under the **Script** tab. This has already been discussed in Chapter 2, *Firebug Window Overview*.

Conditional breakpoints

Sometimes we have an error inside a loop that can be really difficult to get to. We definitely don't want to put a breakpoint inside a loop and hit *F10* (**Step Over**) a few thousand times until we get to the error condition. Thankfully, Firebug provides us with a utility we can use to insert breakpoints on the basis of certain conditions.

Perhaps the most important tool for debugging inside the loops is the conditional breakpoint. We can set a condition on a breakpoint, so that it will break only when a specified condition is true.

To see conditional breakpoints in action, type the following code in some text editor, save it as an HTML file, open in Firefox, and open Firebug:

```
<html>
<head>
<title>Javascript Debugging-Conditional Breakpoint</title>
<script>
   var myArray = new Array(9);
   function printTableOf(num){
       for(i = 1; i<=9; i++){
      myArray[i] = i*num;
      document.getElementById("myId"+i).innerHtml = myArray[i];
       }
   }
</script>
</head>
<body>
   <div id="myId1"></div>
   <div id="myId2"></div>
   <div id="myId3"></div>
   <div id="myId4"></div>
   <div id="myId5"></div>
   <input type="button" value="Click Me!" onclick="printTableOf(2);"
/>
</body>
</html>
```

When we click on the **Click Me!** button, we will see the following error on Firebug's console:

The error contains very useful information that can be of great help while debugging the code. It shows line number where the error occurs, cause of error, and stack.

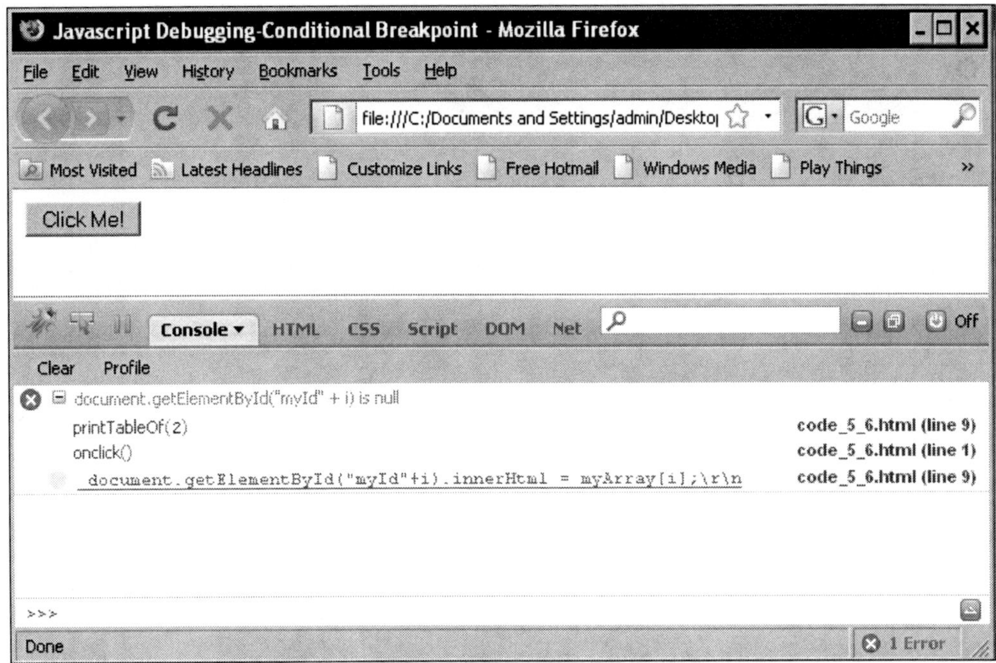

Now, refresh the page and go to the **Script** tab. Right-click on the *line number* where the error occurred. Firebug will show us a blue balloon where we can give condition, and when to pause the execution. Generally, the condition is decided by the cause of the error. In our case the cause is:

```
document.getElementById("myId"+i) is null
```

So, the condition would be:

```
document.getElementById("myId"+i) == null
```

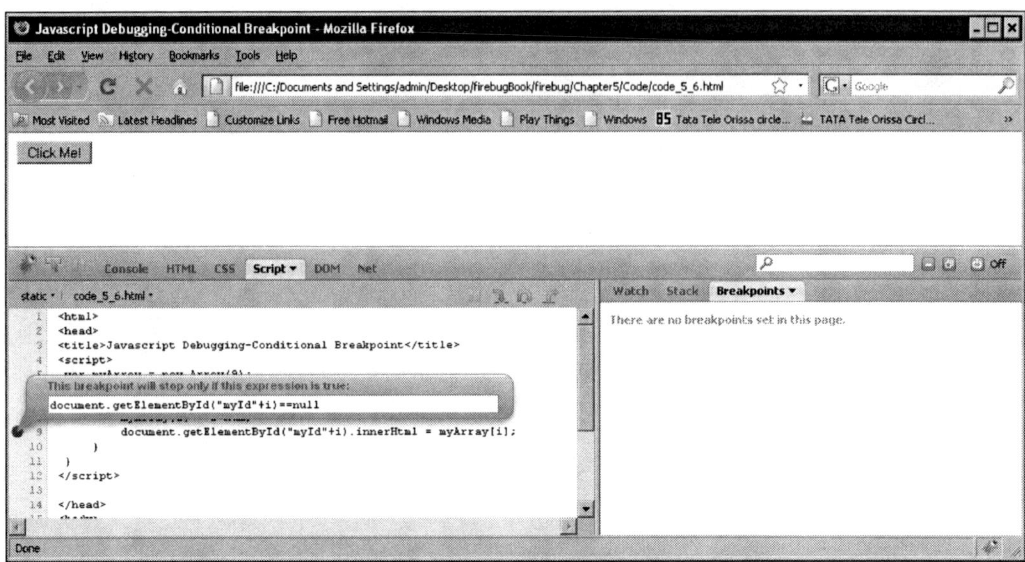

As soon as we hit *Enter,* we can see the breakpoint is inserted on the **Breakpoints** panel.

[**Removing breakpoints**: To remove breakpoints, uncheck the checkbox(es) in the **Breakpoints** panel or simply click on the big red dot.]

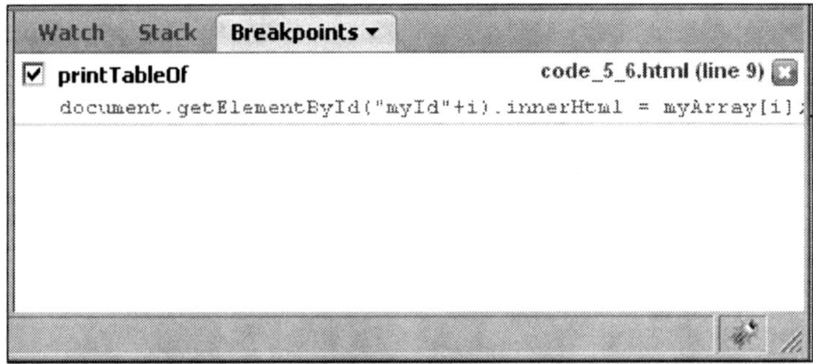

Now, let's click on the **Click Me!** to start the execution of the script. As soon as we click, we will notice that the execution of the JavaScript is paused on the line where we inserted a conditional breakpoint.

To see the current values of variables in the current scope, check the **Watch** panel. Notice that the value of variable **i=6** when the execution is paused.

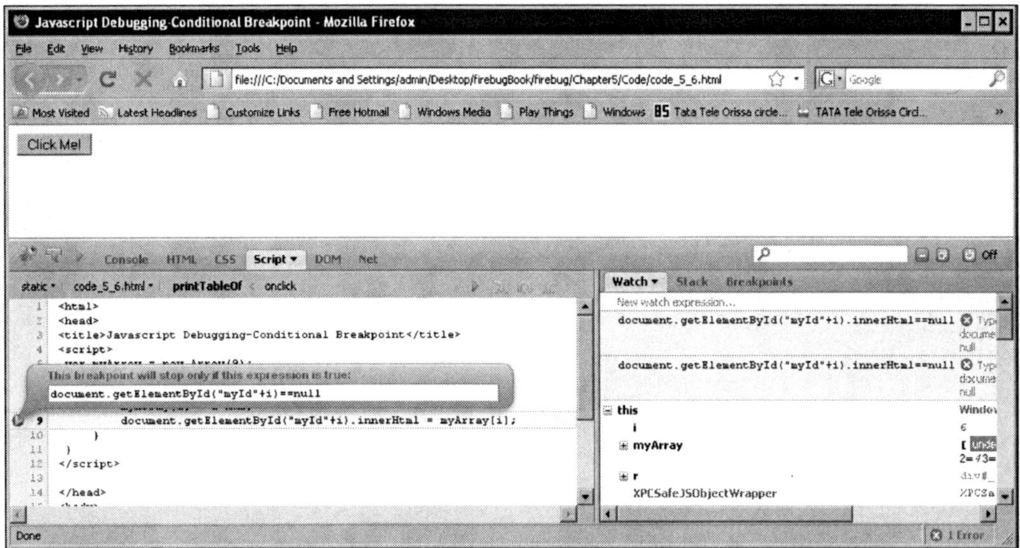

Summary

In this chapter, we discussed the command line API, the console API, and debugging JavaScript with Firebug in detail.

We discussed how to insert conditional and unconditional breakpoints, and how one to use the step debugger of Firebug to debug the script (internal or external). We also focused on watches, stack trace, and the error console, which can all be of great help in the debugging process.

You may be wondering why we haven't discussed debugging JavaScript with the console and the command line API. Well, the answer is, we'll discuss all this once again in Chapter 8. There, we'll see how one can debug an AJAX call by using the console and the command line API.

6

Knowing Your DOM

Document Object Model (**DOM**) is a cross-platform and language-independent convention for representing and interacting with objects in HTML. DOM supports navigation in any direction (such as parent and previous sibling) and allows for arbitrary modifications. Through JavaScript, one can easily traverse within the DOM. Browsers rely on layout engine (for example, Gecko, Trident/MSHTML, Presto, and so on) to parse HTML into DOM. In other words, DOM is a huge hierarchy of objects and functions, just waiting to be tickled by JavaScript. Firebug helps us find DOM objects quickly and then edit them on the fly.

We will be discussing the following features of Firebug in this chapter:

- Inspecting DOM
- Filtering properties, functions, and constants
- Modifying DOM on the fly
- JavaScript code navigation

Inspecting DOM

The DOM inspector allows for full, in-place editing of our document structure, not just text nodes. In the DOM inspector, Firebug auto completes property value when we press the *Tab* key. The following are the steps to inspect an element under the **DOM** tab:

1. Press *Ctrl+Shift+C*—the shortcut key to open Firebug in inspect mode.
2. Let's move the mouse pointer over the HTML element that we want to inspect and click on that element. The HTML script of that element will be shown in Firebug's **HTML** tab.

3. Right-clicking on the selected DOM element will open a context menu. Let's select the **Inspect in DOM Tab** option from the context menu.

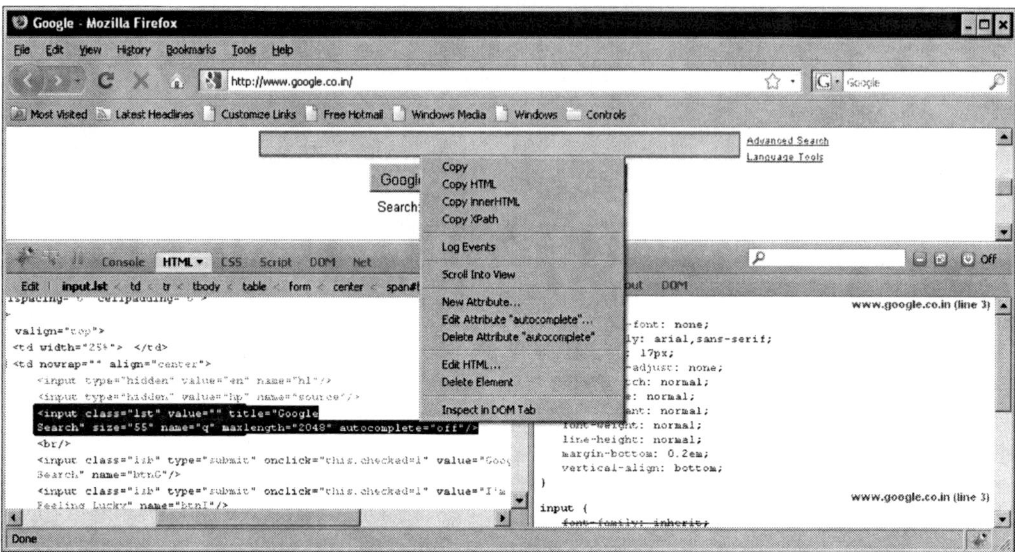

4. As soon as we do that, Firebug will take us to its **DOM** tab.

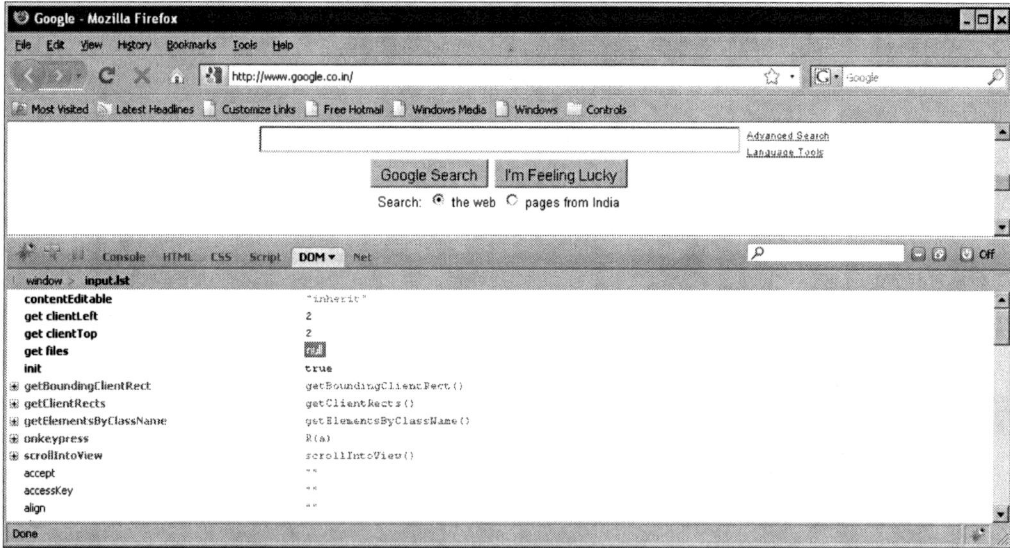

Filtering properties, functions, and constants

Many times we want to analyze whether a function written by us is associated with an HTML element. Firebug provides us an easy way to figure out whether an event, listener, function, property, or constants are associated with a particular element.

The **DOM** tab is not only a tab but also a drop-down menu.

When we click on the down arrow icon on the **DOM** tab, Firebug will show a drop-down list from which one can select the filtering options and inspect the element thoroughly. The following are the options provided by this menu:

- **Show User-defined Properties**
- **Show User-defined Functions**
- **Show DOM Properties**
- **Show DOM Functions**
- **Show DOM Constants**
- **Refresh**

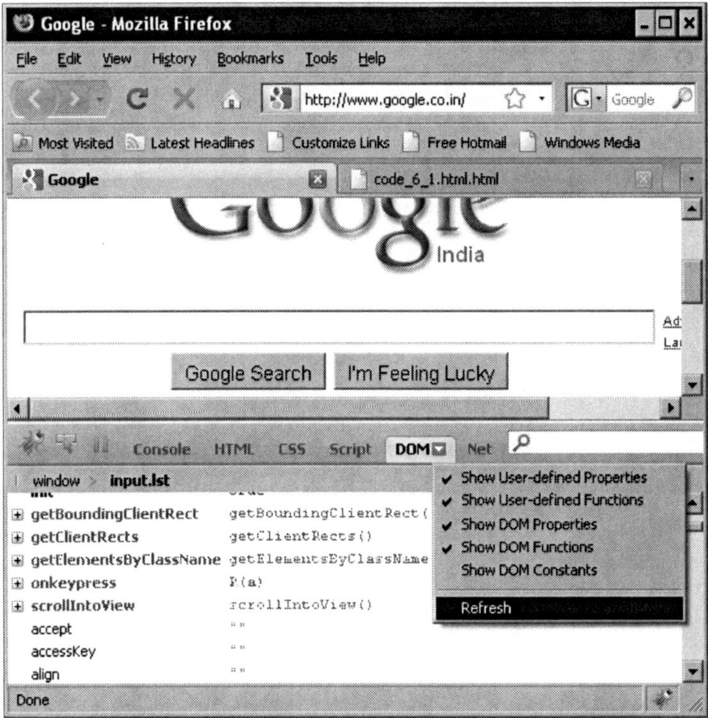

There are two kinds of objects and functions:

- Part of the standard DOM
- Part of our own JavaScript code

Firebug can notify the difference, and shows us our own script-created objects and functions in bold at the top of the list.

- The text that is **bold** and **green** is a user-defined function.
- The text that is **bold** and **black** is a user-defined property.
- The text whose size is **normal** and is **green** in color is a DOM-defined function.
- The text whose size is **normal** and is **black** in color is a DOM-defined property.
- The upper case letters (capital letters) are the DOM constants.

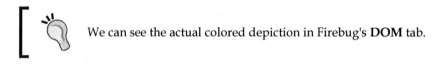

We can see the actual colored depiction in Firebug's **DOM** tab.

In the following code, the `onkeyup()` event is a user-defined function for `<input/>` and `calculatefactorial()` is a user-defined function for the current window. To test this code, let's type the code in an HTML file, open it with Firefox, and enable Firebug by pressing the *F12* key. Inspect the input element in the DOM.

```
<html>
    <head>
            <script>
                    function calculateFactorial(num,event){
                            if(event.keyCode!=13){
                                    return;
                            }
                            var fact=1;
                            for(i=1;i<=num;i++){
                                    fact*=i;
                            }
                            alert ("The Factorial of "+ num + " is: " +
                                                                    fact)
                    }
            </script>
<title>code_6_1.html.html</title>
</head>
<body><font face="monospace">
            Enter a number to calculate its factorial
```

```
        <input type = "text" name="searchBox" onkeyup="calculateFact
orial(this.value,event)"/>
</font>
</body>
</html>
```

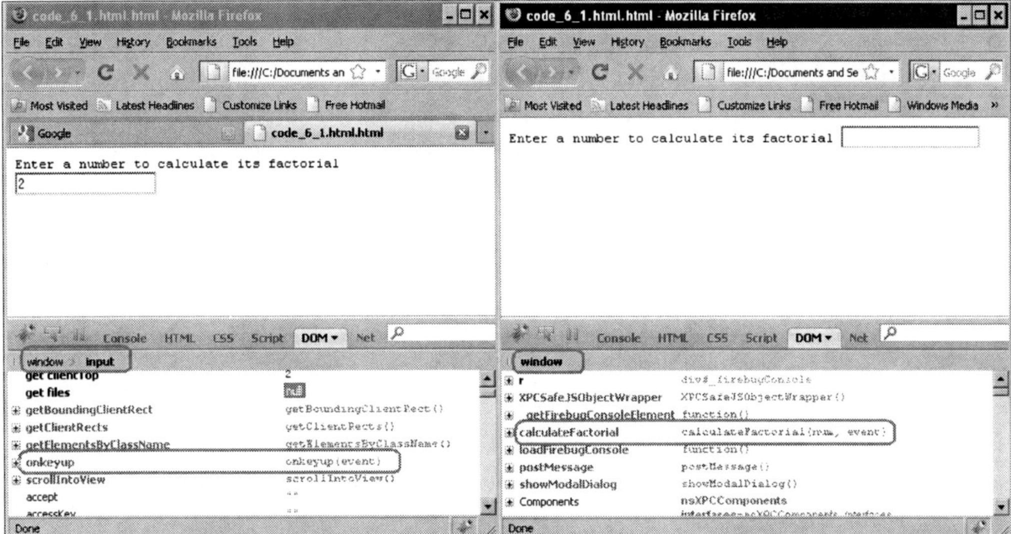

Intuitive DOM element summaries

There are many different kinds of DOM and JavaScript objects, and Firebug does its best to visually distinguish each, while providing as much information as possible. When appropriate, objects include brief summaries of their contents so that we can see what's there without having to click. Objects are color coded so that HTML elements, numbers, strings, functions, arrays, objects, and nulls are all easy to distinguish.

Modifying DOM on the fly

There are lots of great features of Firebug, one of them being editing the DOM element's properties and constants on the fly.

It's no fun to just look at the DOM; many times we want to change it. The reason for changing it could be related to debugging JavaScript. Consider a scenario where we have an `<input/>` element in our DOM whose `disabled` attribute is set to `true` (that is, the input box is locked and no event would be fired for that element). Now, we have written a JavaScript code that expects the `<input/>` element is not disabled. Firebug notifies us on the error console that this particular element is disabled and access to the element is denied. What will we do here?

We can edit our source code and reload the page to test the JavaScript code or inspect the `<input/>` element by double-clicking the white space of the row in the tree where the `disable` attribute is written. Firebug is smart enough to toggle between `true` and `false`. Therefore, if the value for `disable` is `true`, Firebug will automatically make it `false`.

If the property or constant value is string/integer/decimal type (that is, non-Boolean) then a little editor will appear that will let us change the value of the variable in question.

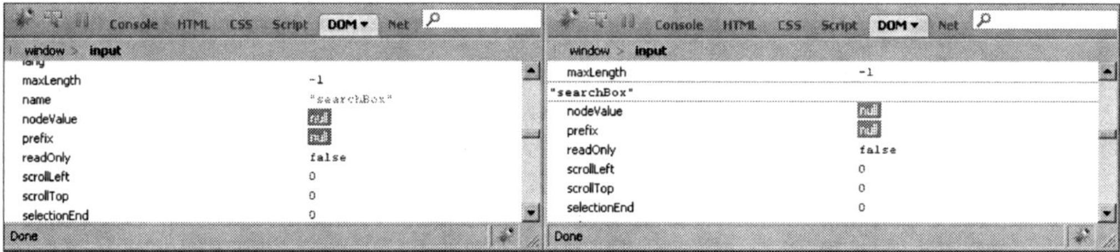

Never forget

The DOM editor is a miniature JavaScript command line. This means we can write any JavaScript expression we want. When we press *Enter*, the expression will be evaluated and the result will be assigned to the variable.

Auto-complete

Editing the DOM is a lot easier with auto-complete. Using the *Tab* key we can complete the name of object properties. Keep hitting it to cycle through the complete set of possibilities, and use *Shift+Tab* to go backwards.

As the mini editor on the **DOM** tab is a JavaScript command line, we can always enjoy the auto-complete feature while editing the values in the **DOM** tab. Auto-complete works like a charm at many levels. We can start pressing the *Tab* key before we type anything to cycle through global variables. We can press the *Tab* key after typing `document.b` to cycle through all properties that start with `b`. We can even press the *Tab* key after a complex expression such as `document.getElementsByTagName('a')[0]` to see all properties of the first link in the document.

Sometimes while editing a value, we may realize that it is not supposed to be edited. In this case simply use the *Esc* key to cancel editing.

Losing the starting element

Some of the properties of the DOM tree are expandable. We can see a **+** symbol next to some properties. If we click on the **+** (expandable column) of the explorer, Firebug will expand the object within the current view, but if we want to give an object the full view, just click the link (that appears in the right column) to the object.

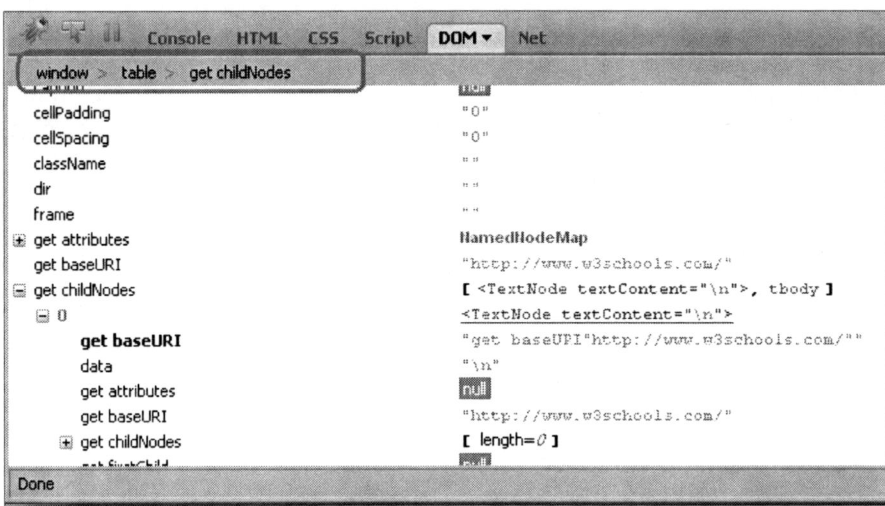

Each time we click an object, Firebug will append to the path in the toolbar. That shows us the breadcrumb trail of properties that were accessed on the way to locating that object. We can click any part of the path to jump back to it.

Adding/removing the DOM elements' attributes

We can add or remove the attributes (and their values) of an element on the fly. And for doing this we don't need to dig in the **DOM** tab. Adding and removing the attributes of any element in the DOM is very simple. Let's see an example of how to add/remove the elements' attributes.

Here we used `http://www.google.com` as a sample to discuss adding and removing attributes.

Removing attributes

To remove attributes from a particular DOM element, just follow these steps:

1. First, let's open Firebug in inspect mode by pressing *Ctrl+Shift+C*, and then select the element whose attributes are to be altered. (In our case we will choose the big input box of Google.)

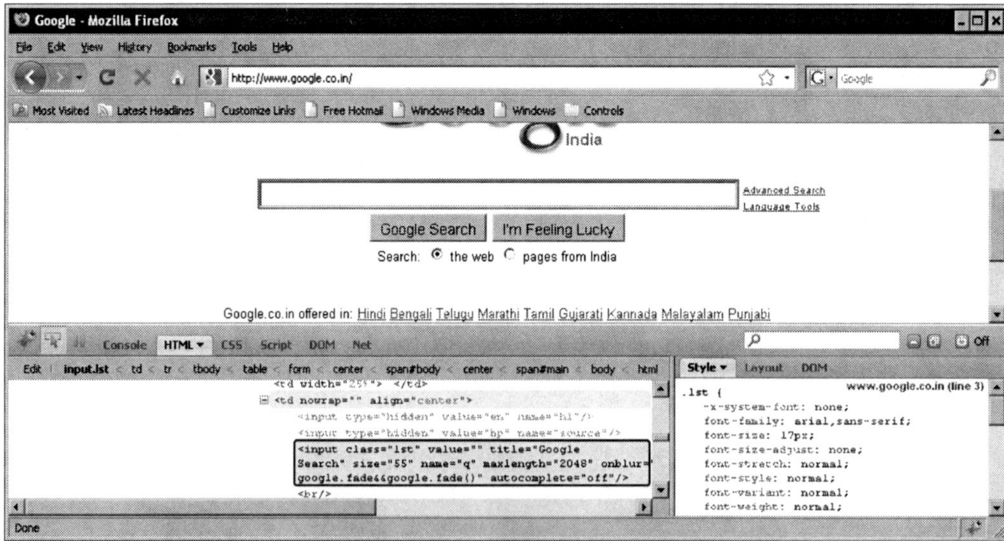

2. Let's drag our mouse pointer over the selected element in the **HTML** tab and click on the attribute that we want to remove. As soon as we do that, a mini text editor will pop up.

3. Now we can remove the attribute by pressing *Delete* or the *Backspace* key followed by the *Enter* key.

If at any point we don't want to remove/modify the attribute, we can always press the *Esc* key to cancel modifications.

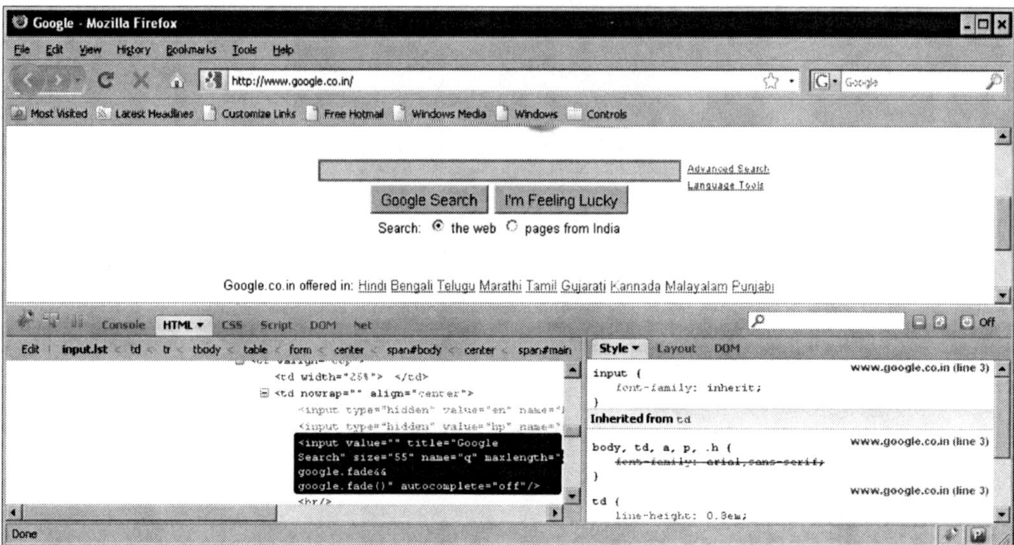

Adding attributes

Adding new attributes to any DOM element is very simple. To add attributes from a particular DOM element, just follow these steps:

1. We need to open Firebug in inspect mode and choose the element from DOM.
2. Now, let's right-click on the selected element in the **HTML** tab.
3. When we right-click on the DOM element, a context menu will open. Let's select the **New Attribute...** option from it.

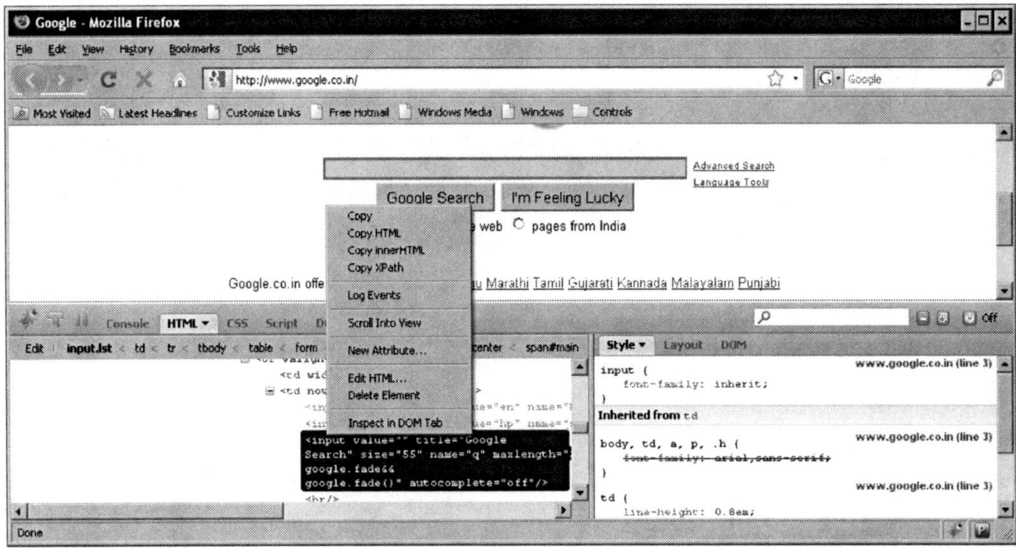

4. Again, the mini text editor will pop up. Let's start typing the attribute's name (in our case "`class`" is the attribute name).

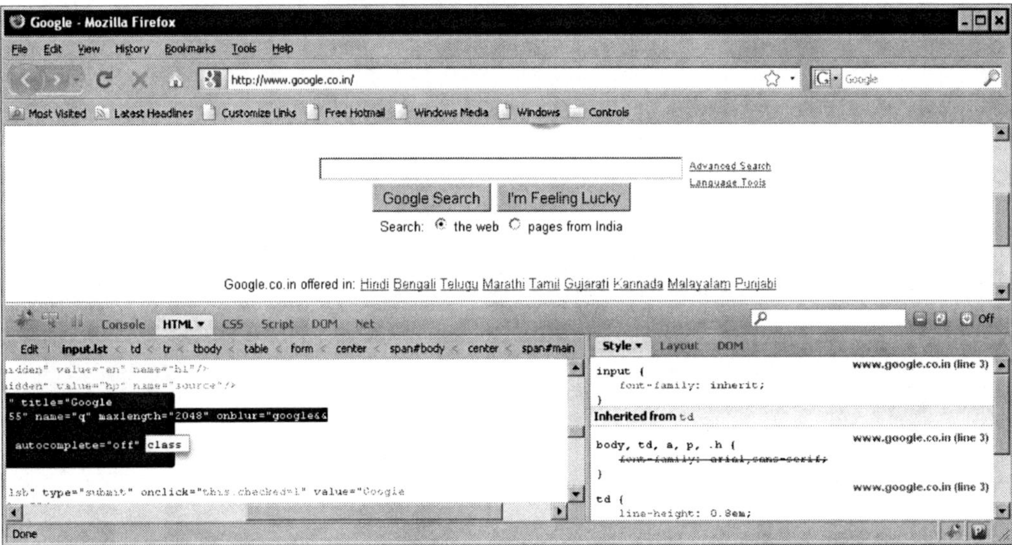

5. Press the *Tab* key to input the value of this attribute. When we press the *Tab* key, our smart Firebug automatically adds an equal symbol = between the attribute's name and value.

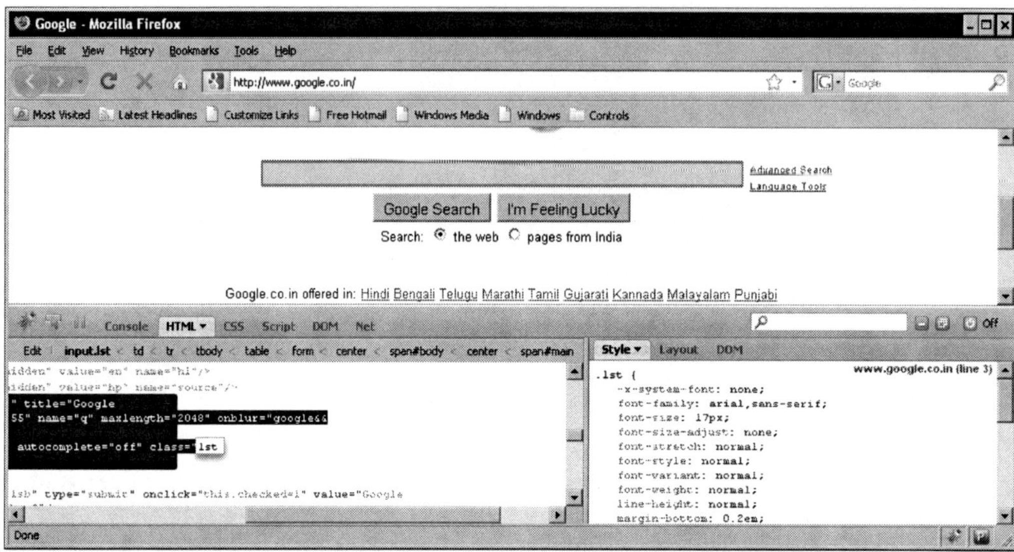

6. Now we can give value to our new attribute.

If we want to continue adding more attributes, Firebug provides a very easy way for doing this. All we need to do is press the *Tab* key when we are done with the attribute's value part.

JavaScript code navigation

The DOM tree explorer is also a great way to find JavaScript functions that we wish to debug. If we click on a function in the DOM explorer, Firebug will take us right to the **Script** tab and highlight that function.

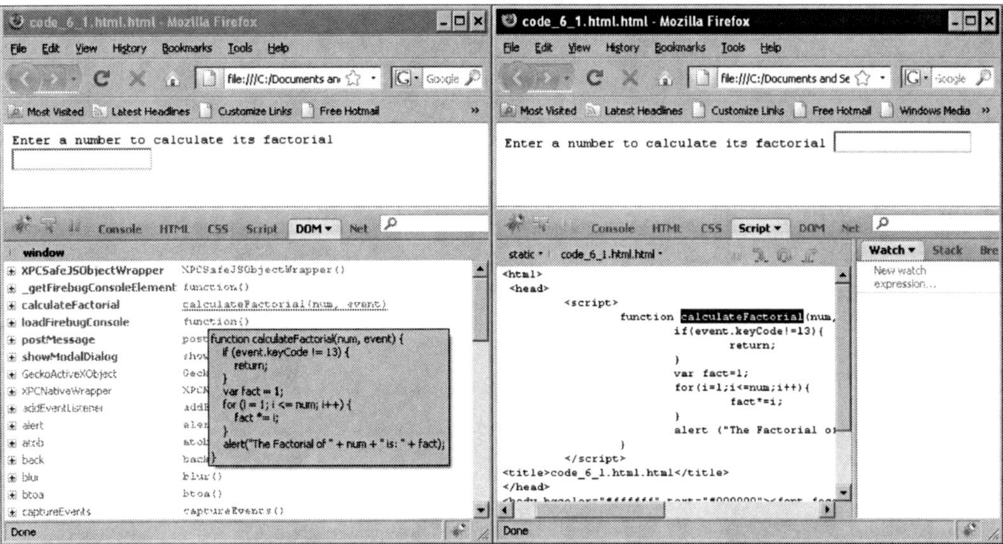

Now in **Script** tab, we can insert conditional/unconditional breakpoints in that function and debug our code.

If we move our mouse pointer over the function name on the DOM tree, then it will show a preview of the code that is written inside the definition of the function.

Summary

Let's recall what we discussed in this chapter. DOM is just a big hierarchy of objects. Objects can be HTML objects or JavaScript objects. We saw how Firebug shows the difference between user-defined and DOM-defined properties and functions. We can also filter the DOM tree by simply selecting the drop-down options from the list in the **DOM** tab.

We discussed how we can modify/edit the values of properties and constants of any DOM object. We also saw how smart Firebug is in differentiating between values of different properties based on their types, such as `String`, `Boolean`, and so on.

We also saw how Firebug helps us to easily add and remove the attributes of any particular DOM element.

7
Performance Tuning Our Web Application

This chapter explains various ways to analyze the performance of our web application on the browser. There are plenty of tools available to measure and analyze the performance of a web application on the server side; most of the databases provide tools to profile the time taken by database queries. Similarly, almost all application servers provide various statistics about the time taken to serve each request (along with a break up of the time into various components).

However, most web developers don't give much attention to the performance of the application from the browser's perspective. Not only it is important that the server serves a request in the minimum possible time, but it is also important that the response is rendered on the browser in the minimum time.

In this chapter, we will learn how to do the following things to analyze and tune the performance of our web applications:

- Network monitoring
- Breaking down various requests by type
- Examining HTTP headers
- Analyzing the browser cache
- `XMLHttpRequest` monitoring

Network monitoring

Even if the server does not take much time to process a request, a web application might appear slow to an end user because of various reasons, such as:

- Network latency
- The order in which the files are loaded
- The number of requests made to the server
- Browser caching (or the absence of it!)

Firebug's **Net** panel helps us detect such problems very easily.

The **Net** panel is set to **Disabled** by default in Firebug. In order to use it, we must first set the option to **Enabled**.

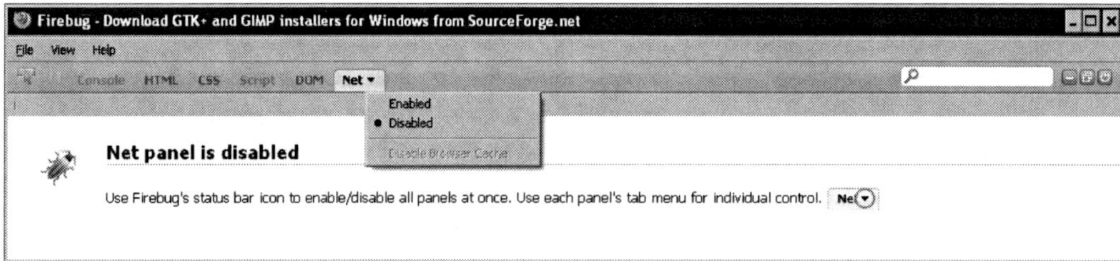

The main purpose of the **Net** panel is to monitor HTTP traffic initiated by a web page and simply present all collected and computed information to the user in a graphical and intuitive interface.

The following screenshot shows various requests made by the browser to load the homepage of the Packt website (`www.packtpub.com`):

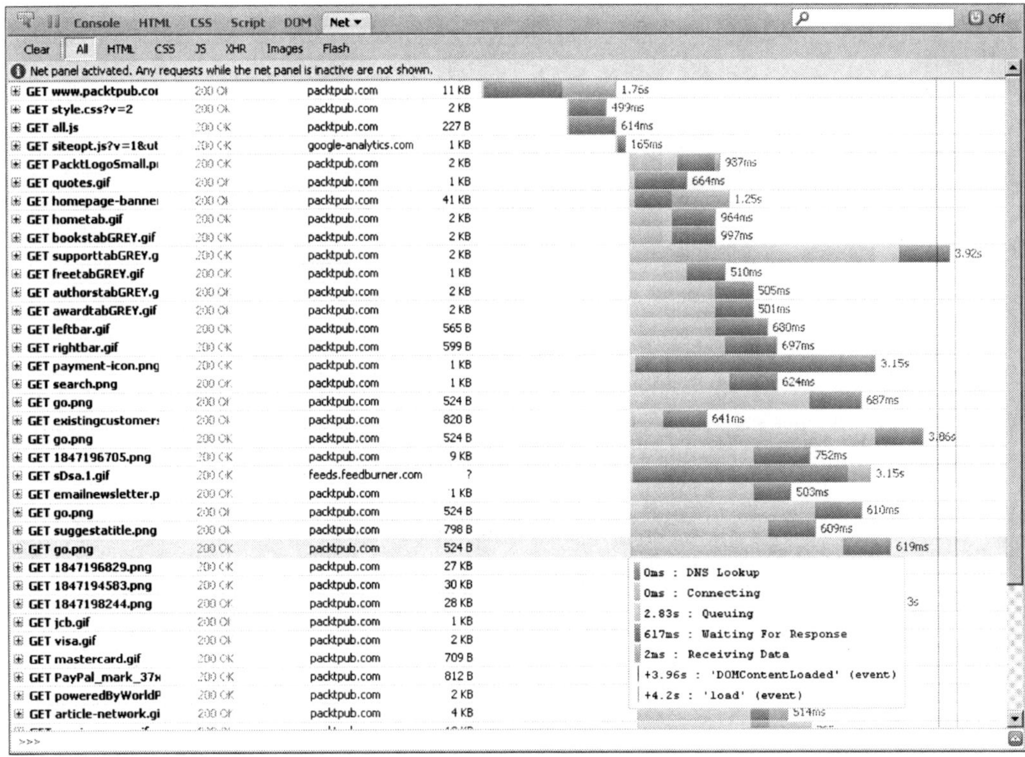

Description of information in the Net panel

Each entry/row in the **Net** panel displays basic information about the request and a graphical *timeline* that depicts load phases in time.

The files shown in the **Net** panel are sorted based on the order of how the files were loaded by Firefox.

Column name	Description
URL	The URL of the file that was loaded as part of the request. The `GET` prefix for most of the requests depicts the method of the request (`GET`, `POST`, and so on).
Status	The status of the HTTP request and the code. For example, code 200 denotes a successful HTTP request and code 304 denotes that the file was not modified since the last request (based on some caching time limit).

Column name	Description
Domain	The domain to which the request is sent. If we are loading files from other sites (for example, linking images from other sites, putting ads from an ad server), then a different Domain will be shown for that particular file/request.
Size	The size of the response data.
Timeline	The time it took to load the particular file/request. It also shows whether or not the file is loaded from the cache. The bar shows us when the file started and stopped loading relative to other files.

It is possible to hide certain columns that **Net** panel shows us by default. In order to customize the columns that we want to see in the **Net** panel, simply right-click on the table header and choose the columns that we want to see.

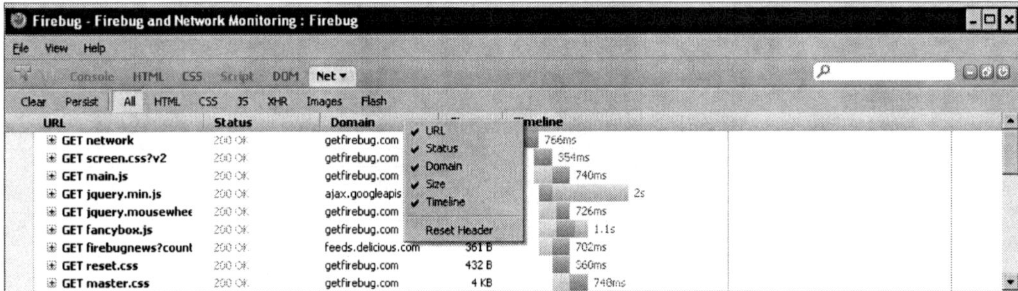

Load-time bar color significance

The different colors used in the timeline bar are significant. The following table describes what each color means in the timeline bar:

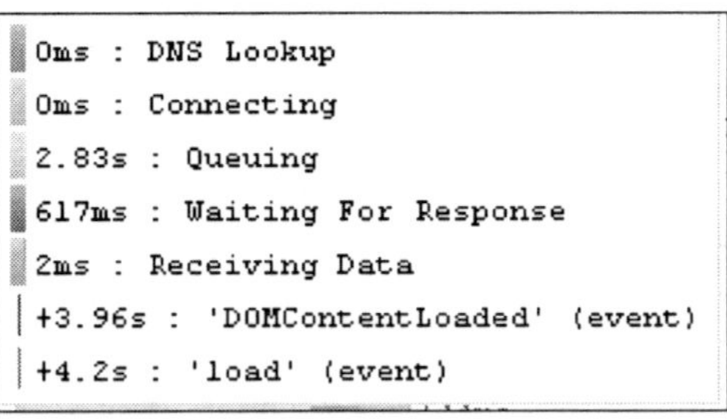

We can see the actual colored image in Firebug's **Net** panel.

Color	Description
Green	Time for DNS Lookup
Light Green	Time to connect to the server
Light Brown	Time the request had to wait in the queue.
Purple	Time waiting for a response from the server
Dark Grey	Request was sent to server, request served by the server and not from browser cache.
Light Grey	Request was sent to the server, "304 Not Modified" received from server, response loaded from the browser cache.

In order to understand information provided by the **Net** panel of Firebug, it is important to understand the various steps between requesting for a page and when the page has been fully rendered on the browser.

At a higher level, the following steps are involved in serving a "page request" at the browser end:

- Resolving DNS names
- Setting up TCP connections
- Transmitting HTTP requests
- Downloading resources
- Fetching resources from cache
- Parsing and executing scripts
- Rendering objects on the page

Browser queue wait time

There can be multiple reasons for a request to wait in the browser queue before it is sent to the server. The two most common reasons are:

- If there are multiple JavaScript files on a web page, they are loaded one after the other by the browser and not loaded simultaneously. They are loaded in the same sequence as they are present on the web page. A web developer should always consider if it is possible to convert multiple JavaScript files on a page into a single JavaScript file.
- Each browser has a limit on the number of concurrent requests that can be made to a single domain by a web page. For example, this limit is six for Firefox 3. If there are eight images on a web page that have to be loaded from the same domain, six requests will be made simultaneously, and the request for two images has to wait before a response for any of the previous two requests is received from the server.

When optimizing the performance of a web application from the browser's perspective, *browser queue wait time* is a very important consideration.

How to bypass the maximum concurrent requests limit by the browser

If, for whatever reason, a web page needs to make a lot of requests to the server to get images, CSS files, AJAX responses, and so on, then one common technique is to host the image files on a separate subdomain. For example, host all the images for the Packt site on `images.packtpub.com` instead of the `www.packtpub.com` subdomain. However, it is important to keep in mind that every subdomain that is added also requires a DNS lookup. Based on a study by Yahoo, having two to four subdomains for a site is a good compromise between parallel requests and DNS lookups.

Breaking down various requests by type

If there are a lot of requests shown on the **Net** panel and we wish to view requests only for a particular type of file, we can filter the requests based on that particular type. This also allows us to find out the total size and download time for a particular type of file.

For example, if we like to check the requests for only images, we can click the **Images** button on the toolbar to filter the requests for images.

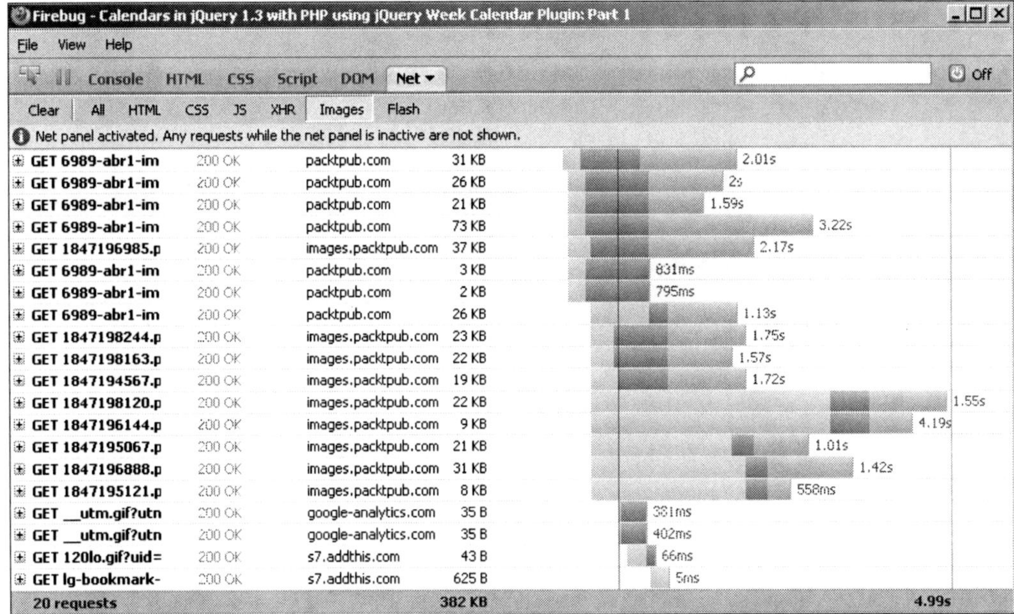

Similarly, clicking on the **CSS** button shows requests for the CSS files only.

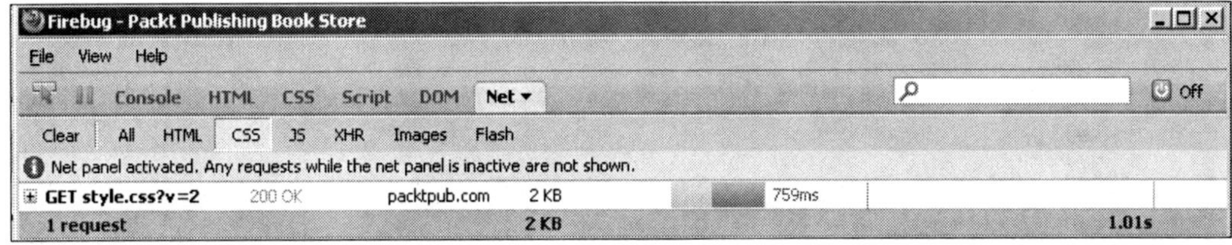

Examining HTTP headers

HTTP headers contain a wealth of interesting information, such as the MIME type of the file, the type of web server, caching directives, the cookie, and lots more. To see the HTTP headers, just click the arrow to the left of each request to expand it.

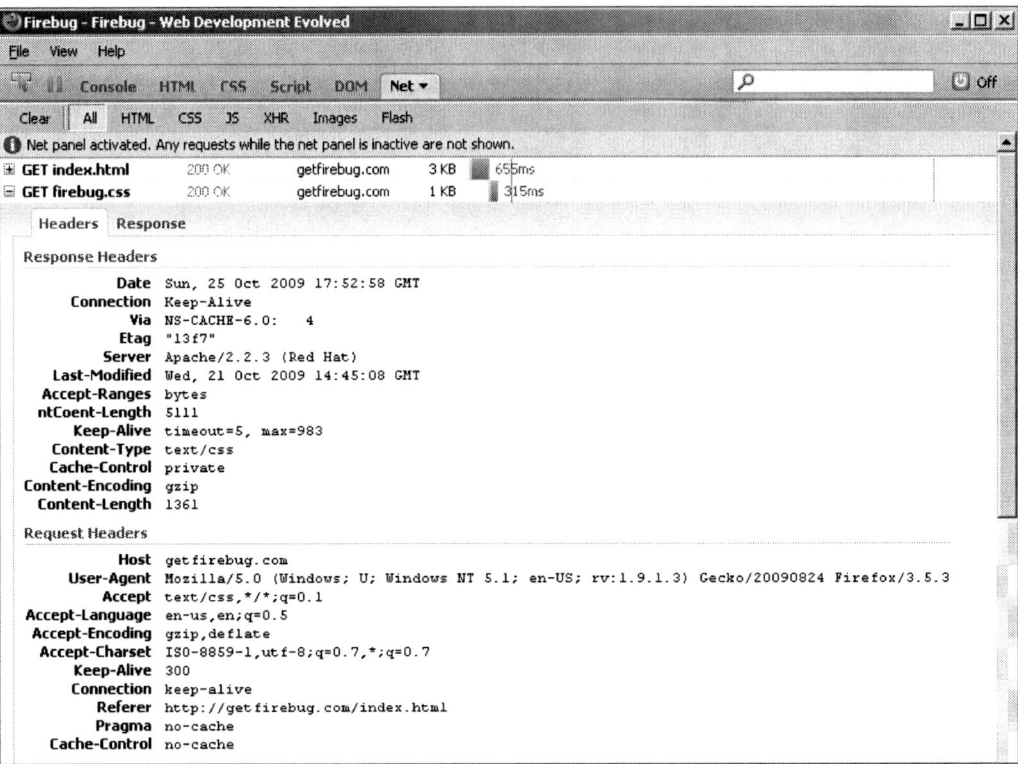

For each HTTP request, Firebug displays the following tabs when we click on the **+** button:

- **Headers**
- **Response**

In addition to the previously mentioned tabs, Firebug displays the following tabs if applicable:

- **HTML**
- **Params**
- **Cache**
- **Post**

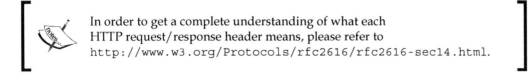

In order to get a complete understanding of what each HTTP request/response header means, please refer to `http://www.w3.org/Protocols/rfc2616/rfc2616-sec14.html`.

Analyzing the browser cache

Not all network requests are equal—some of them are loaded from the browser cache instead of the network. Firebug color code requests are served by the cache in a lighter gray shade so that we can quickly scan and see how effectively our site is using the cache to optimize page load times.

The following screenshot shows the **Net** panel view when the `http://www.getfirebug.com` page is loaded for the first time by the browser:

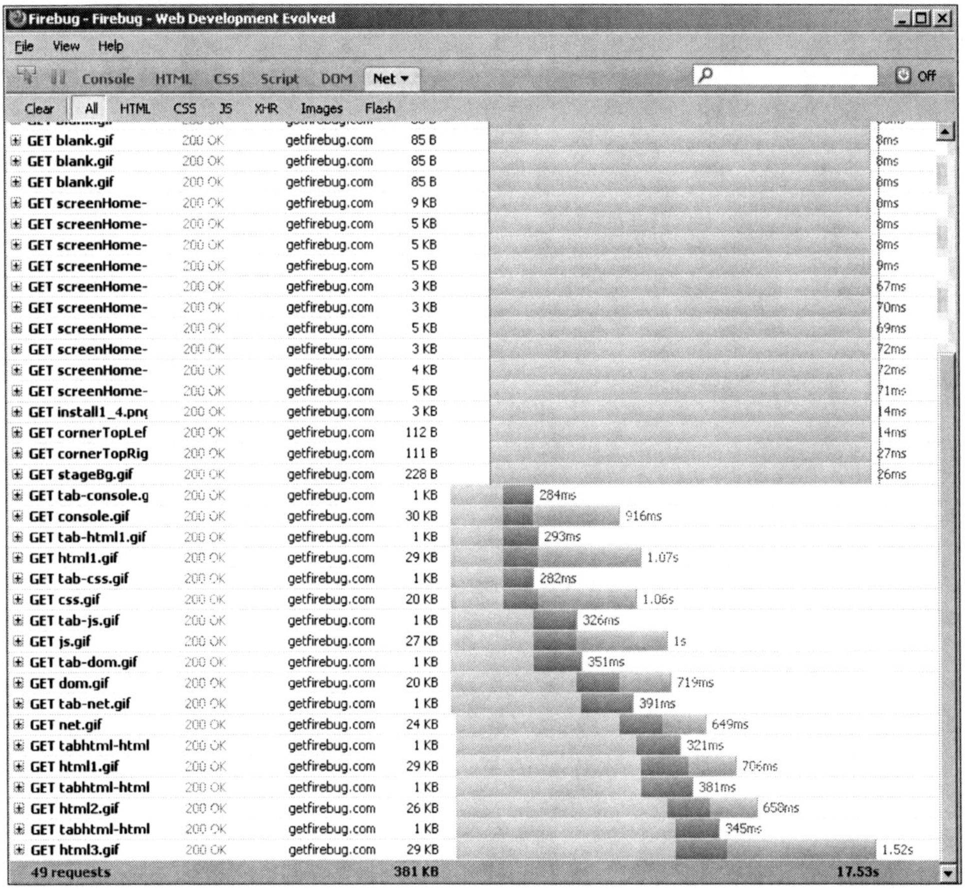

Firebug - Firebug - Web Development Evolved

File View Help

Console HTML CSS Script DOM Net ▾ Off

Clear All HTML CSS JS XHR Images Flash

Request	Status	Domain	Size	Timeline
GET blank.gif	200 OK	getfirebug.com	85 B	8ms
GET blank.gif	200 OK	getfirebug.com	85 B	8ms
GET blank.gif	200 OK	getfirebug.com	85 B	8ms
GET screenHome-	200 OK	getfirebug.com	9 KB	8ms
GET screenHome-	200 OK	getfirebug.com	5 KB	8ms
GET screenHome-	200 OK	getfirebug.com	5 KB	8ms
GET screenHome-	200 OK	getfirebug.com	5 KB	9ms
GET screenHome-	200 OK	getfirebug.com	3 KB	67ms
GET screenHome-	200 OK	getfirebug.com	3 KB	70ms
GET screenHome-	200 OK	getfirebug.com	5 KB	69ms
GET screenHome-	200 OK	getfirebug.com	3 KB	72ms
GET screenHome-	200 OK	getfirebug.com	4 KB	72ms
GET screenHome-	200 OK	getfirebug.com	5 KB	71ms
GET install1_4.pn(	200 OK	getfirebug.com	3 KB	14ms
GET cornerTopLef	200 OK	getfirebug.com	112 B	14ms
GET cornerTopRig	200 OK	getfirebug.com	111 B	27ms
GET stageBg.gif	200 OK	getfirebug.com	228 B	26ms
GET tab-console.g	200 OK	getfirebug.com	1 KB	284ms
GET console.gif	200 OK	getfirebug.com	30 KB	916ms
GET tab-html1.gif	200 OK	getfirebug.com	1 KB	293ms
GET html1.gif	200 OK	getfirebug.com	29 KB	1.07s
GET tab-css.gif	200 OK	getfirebug.com	1 KB	282ms
GET css.gif	200 OK	getfirebug.com	20 KB	1.06s
GET tab-js.gif	200 OK	getfirebug.com	1 KB	326ms
GET js.gif	200 OK	getfirebug.com	27 KB	1s
GET tab-dom.gif	200 OK	getfirebug.com	1 KB	351ms
GET dom.gif	200 OK	getfirebug.com	20 KB	719ms
GET tab-net.gif	200 OK	getfirebug.com	1 KB	391ms
GET net.gif	200 OK	getfirebug.com	24 KB	649ms
GET tabhtml-html	200 OK	getfirebug.com	1 KB	321ms
GET html1.gif	200 OK	getfirebug.com	29 KB	706ms
GET tabhtml-html	200 OK	getfirebug.com	1 KB	381ms
GET html2.gif	200 OK	getfirebug.com	26 KB	658ms
GET tabhtml-html	200 OK	getfirebug.com	1 KB	345ms
GET html3.gif	200 OK	getfirebug.com	29 KB	1.52s
49 requests			381 KB	17.53s

The following screenshot shows the **Net** panel view for subsequent requests to the `getfirebug.com` homepage. Note the difference in the number of requests made by the browser to load the same page. The difference is because of the images and CSS, along with JavaScript and some other files that are cached by the browser.

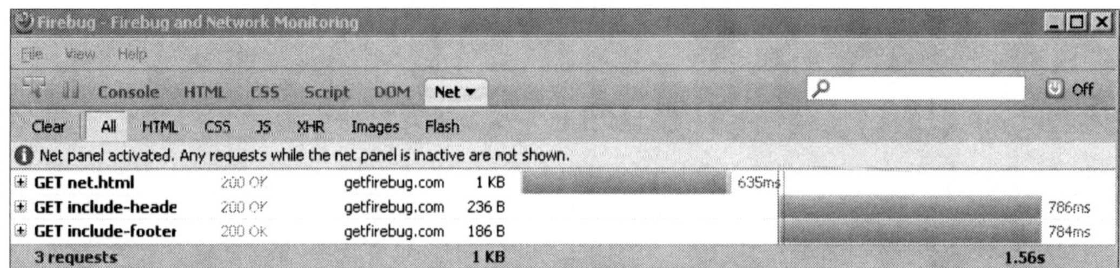

In order to dig deeper into how browser caching works, it is important to understand the following HTTP response headers:

Header name	Description
`Last-Modified`	This entity-header field indicates the date and time at which the origin server believes the variant was last modified.
`ETag`	This response-header field provides the current value of the entity tag for the requested variant.
`Expires`	This entity-header field gives the date/time after which the response is considered stale. A stale cache entry may not normally be returned by a cache (either a proxy cache or a user agent cache) unless it is first validated with the origin server (or with an intermediate cache that has a fresh copy of the entity).
`Cache-Control`	This general-header field is used to specify directives that MUST be obeyed by all caching mechanisms along the request/response chain. The directives specify behavior intended to prevent caches from adversely interfering with the request or response.

The following screenshot shows the HTTP response header for a CSS file that is loaded from the cache by the browser for rendering a page instead of fetching the file from the web server:

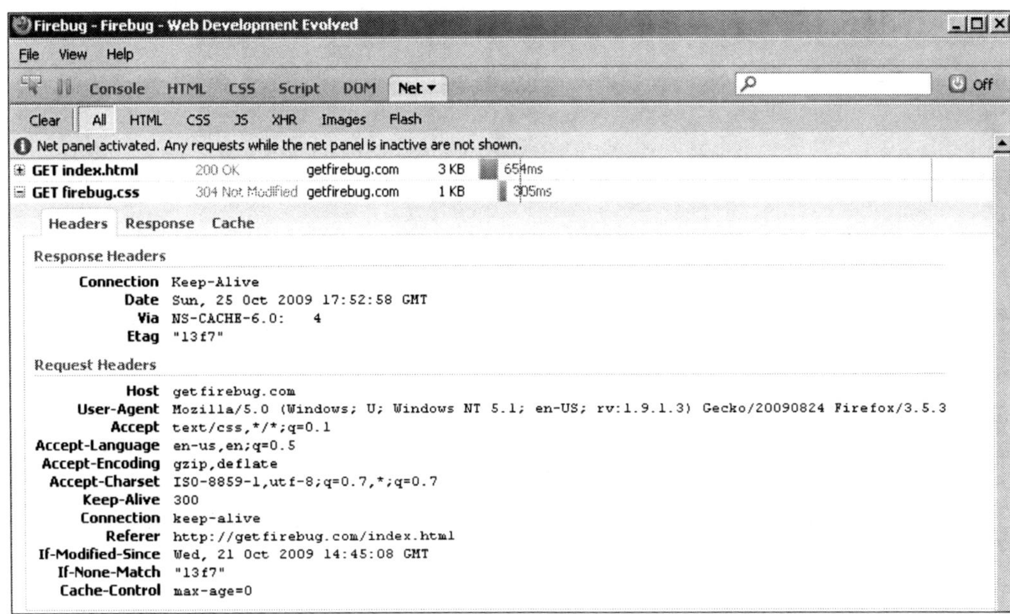

Clicking on the **Cache** tab shows various statistics related to the cache usage by the browser:

Last Modified	Mon Oct 26 2009 01:02:25 GMT+0530 (India Standard Time)
Last Fetched	Mon Oct 26 2009 01:02:25 GMT+0530 (India Standard Time)
Expires	Mon Oct 26 2009 01:02:50 GMT+0530 (India Standard Time)
Data Size	20
Fetch Count	63
Device	disk

XMLHttpRequest monitoring

Until now, we have talked about how to analyze the requests and responses that are made and received when a page is loaded by the browser. However, current web applications make a lot of asynchronous XML requests (yes, we are talking about AJAX requests). In order to view the AJAX requests that are made by a web page, take a look at Firebug's **XHR** tab.

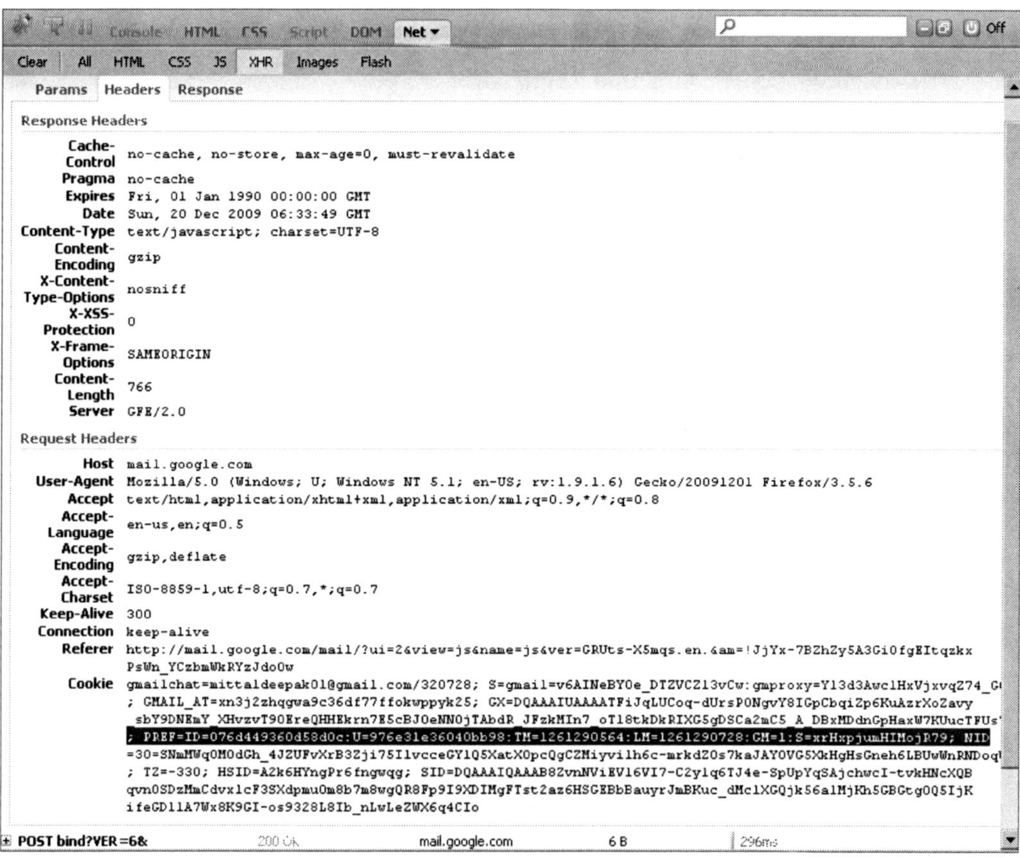

The **XHR** tab displays the AJAX requests made and the responses received by the web page that we are currently viewing. We can see the start and completion of these AJAX requests and whether they were successful and what is returned from the server.

As we will notice, an `XMLHttpRequest` is not much different from a normal request. The previous image shows the AJAX requests made by Gmail when the user clicks on the **Inbox** link.

The **XHR** tab displays the AJAX events as they happen on a page. If our view becomes too crowded while viewing and analyzing AJAX events, simply click on the **Clear** button to remove the events that are currently being displayed.

How to find out the download speed for a resource

The download speed of a web resource (CSS, HTML, image, JavaScript) plays an important part in the overall perceptible performance of the web page. If the download speed of a resource from the server is slow (because of the speed of the connection between the client and the server machine), then no amount of performance tuning at the server level or HTML level will result in a fast page response.

Firebug's **Net** panel displays the size of the resource and the amount of time it took to simply download the resource from the server.

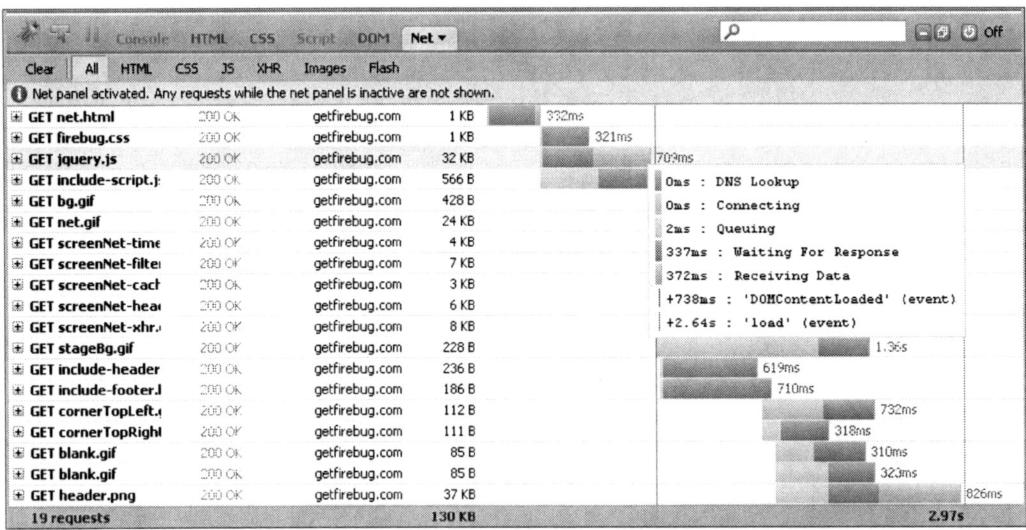

For example, the previous screenshot shows the following information that is required to find out the download speed of the `jquery.js` file from the `firebug.com` server:

- Size of the file: 32 KB
- Time it took for download of the file: 372 ms

Using this information, we can calculate that the download speed of the file is 86 KB/second. It becomes especially important when we are fetching images or JavaScript files from external servers. In those cases, it becomes important to determine if the upload speed of the external servers is good enough and does not slow down the performance of our web application.

Firebug extensions for analyzing performance

Firebug packs a lot of features right out of the box, to monitor, analyze, and fine tune the performance of our web application at the browser layer. There are some very useful plugins/extensions that provide additional information and features to make it even easier to analyze web application performance. The two most important extensions are:

- Yahoo YSlow
- Google Page Speed

These extensions will be discussed in detail in subsequent chapters dedicated to the most useful Firebug extensions. It is strongly recommended to make use of one or both of these extensions in order to supplement the features available out of the box from Firebug.

Summary

In this chapter, we looked at ways to analyze the time taken by a web page to load on the browser using Firebug. We also saw how Firebug's **Net** panel can provide insights into various bottlenecks in a web application. Firebug provides an easy way to study the HTTP headers of the requests made by the web page and responses received from the server.

8

AJAX Development

JavaScript has always been an extremely difficult language to debug, due to the fact that it's loosely typed and no good tools have been made available for debugging. Therefore, it's difficult to debug **AJAX** (**Asynchronous JavaScript and XML**) because the requests and the responses are all handled by JavaScript. Luckily, Firebug is extremely useful for debugging JavaScript and AJAX requests/responses. In this chapter, we'll discuss the features that Firebug offers to help us debug any AJAX requests we make.

In this amazing chapter, we'll discuss the following ways that help debug AJAX:

- Tracking `XmlHttpRequest`
- `GET` and `POST` methods
- Viewing live modifications on DOM
- Debugging AJAX calls using properties of Firebug's console object

Tracking XmlHttpRequest

The most relevant part of the Firebug tool in terms of AJAX is the option to show XML HTTP requests and responses. This feature allows us to view all requests made on the web. We can see whether this feature is active/enabled by clicking on the drop-down list of the **Console** tab and making sure that the **Show XMLHttpRequests** option is checked. Once it's working, we'll see all XML HTTP requests that are made.

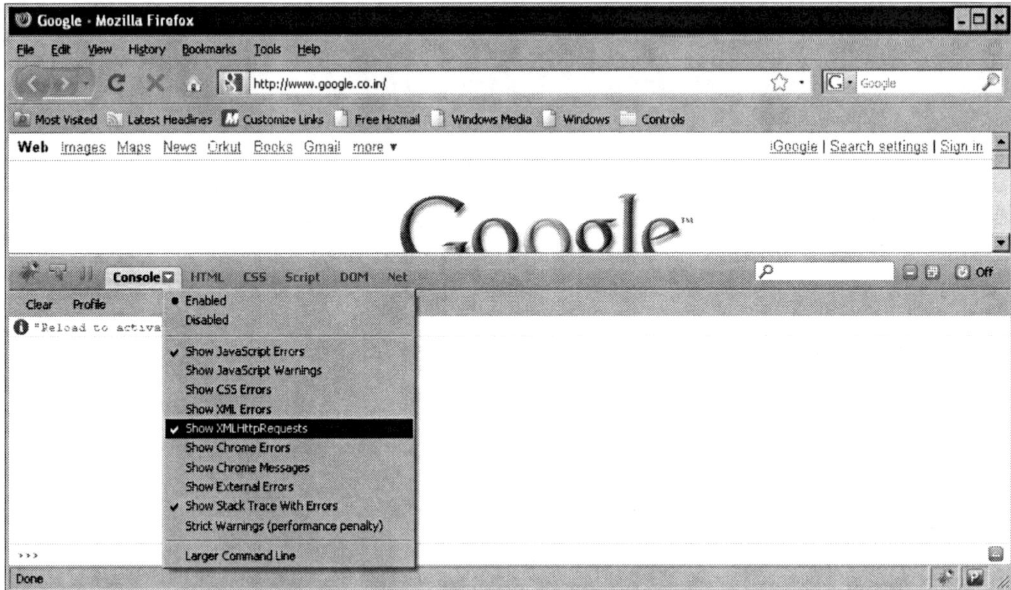

Request/response headers and parameters

After enabling **Show XMLHttpRequests** option on the **Console** tab, the **Console** tab acts like an AJAX spy. Each `XMLHttpRequest` will be automatically logged to the console, where we can inspect its response as text, JSON, or XML. This is extremely useful for debugging any AJAX code, and it's also quite fun to analyze how other web pages use AJAX.

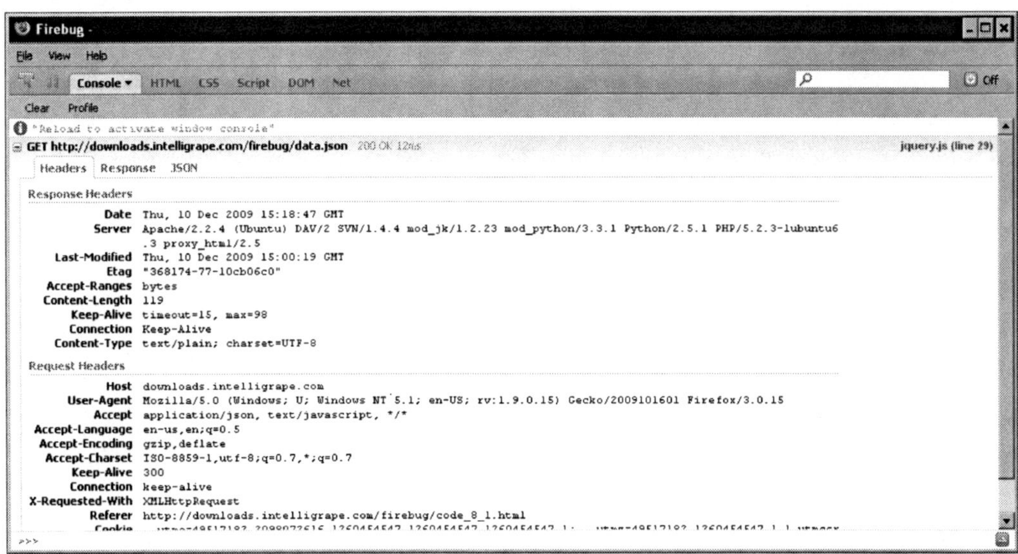

We'll discuss all of this with the help of an example. Let's write the following HTML code in a file and save it with `.html` extension (that is, create an HTML file and write this following code to that file):

This code uses the jQuery (a framework over JavaScript). We can download jQuery framework from `http://jquery.com` and include that `jquery.js` file in the same way that we include any other JavaScript file.

```
<html>
<head>
<script src="jquery.js"></script>
<script>
    $(document).ready(function(){
        $('#btn_json').click(function(){
            $.getJSON('data.json',function(data){
                var htmlString = "<strong>Name:</strong> " +
                                                    data[0].name;
                htmlString += "<br/><strong>Occupation:</strong> " +
                                              data[0].occupation;
                htmlString += "<br/><strong>Company:</strong> " +
                                                 data[0].company;
                $('#result').html(htmlString);
            })
        })
    })
```

```
</script>
</head>
   <body>
      Click this button to get JSON response
      <input type="button" value="JSON Request" id="btn_json"/>
   <div id="result"></div>

   </body>
</html>
```

Let's place the `jquery.js` file in the same folder where we saved the HTML file.

The jQuery's function, `getJSON(URL, callback)`, sends a request to the server and expects the server to respond in the JSON format.

JSON (JavaScript Object Notation) is a way of representing an object's value in a key-value form. The term JSON was coined by Douglas Crockford to capitalize on this simple syntax. The following notation can offer a concise alternative to the sometimes-bulky XML format:

```
{
"key": "value",
"key 2": ["array","of","items"]
}
```

For information on some of the potential advantages of JSON, as well as implementations in many programming languages, refer to `http://json.org/`.

There are two parameters of `getJSON(URL, callback)`. The first parameter, `URL`, is used to specify the URL of the server to which the request is to be made. The second parameter, `callback`, comes into the picture with server responses. The callback is again a function or a closure to which the JSON response is passed. The manipulation or processing of the JSON is done here.

Now, let's install the Apache server on our machine to simulate the client-server scenario locally and view the request header and parameters along with response header and data, which can be in different forms such as text, JSON, or XML.

Apache is used to serve the static contents of the website. To download, install, and know more about Apache, visit `http://httpd.apache.org/download.cgi`.

Let's create a file, say `data.json`, with the following contents and place that file, along with other HTML file(s), into the static directory under Apache's installation directory:

```
[
   {
      "name"    : "Chandan Luthra",
      "occupation"    : "Software Developer",
      "company"    : "Intelligrape Softwares"
   }
]
```

All the files, that is HTML, JSON, and JavaScript files, should be in the same folder.

After placing the files in Apache, let's start our server (Apache).

Now the playground is set for shooting AJAX calls/requests from the browser using JavaScript.

Let's run the HTML file (by typing its URL in the browser) in which we have written the code for firing AJAX call in the Firefox, and enable the Firebug.

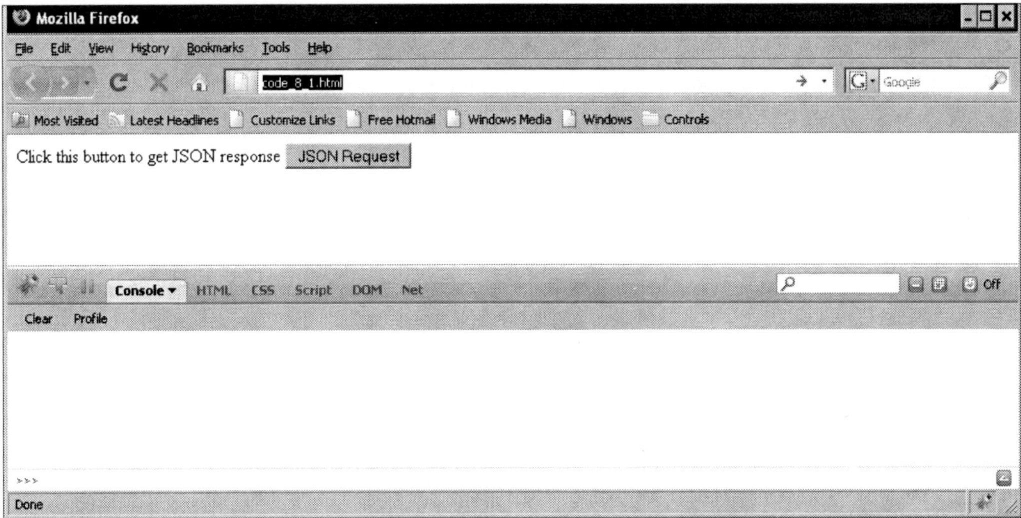

Let's click on the **JSON Request** button to make an AJAX call/request to the server. As soon as we click the button, a `GET` request is made to the server in the **Console** tab , as shown in the next screenshot. If we expand the `GET` request by clicking the **+** button we'll see three tabs.

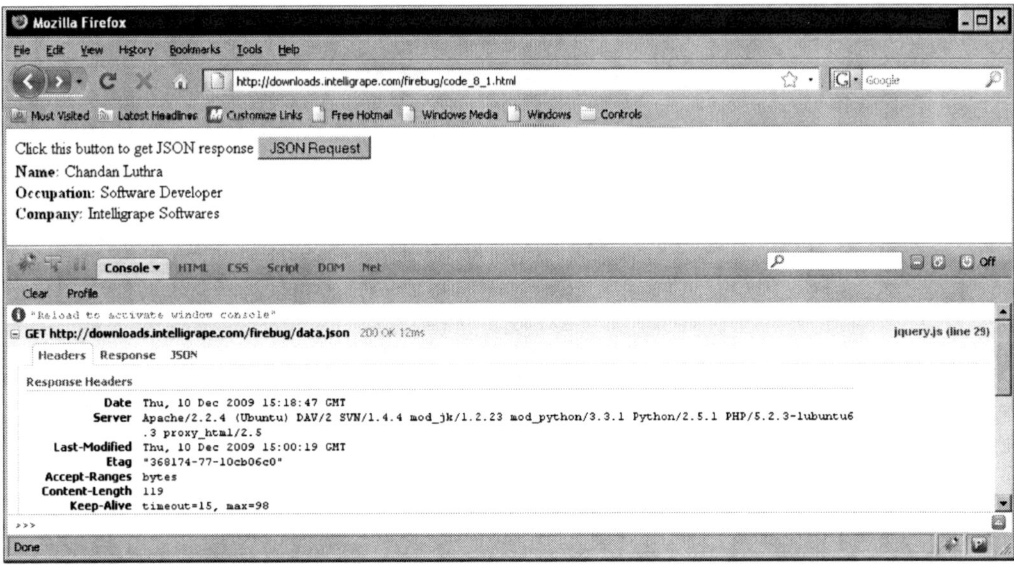

- **Headers**:

  This tab will show all the request and response headers and their values for a particular HTTP protocol transaction.

For more information on HTTP headers, visit `http://www.w3.org/Protocols/rfc2616/rfc2616-sec14.html`.

- **Response**:

  This tab shows the response returned from the server. The response could be in any type; it could be in XML, JSON, or plain text. In our case it is JSON response. We can also see the response code (for example, `200`, `404`, `500`, `304`, and so on) just next to the bold request URL in the **Console** tab.

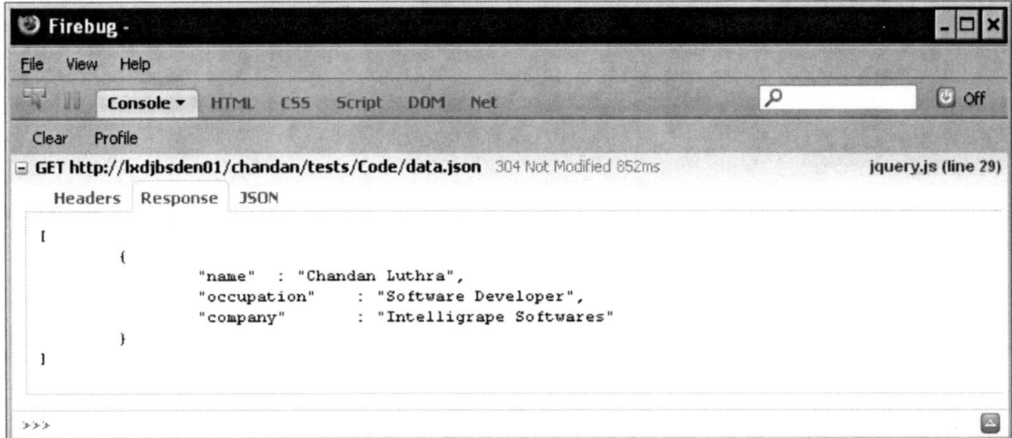

- JSON:

  In our example, the server returned a JSON string. Therefore, Firebug shows an extra tab, that is, the **JSON** tab, for this special response. This tab shows how Firefox/Firebug parses this JSON response into a JavaScript object that can be used and interpreted by JavaScript.

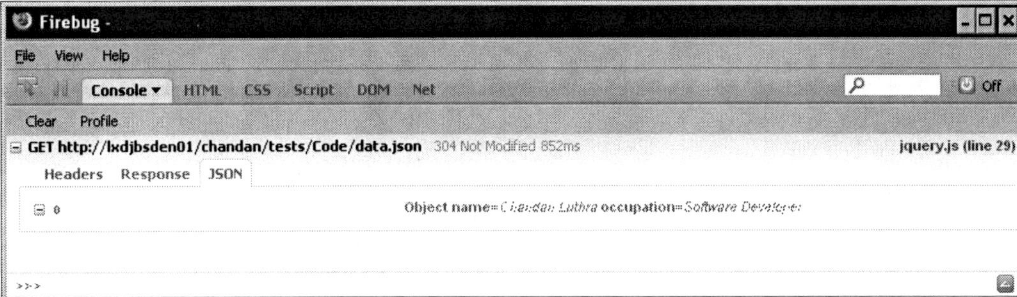

GET/POST request

GET and POST methods act as the carrier of the data from client side to server side. HTTP requests using the POST method are almost the same as those using GET. The difference between the methods is that GET is insecure and limited data can be transferred, whereas through POST, one can transfer unlimited data and the method is more secure. One of the most visible differences is that GET places its arguments in the query string portion of the URL, whereas POST requests do not. However, in AJAX calls, even this distinction is invisible to the average user. Generally, the only reason to choose one method over the other is to conform to the norms of the server-side code, or to provide for large amounts of transmitted data; GET has a more stringent limit.

We have already seen an example of a `GET` request in the previous section; we will now focus on the `POST` request. Let's try the following example to make a `POST` call to the server and see the differences between `GET` and `POST`:

```
<html>
<head>
<script src="jquery.js"></script>
<script>
   $(document).ready(function() {
      $('#btn_post').click(function() {
         $.post('data.json', {'q': 'test'}, function(data) {
            $('#result').html(data);
         });
      return false;
      });
   });


   </script>
</head>
   <body>
      Click this button to make a POST request
      <input type="button" value="POST Request" id="btn_post"/>
   <div id="result"></div>

   </body>
</html>
```

In the preceding code, the jQuery's `post()` is used to post the data to the server in AJAX fashion. It has three parameters. The first parameter defines the URL of the server to which the data is posted. The second parameter is a key-value pair of the actual parameter (that is, parameters and values that are sent to the server) name, and their values. The third parameter is a jQuery's closure/callback function, which would be executed when the response is received from the server.

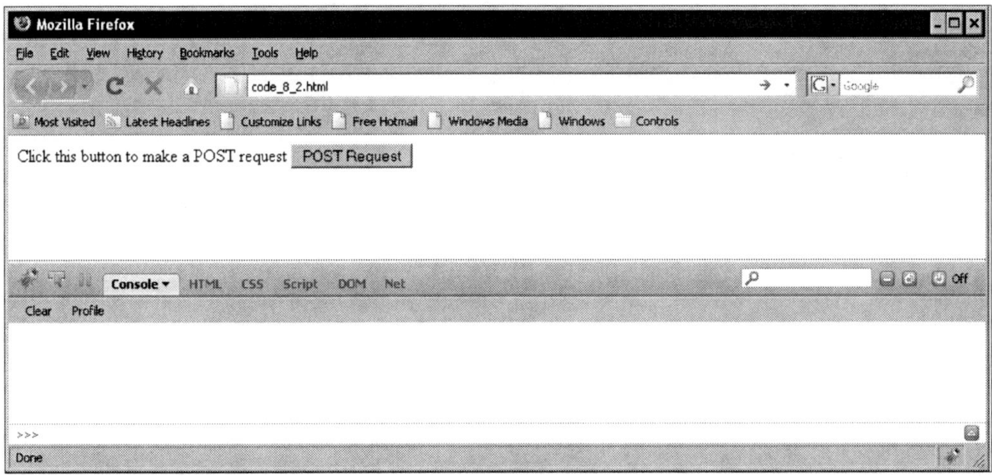

Now, let's click on the **POST Request** button to mock the post request via AJAX. Here we will find that the request is a `POST` request and one new tab, the **Post** tab, can be seen. Under the **Post** tab, all the parameters and values that we sent to the server can be seen.

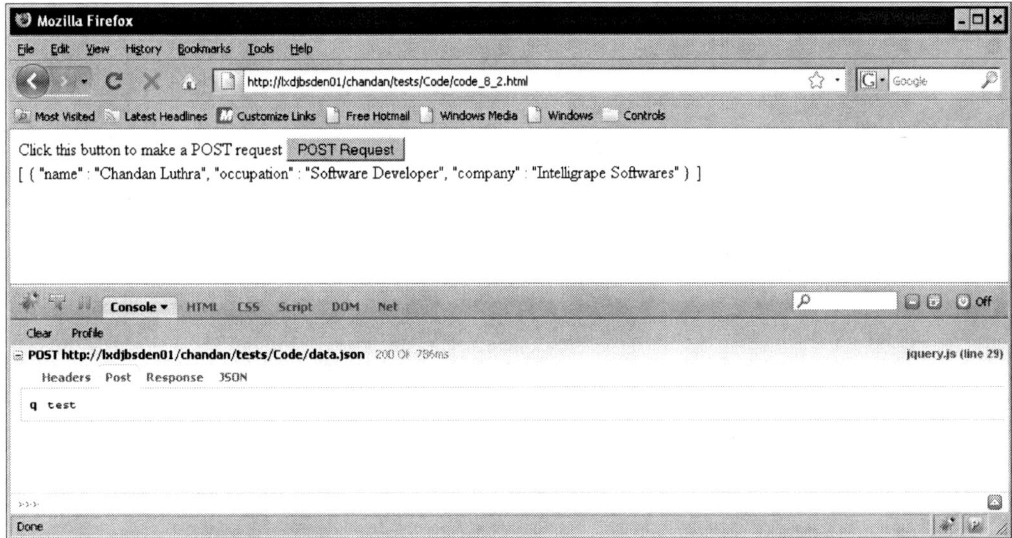

Viewing live modifications on DOM

Firebug allows us to view the current DOM. The current DOM here means that if we have written a JavaScript code that changes the DOM, then we can't see the modified DOM by viewing the page source. The **Page Source** option of Firefox will only show us the initial DOM, not the modified one.

Thankfully, Firebug provides us with an **HTML** tab that allows us to view the live modifications of the DOM. To explain this section, we'll pick the first example of this chapter, in which we populate a `<div>` to show the information returned by the server after successful completion of an AJAX call. The following screenshot shows the **HTML** tab, in which the `<div id="result" />` is an empty element:

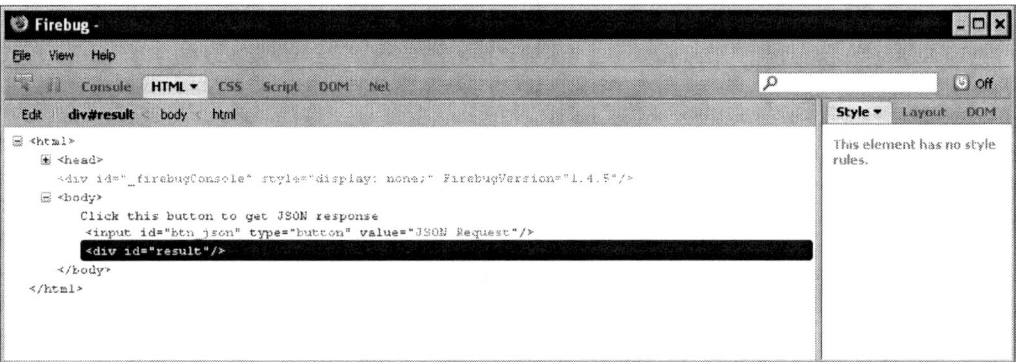

Now, as soon as we click the **JSON Request** button on the page, an AJAX call is made to the server and it returns the data to the client. Our JavaScript code manipulates that data and populates the empty `<div>`. Here, Firebug keeps an eye on the DOM and tracks the changes that are made.

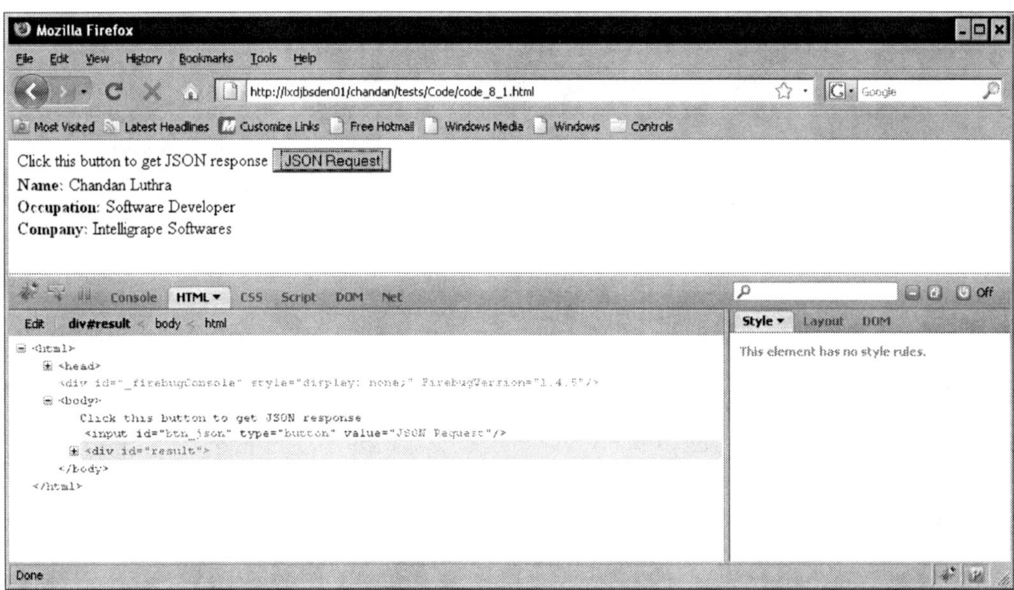

Firebug highlights that `<div>` (and all the area that is modified) and we can see a **+** (expand) button beside the `<div>`, which means that the `<div>` can be expanded now. In other words, the `<div>` is populated with some HTML or child elements.

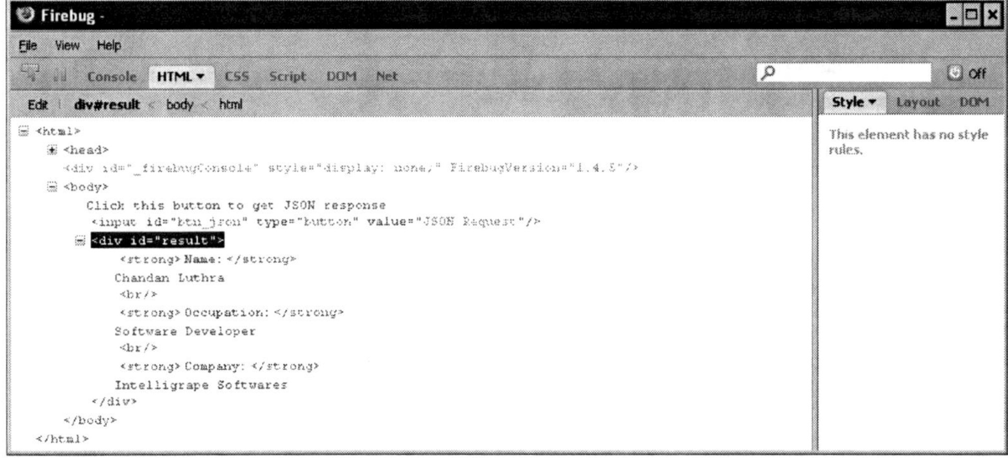

To see the inner HTML of the populated `<div>`, click on the **+** (expand) button. We will see that there is some HTML within that `<div>`. This new HTML was not on our DOM before. It can be seen only through Firebug and not by the normal **Page Source** option of Firefox.

Debugging AJAX calls using properties of a console object

Debugging the AJAX calls was never easy. Thanks to Firebug and its console API that blesses us with many methods or functions, we can debug our JavaScript code. To know more about the console object and its API, refer to Chapter 5, *JavaScript Development*.

For now let's discuss a typical case where one can never debug a code without Firebug. Consider a case where the function `foo()` requests the JavaScript function `bar()` using AJAX; that is, `foo()` is on the client side (browser). The function `foo()` requests a JavaScript function `bar()` from the server and executes the `bar()` without refreshing the page. Now, suppose there is some bug in `bar()`, how can we debug that code and how can we place the breakpoints on it?

Firebug has the solution for these types of weird bugs.

console.debug(object[, object, ...])

As we already know that `console.debug()` writes a message to the console, including a hyperlink to the line where it was called, we'll take a look at its usage while debugging an AJAX call.

Consider the following example. This example does the same as our first example in this chapter, but in a different manner. Here we have invoked another JavaScript that we fetched from the server using AJAX.

```
<html>
<head>
   <script src="jquery.js"></script>
   <script>
      $(document).ready(function(){
         $('#btn_js').click(function(){
            $.getScript('myScript.js')
         })
      })
   </script>
</head>
   <body>
      Click this button to fetch a JAVASCRIPT from the SERVER
      <input type="button" value="Get Script" id="btn_js"/>
   <div id="result">
</div>
   </body>
</html>
```

The jQuery's function `getScript()` fetches a JavaScript from the server over AJAX and executes that code in the browser.

Save the preceding code as an HTML file, and the following JavaScript code in a separate file, `myScript.js`:

```
function populateDiv(){
var htmlString = "<strong>Name:</strong>Chandan Luthra" ;
htmlString +="<br/><strong>Occupation:</strong> Software Developer" ;
htmlString +="<br/><strong>Company:</strong> IntelliGrape Softwares";
$('#result').html(htmlString)
}
console.debug(populateDiv);
populateDiv();
```

Let's place both the files in the same folder and host them on any server that serves static content, such as Apache or IIS.

Hit the URL of the HTML file from Firefox and enable Firebug. We will see something like the following screenshot:

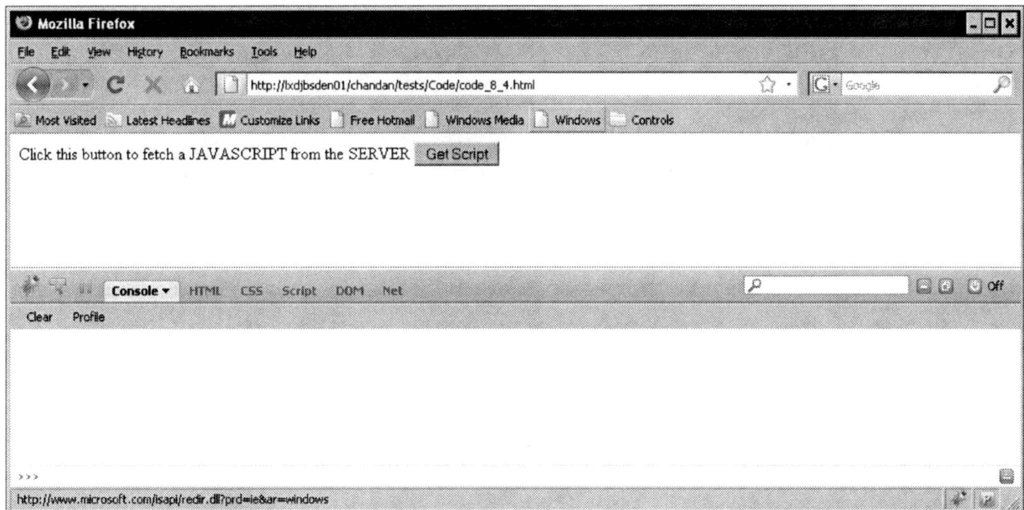

Now, the playground is set to fire an AJAX call to the server to fetch a JavaScript. Let's click the **Get Script** button on the page and keep our eyes on the **Console** tab.

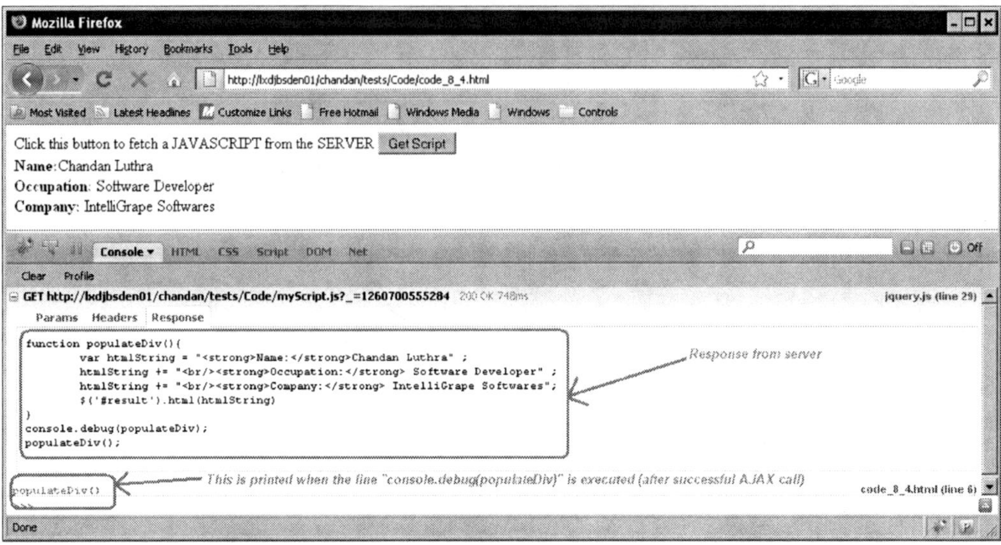

Now if we move our mouse cursor over the `populateDiv()` link on the console, then a small pop up will open that shows us the definition of the function.

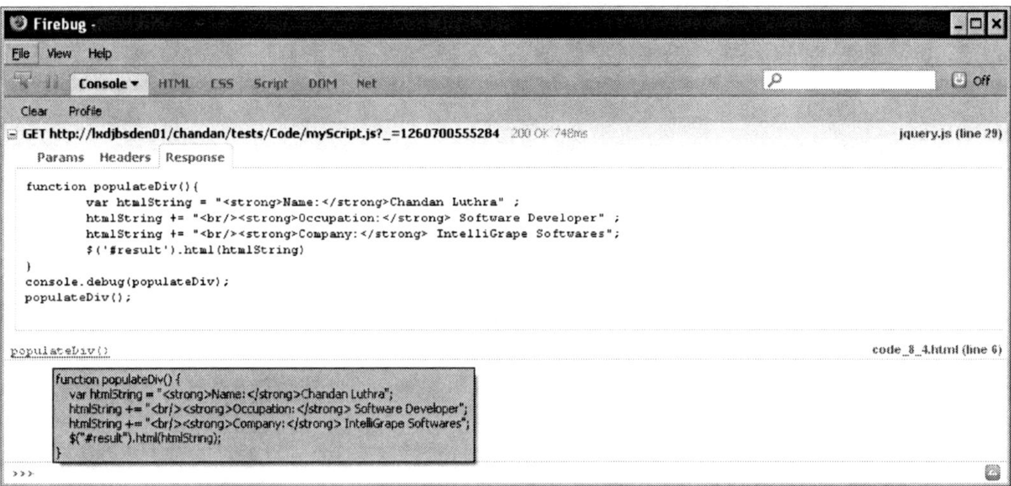

We can also insert some `assert` statements to debug our JavaScript code.

console.assert(expression[, object, ...])

This function is also covered in Chapter 5. But we didn't discuss it in detail there as we all know that we use `assert` statements to write a bug-free code. Asserts are very powerful and useful while doing **Test-driven developments** (TDD).

In AJAX development, these `assert` statements play a very significant role in debugging the JavaScript code easily. Let's continue with our previous example and include some `assert` statements between the lines. Our new `myScript.js` will look something like the following:

```
function populateDiv(){
var htmlString = "<strong>Name:</strong>Chandan Luthra" ;
console.assert(htmlString!=null);
htmlString +="<br/><strong>Occupation:</strong> Software Developer" ;
console.assert(htmlString!=null);
htmlString +="<br/><strong>Company:</strong> IntelliGrape Softwares";
console.assert(htmlString==null); //Assertion would fail here
$('#result').html(htmlString)
}
console.debug(populateDiv);
populateDiv();
```

The following screenshot shows an **Assertion Failure**:

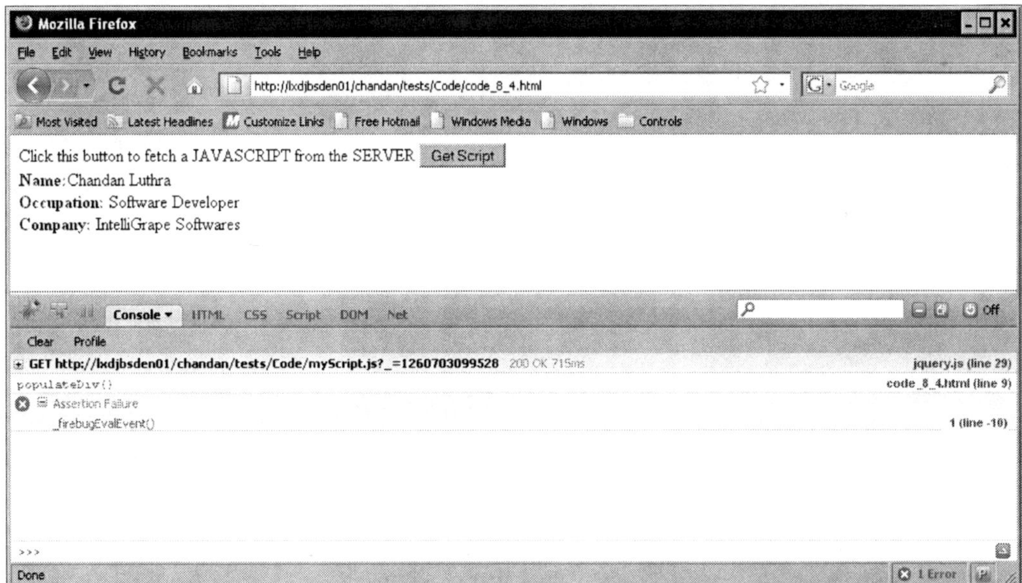

console.dir(object)

This one is interesting because it prints an interactive listing of all properties of the object. This looks identical to the view that we would see in the **DOM** tab. We have included a new statement, `console.dir()`, in our example.

```
function populateDiv(){
var htmlString = "<strong>Name:</strong>Chandan Luthra" ;
htmlString +="<br/><strong>Occupation:</strong> Software Developer" ;
htmlString +="<br/><strong>Company:</strong> IntelliGrape Softwares";
console.dir($(htmlString));
$('#result').html(htmlString)
}
console.debug(populateDiv);
populateDiv();
```

The `console.dir()` function of Firebug will display all the nodes that would be attached under the `<div id="result">`.

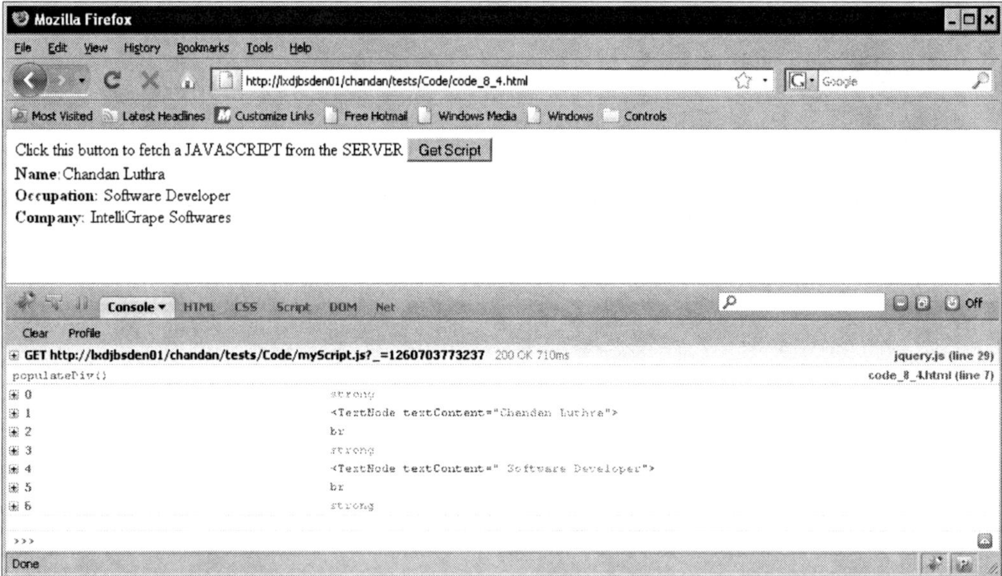

We can see that each node that is represented by **0**, **1**, **2**, **3**, **4**, **5**, can be expanded. On expanding each node, we find something familiar. Try this yourself and see what would happen and what information is hidden beneath these nodes.

Summary

In this chapter, we learned how to track `XmlHttpRequest`. We understood the request and response headers by making `GET` and `POST` requests.

We saw how console API helps us debug the AJAX calls. If our JavaScript code modifies our current DOM, then we can view those modifications on HTML source, live on the **HTML** tab. We can also dig deeper into the console API to find all the functions of the API that can help us debug AJAX.

9

Tips and Tricks for Firebug

In this chapter, we'll discuss a few tips and tricks that can be very useful while debugging and developing. We'll learn how to play with the features that Firebug provides and what else we should know about Firebug.

We will discuss the following in this chapter:

- The magical `cd()` function
- How `console.group()` and `console.groupEnd()` can be useful
- Configuring Firebug and shortcuts

Magical cd()

We already know a fact about the command line—all the expressions and functions that we execute in the command line are relative to the top level window of the page. For example, we cannot invoke any function from Firebug's command line if that function is defined in an iFrame within a page.

Don't worry, Firebug provides us with solutions for such a situation. Let's discuss this scenario with an example.

Here we have two iFrames within the main container page.

The following is the main page code:

```
<html>
<head>
</head>
<body>
    <script>
            function printMe(){
                    console.log("In the Page")
```

```
        }
    </script>
    This is Main Container Page <br/>
    <iframe name="myFrame1" id="myFrame1"
                  src="code_9_1_frame1.html">

    </iframe>

    <iframe name="myFrame2" id="myFrame2"
                  src="code_9_1_frame2.html">

    </iframe>
</body>
</html>
```

The following is the first iFrame code:

```
<html>
    <body>
        <script>
            function printMe(){
                console.info("Context Changed to 'myFrame1'")
                console.log("In Frame One")
            }
        </script>
        This is Frame one
    </body>
</html>
```

The following is the second iFrame code:

```
<html>
    <body>
        <script>
            function printMe(){
                console.info("Context Changed to 'myFrame2'")
                console.log("In Frame Two")
            }
        </script>
        This is Frame two
    </body>
</html>
```

The three code snippets that we just saw are three *different* HTML files. The main page file contains the two iframes—`myFrame1` and `myFrame2`. The `src` attribute (source) for iFrames—`myFrame1` and `myFrame2`—will be the other two files.

All the three files should be placed in the same folder and the name should be given to both iFrames as the one we have used in the code of the main page. When we are done setting the playground for the magic to begin, let's open the file in Firefox and enable Firebug.

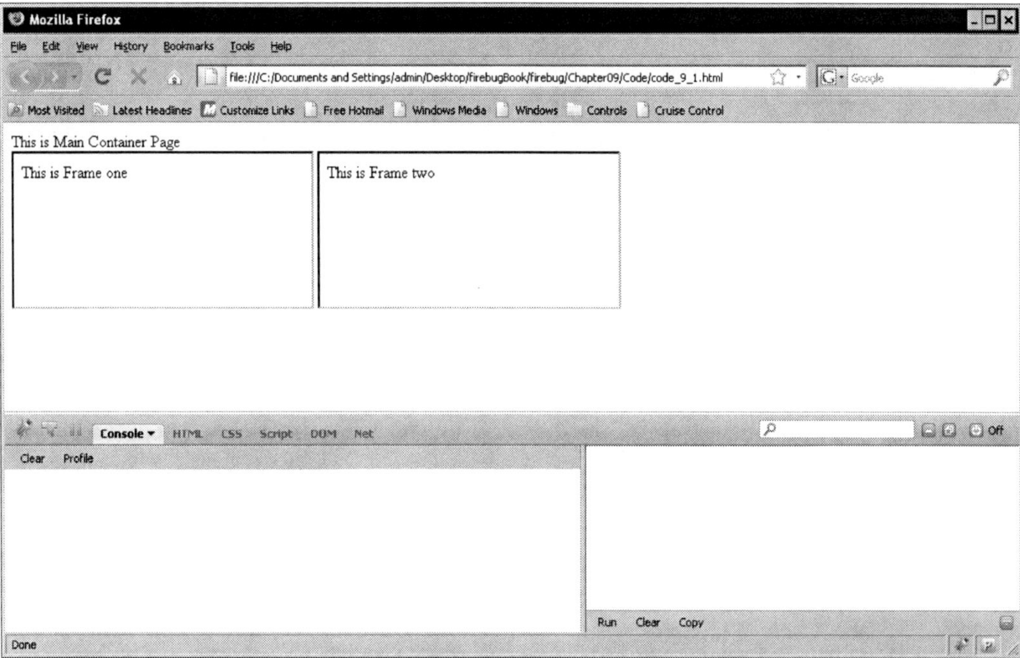

Let's press *Ctrl+Shift+L*; this keyboard shortcut will take us directly to the command line of Firebug. Next we open the command line of Firebug in the multiline mode by clicking the (icon) on the bottom right-hand side of Firebug, and then type the following code in that editor and click **Run**:

```
printMe();
cd(window.frames[0]);
printMe();
cd(window.parent.frames[1]);
printMe();
cd(window.parent);
printMe();
```

As the `cd()` method takes some time to change the context of the window, in order to see the workings of the `cd()` function, please type and execute the previously mentioned code, line by line.

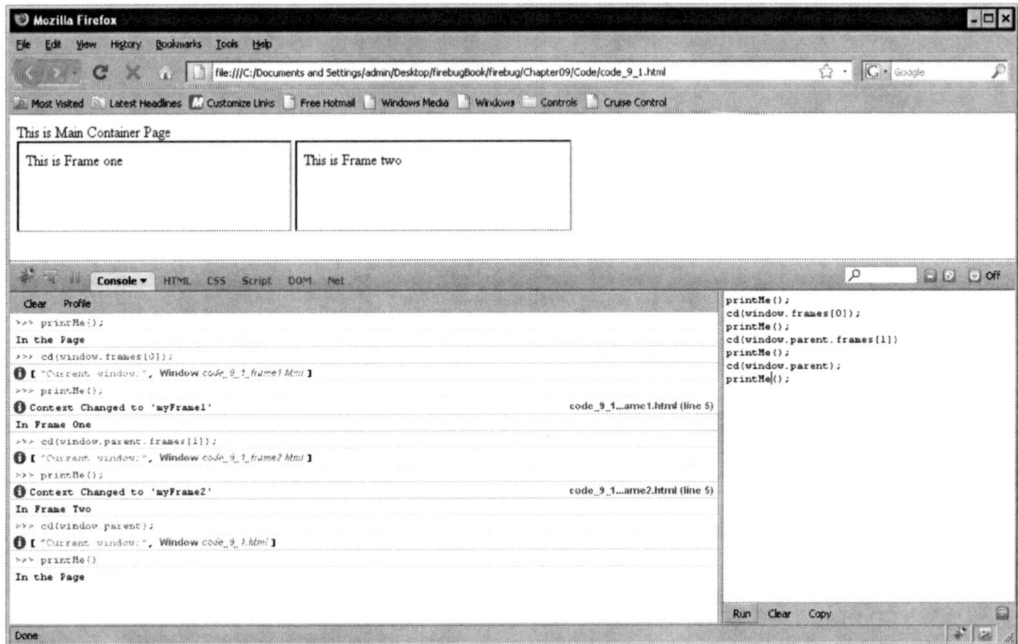

You must be wondering what the code is doing and how the context is being changed? Let's discuss the code line by line.

The `printMe()` function is defined at three different places:

- On the main page
- In the first frame, that is, `myFrame1`
- In the second frame, that is, `myFrame2`

The `printMe()` function prints some information on the console about its parent window.

To access the first frame of the window or page, `window.frames[0]` is used. When `cd()` is invoked with this frame as a parameter, the context of the expressions of the command line is changed to `myFrame1`.

Similarly, `window.parent.frames[1]` is used to access the second frame within the first frame. The `cd(window.parent)` function is used for switching Firebug's command line context back to the default page (the main container page).

This `cd()` function is very useful when we want to fire JavaScript code against some other window or frame that is an element of the parent page.

The hierarchical console

We can always group the output in the console window by using the following two console functions:

- `console.group()`
- `console.groupEnd()`

The `console.group()` function creates a new group in the output console, and all the log, warning, debug, and error statements' output are shown in a new group. The following code explains the use of this function:

```
<html>
<head>
</head>
<body>
    <script>
    function groupedOutput(){
        console.group("group level 1");
            console.log("level 1 log")
             console.group("group level 2");
                console.warn("level 2 warn")
                 console.info("level 2 info")
                console.error("level 2 error")
            console.groupEnd();
             console.log("level 1 log");
        console.groupEnd();
        console.log("ungrouped log");
    }
    </script>
    <input type="button" onclick="groupedOutput()" value="Show grouped
output"/>
</body>
</html>
```

We already know what we have to do with this code. Let's write the preceding code in a file, save it as an `.html` file, and then open this HTML file in Firefox with Firebug enabled.

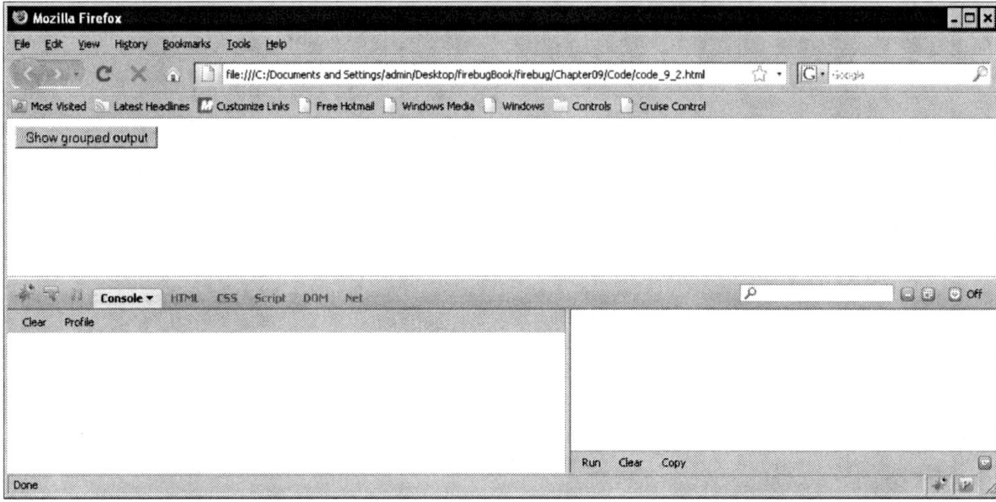

When we open this HTML file in Firefox, we can see a button called **Show grouped output**. A click on this button will invoke the `groupedOutput()` function of the JavaScript written in the file.

Wow, we can see the output now in a well formatted and grouped fashion:

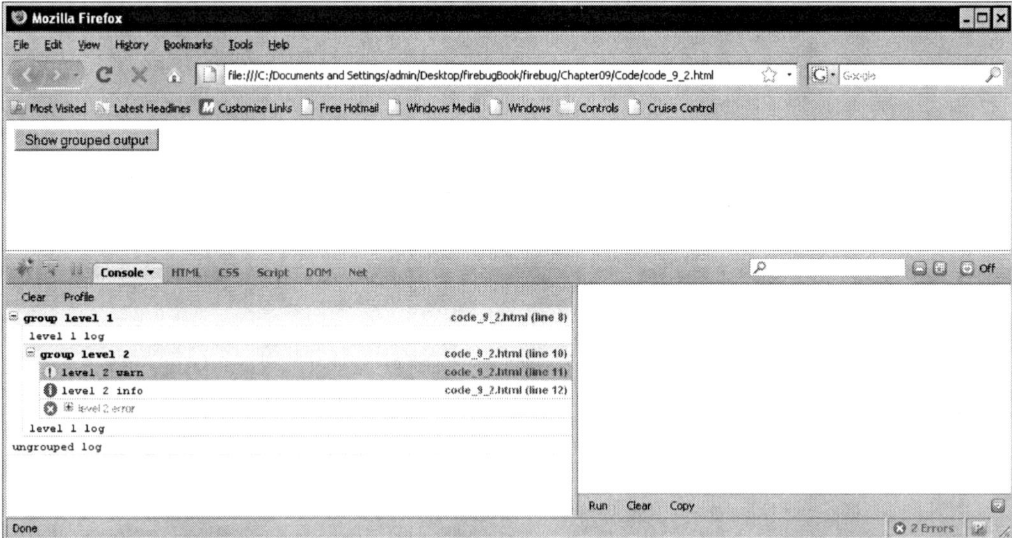

Configuring Firebug to our taste

If we don't want to remember the default shortcut keys provided by Firebug, we can always configure it to remember our set of keys.

On the top left-hand side of the Firebug window, we will find a button, and clicking on it will open the Firebug menu. Now, let's select the **Customize Shortcuts** option from the menu.

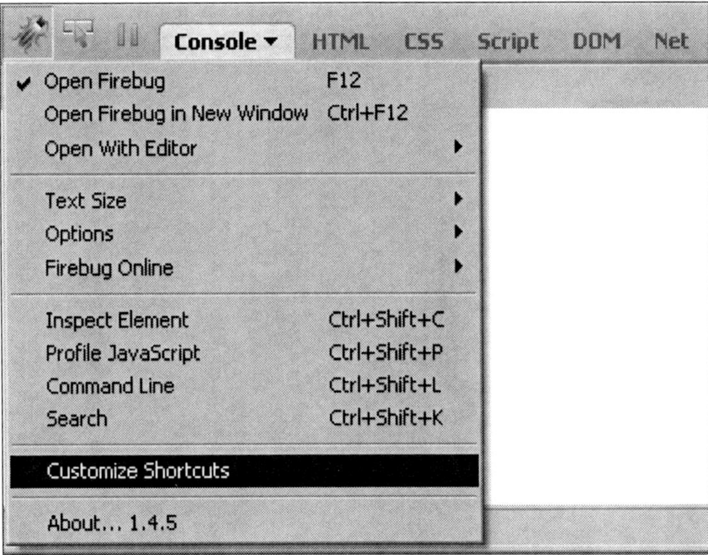

A modal window will open and now we can easily customize our keyboard shortcuts.

There is a list of the shortcut keys that we can use on Firebug. If we want to change the combination of the keys, we can move the cursor to the respective textbox whose shortcut we want to change, and press our favorite combinations of keys that we want to set for that functionality.

Firebug also provides us with a **reset** button for each keyboard shortcut. If we messed up the combinations, we can always reset the key combinations to the defaults.

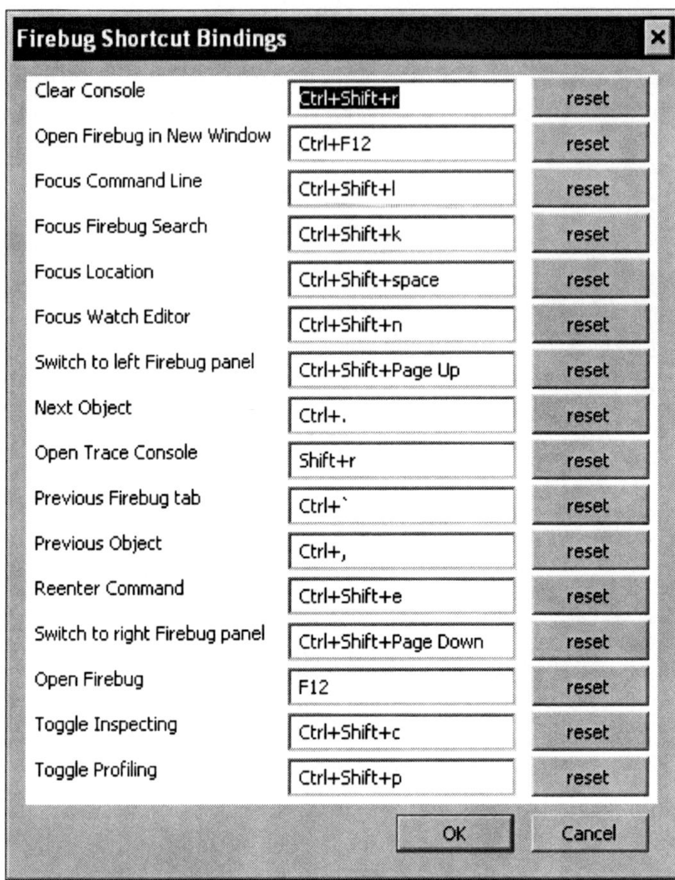

Summary

In this chapter, we discussed some tips and tricks, which we can use to format our output in the console window. We saw how to use the `console.group()` function and how useful it can be for debugging the code. This function could also be very useful for debugging the recursive functions and in loops.

We also looked at how to use the command line's `cd()` function to change the context of the window. By default the context of the expressions executed from the command line is the main parent page. If we want to debug and fire JavaScripts command against any other frame in the page, we need to change the context of the Firebug command to that frame.

Firebug also allows us to set our own keyboard shortcut keys if we find the default shortcuts provided by Firebug difficult to use.

10
Necessary Firebug Extensions

Firebug is packed with tons of useful features to make web development an easier task. Firebug also has a plugin architecture that allows developers to write extensions on top of Firebug (just like Firebug is an extension to Firefox browsers), in order to enhance the utility of Firebug and Firefox.

Many developers have written various Firebug extensions and made them publicly available. The Firebug extensions page (`http://getfirebug.com/extensions/`) contains a list of around 30 extensions that are currently available.

In this chapter, we go through the following few extensions, which we consider particularly useful for web development:

- YSlow
- Firecookie
- Pixel Perfect
- Firefinder
- FireQuery
- CodeBurner
- SenSEO
- Page Speed

YSlow

YSlow is a Firebug extension that evaluates a web page for performance and suggests potential places for improvements. YSlow is based on 22 rules that affect the performance of a web page on the browser. These rules are identified by the Yahoo performance team—the team has identified a total of 34 rules, of which 22 are testable by Firebug.

YSlow gives us letter grades on one of the three predefined (or user defined) rule sets. It has a handful of useful features, such as displaying information and statistics about web page components, and integration of optimization tools such as JSLint and Smush.it.

YSlow analyzes web page performance by examining all the components on the page, including components dynamically created by using JavaScript. It measures the performance of the page and offers suggestions for improving it.

The 22 rules on which YSlow is based are listed here in order of importance and effectiveness:

1. Minimize HTTP Requests
2. Use a Content Delivery Network
3. Add an Expires or a Cache-Control Header
4. Gzip Components
5. Put StyleSheets at the Top
6. Put Scripts at the Bottom
7. Avoid CSS Expressions
8. Make JavaScript and CSS External
9. Reduce DNS Lookups
10. Minify JavaScript and CSS
11. Avoid Redirects
12. Remove Duplicate Scripts
13. Configure ETags
14. Make AJAX Cacheable
15. Use GET for AJAX Requests

16. Reduce the Number of DOM Elements
17. No 404s
18. Reduce Cookie Size
19. Use Cookie-Free Domains for Components
20. Avoid Filters
21. Do Not Scale Images in HTML
22. Make favicon.ico Small and Cacheable

When analyzing a web page, YSlow deducts points for each infraction of these rules and then applies a grade to each rule. In YSlow 2.0, users can create their own custom rulesets in addition to the following three predefined rulesets:

- **YSlow (V2)**: This ruleset contains the 22 rules that we have just seen
- **Classic (V1)**: This ruleset contains the first 13 rules
- **Small Site or Blog**: This ruleset contains 14 rules that are applicable to small websites or blogs

After analyzing the performance of the web page based on the chosen ruleset, YSlow shows the report in the following four tabs:

- **Grade**

  This tab (as the name suggests) gives an overall grade to our page for each rule that YSlow suggests.

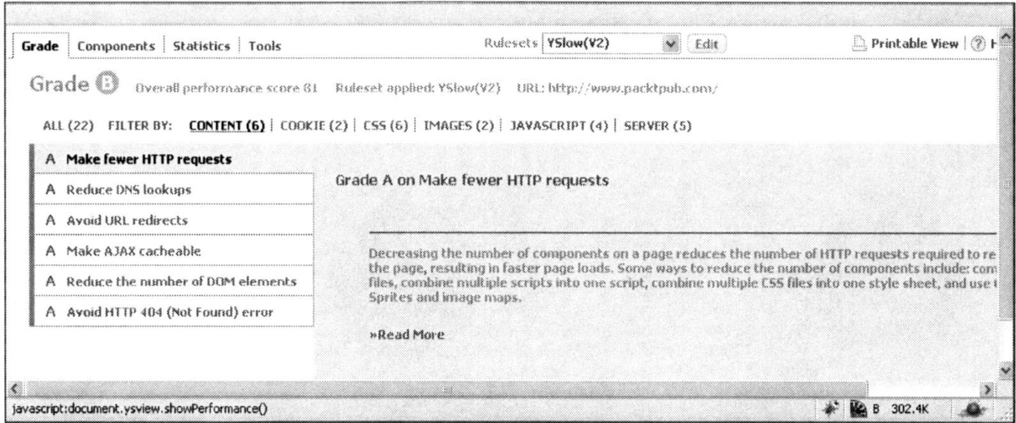

- **Components**

  This tab shows various components that the page consists of and information related to those components, which affect the performance of the page on the browser.

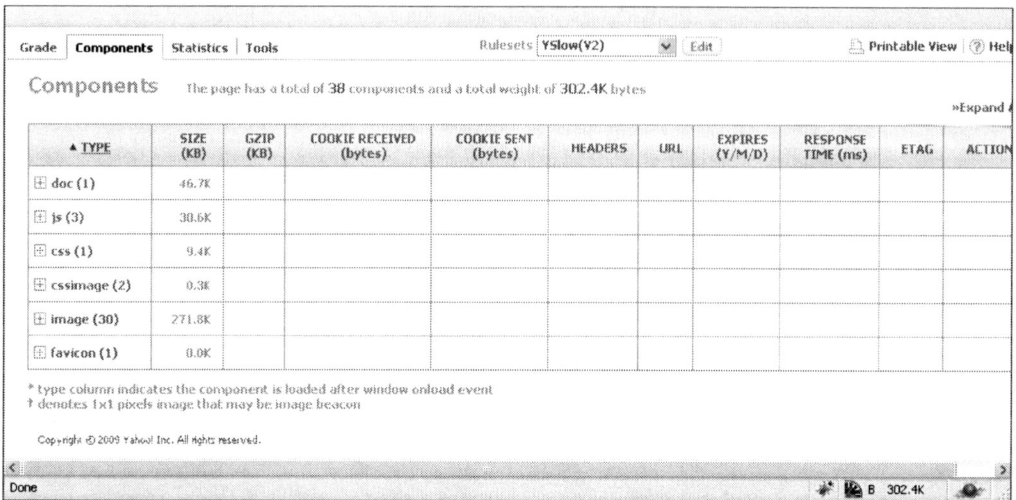

- **Statistics**

  This tab provides a graphical representation of the number of requests made to the server for the page to be served in both cases—when the user browser makes its very first request to the page (without any browser cache) and when the user browser has a cached version of the page.

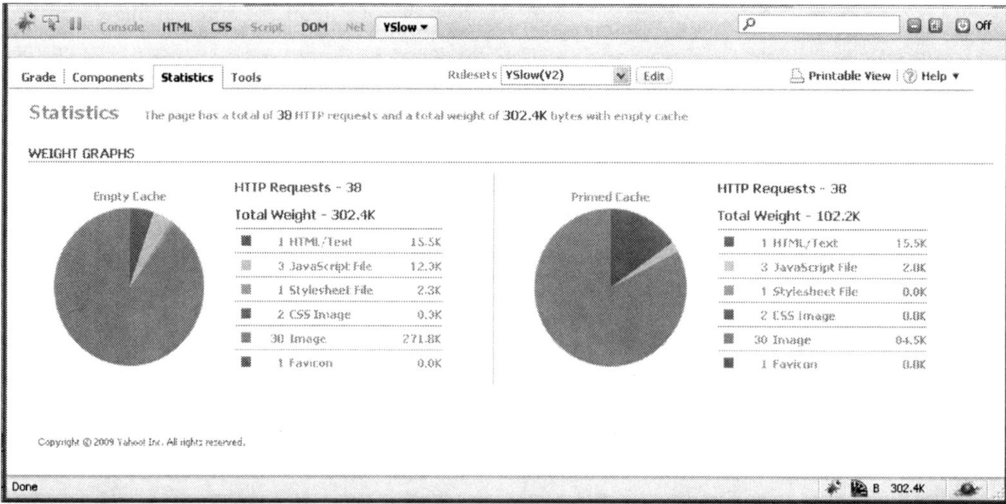

- **Tools**

  This tab shows a listing of various tools that YSlow suggests and that can be used to run on page resources (JavaScript, CSS, image files) to improve the performance of the page.

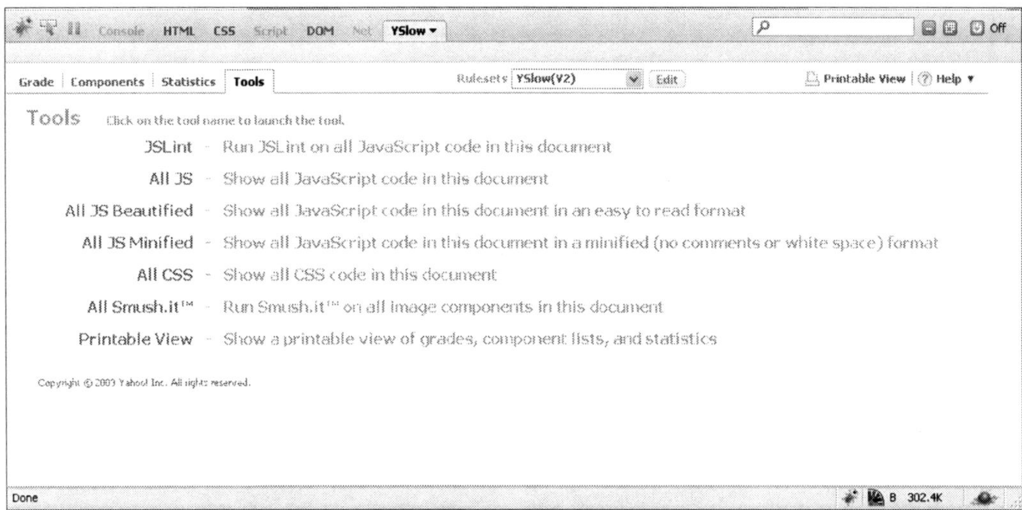

YSlow is an indispensible extension before we launch a new application. Spending some time analyzing the performance of an application using YSlow has always provided us with some very useful insights about increasing application performance for the end users. One of the most common ones is the way the application has been set up on the web server (Apache, IIS, and so on) with regards to caching.

Yahoo has provided comprehensive documentation on various rules that YSlow checks and the reasons behind those rules at `http://developer.yahoo.com/yslow/help/`. The reader is encouraged to go through this documentation in order to understand YSlow and frontend web page performance.

Firecookie

If our web application utilizes cookies to a great extent, then analyzing the cookies that are sent by the application to the browser can become a time consuming and tedious task. The Firecookie extension provides a host of features and options to manage and analyze cookies.

Firecookie helps us view and manage cookies in our browser. It displays a list of all cookies associated with the currently displayed website. It displays basic information about a cookie such as its name, value, domain, expiry date, and so on. We can use it to inspect cookies, view cookie permissions, events, expire time, and much more. Firecookie allows us to do the following (all from within Firebug's panel):

- View cookies
- Create a cookie
- Remove a cookie
- Filter cookies
- Export cookies
- Log cookie events (creation, deletion, and so on)
- Modify cookies' settings (for example, accepting only from a certain site)
- Search for a particular cookie

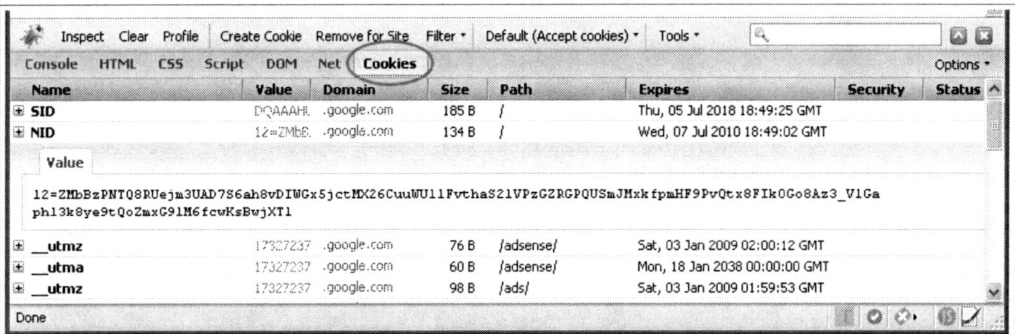

One of the best things about Firecookie is that we can see the cookies change as events on the **Console** tab. With Firecookie installed, the **Console** tab also shows the cookie changes that take place when a page is loaded, or due to any JavaScript code. For example, it is common practice on content websites to store the font preference (smaller or bigger font than usual) using cookies on the user's browser if the user does not have an account on the website, but still wants font preference to be remembered when he/she opens the same website again (on the same machine).

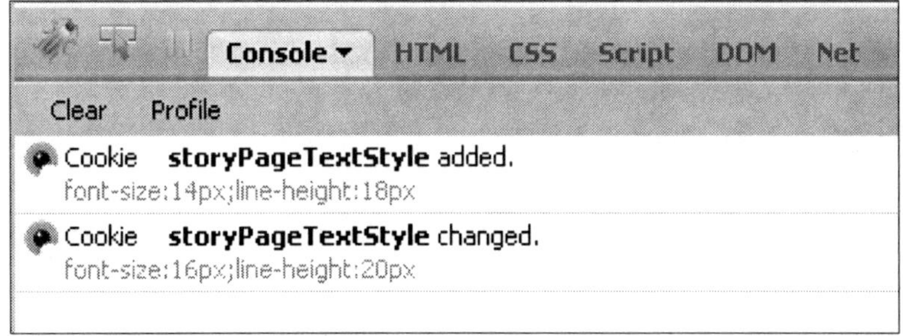

Pixel Perfect

Pixel Perfect is a very useful extension for web developers and web designers. It allows developers and designers to easily overlay a web composition on top of the developed HTML page and compare them minutely instead of relying on subjective visual inspection. Switching the composition on and off allows the developer to see how many pixels they are off while in development.

Pixel Perfect also has an opacity option so that we can view the HTML below the composition. By being able to see both the composition and the HTML we can now simultaneously use Firebug while Pixel Perfect is still in action. Pixel Perfect allows us to adjust the opacity of the overlay and drag it around to make sure it all lines up just right, and then we can measure the accuracy of the position and dimensions of the web page components against the original design.

In order to use Pixel Perfect, let's follow these steps:

1. Load a sample website that we would like to test and click on the icon to launch the Pixel Perfect panel.

2. To load our design compositions into the overlay list, let's click the **Add overlay** button. A standard file browser will appear and we can select any standard graphic format that can be loaded into a regular XHTML page (JPG, PNG, and so on). We can add as many overlay files as we like.

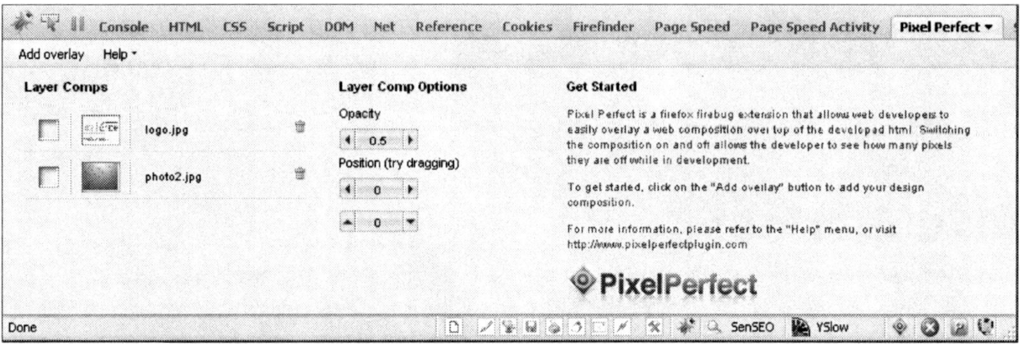

3. Click on the square box located to the left of our overlay icon to toggle the overlay on. The overlay should now appear in the main browser window. By default, the overlay is positioned to absolute top left. We can delete any overlay by clicking on the *trash* icon located to the right of the overlay icon.
4. Change the **Opacity** to make our composition either more transparent or less transparent. Making the composition more transparent will allow us to see our changes on the actual developed HTML code below the composition. Less transparency is useful for toggling the composition on and off to see pixel shifts. By default the **Opacity** is set to **0.5**.
5. We can now move the overlay to the position of our choice by either dragging the overlay using mouse or by manipulating the left/right and up/down arrow keys.

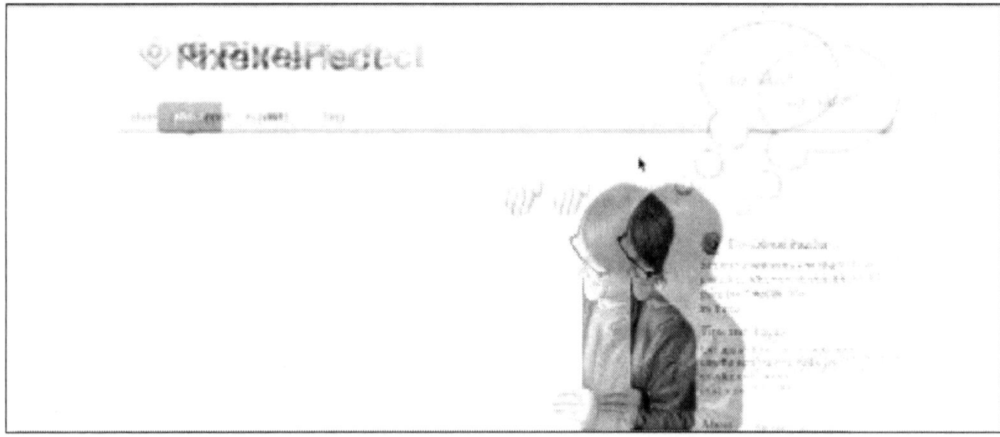

Pixel Perfect options menu

Pixel Perfect provides the following two configuration options:

- **Hide statusbar info**:

  Selecting this option will hide the Pixel Perfect icon in the status bar. This can be useful if we have many plugins installed and our status bar is getting cluttered. We can then access Pixel Perfect by clicking the Firebug icon.

- **Hide overlay when inspecting**:

  By default, our overlay will become invisible when we switch to a Firebug tab (that is, HTML view). This allows us to inspect our HTML and make changes without having the overlay block inspection. However, we can keep the overlay on at all times by turning this option off.

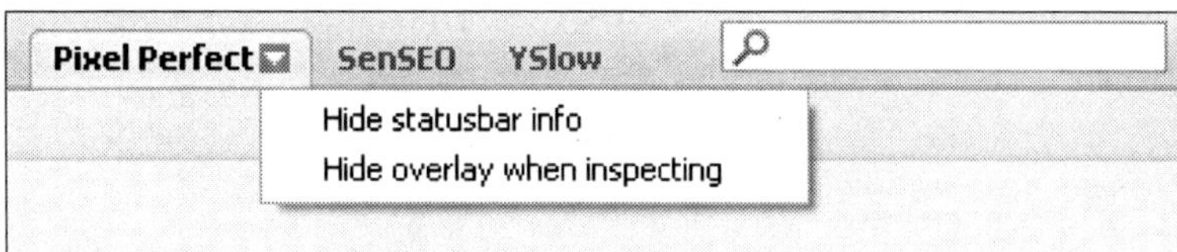

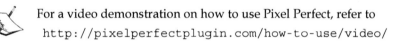

For a video demonstration on how to use Pixel Perfect, refer to `http://pixelperfectplugin.com/how-to-use/video/`

Firefinder

The Firefinder extension allows us to quickly find web page elements that match CSS or Xpath selectors, and that we input as our search criteria. Firefinder is great for testing the page elements that are affected by a CSS style rule as well as for highlighting and finding elements that match our searches.

In order to search for page elements using Firefinder, let's do the following steps:

1. Open the Firebug panel.
2. Click on the **Firefinder** tab.
3. Enter the search expression in the search box (for example, `div`) and click on the **Filter** button.
4. **Matching elements** (with a total count of the elements found) are displayed.

5. In the search results, we can click on the **Inspect** button to jump to the HTML source of the element in the **HTML** tab. We can also share the HTML source of the element with a friend via the **FriendlyFire** button.

If we are jQuery fans, then Firefinder can be a very helpful tool. Most of the jQuery work starts with creating a selector and we can test those selectors very easily with the Firefinder.

Firefinder provides another handy feature called **Auto-select**. We can auto-select elements when hovering or via the context menu. In order to auto-select an element while hovering, click on the **Auto-select** button under the **Firefinder** tab in Firebug panel.

FireQuery

The FireQuery extension extends Firebug with jQuery-focused features. It adds extra functionality to the **HTML** tab and allows us to visually see embedded data elements and event handlers that were added via jQuery.

FireQuery is a collection of Firebug enhancements for jQuery—a very handy extension for jQuery fans. If the page that we are viewing does not make use of jQuery JavaScript library, then it also allows us to inject jQuery into those pages very easily. This enables us to play around with jQuery or extract information for a web page that might not have jQuery installed previously.

The extension provides the following functionalities:

- jQuery expressions are intelligently presented in the Firebug console and DOM inspector
- Attached jQuery data objects are shown as proper JavaScript objects
- Elements in jQuery collections are highlighted when the mouse pointer is hovered over them

- It enables us to inject jQuery into any web page using the **jQuerify** button under the **Console** tab.

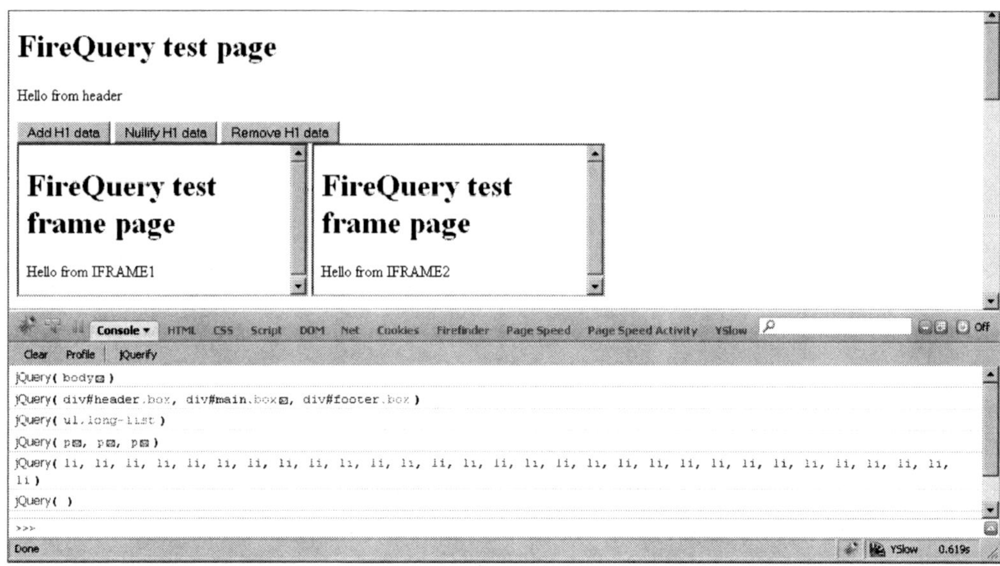

- After we run the jQuery, the **HTML** tab will look like the following screenshot:

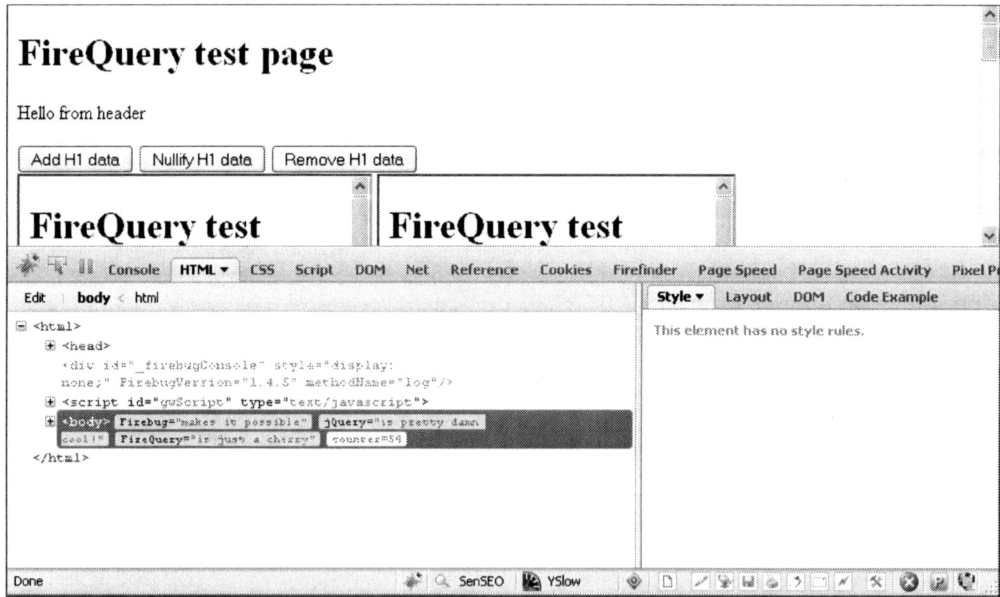

CodeBurner

CodeBurner is a Firefox add-on that integrates with Firebug, to extend it with reference material for HTML and CSS.

The extension's core functionality is centered on a new reference panel, which contains a search tool for looking up HTML elements, attributes, and CSS properties.

This extension also integrates nicely with the context menus in HTML, CSS, and DOM panels. This allows the user to look-up for the selected item via the context menu on the item.

In order to search for help on a particular HTML or CSS element, let's do the following steps:

1. Open the Firebug panel.
2. Click on the **Reference** tab.
3. Enter the element name in the **Search for** textbox on the right-hand side.
4. HTML and CSS elements that match the search criteria are shown on the left-hand side of the window.

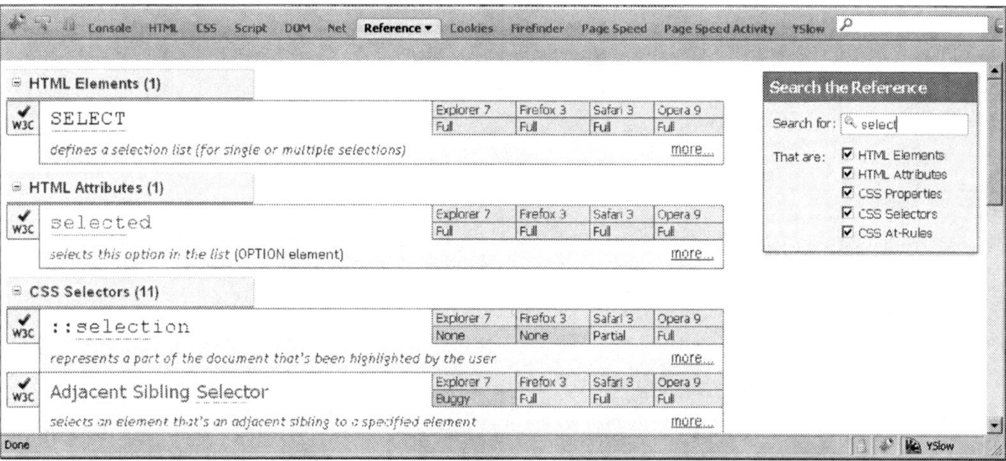

The following screenshot shows what each element depicts:

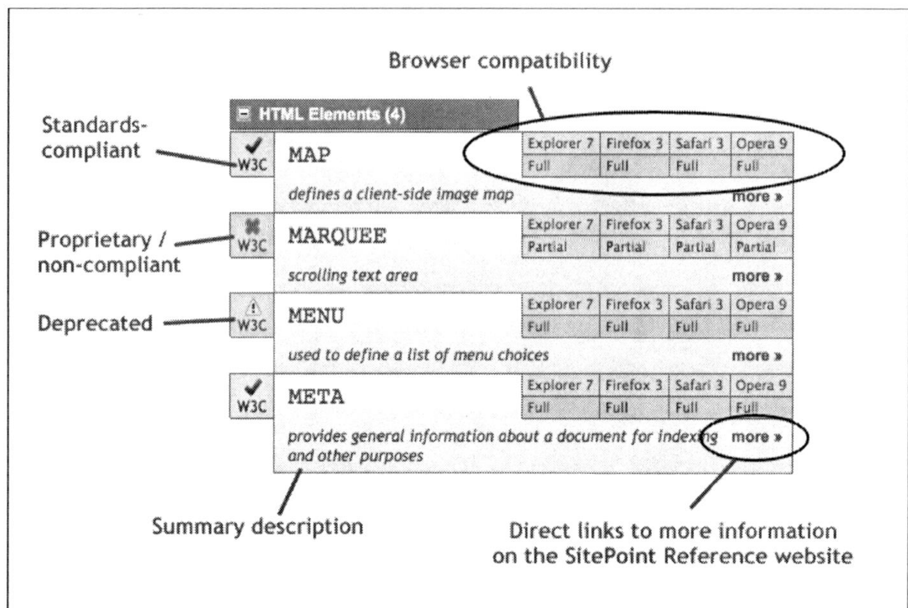

So, overall CodeBurner is a very useful tool for any web developer working on HTML and CSS, and serves as a good and useful reference for HTML and CSS.

SenSEO

The SenSEO extension checks the most important on-page SEO criteria and calculates a grade of how good our page fulfills these criteria. SenSEO evaluates our page with respect to Google's webmaster guidelines for search engine optimization, just like YSlow evaluates the page with respect to Yahoo's best practices for performance optimization.

SenSEO provides an overview of SEO-important web page components and analysis of on-page SEO criteria such as the document title, meta description, meta keywords, headings, and many more. SenSEO can be very handy before a launch to catch any simple tweaks that we may have overlooked during development. The rules that SenSEO checks our page against are:

- Use Title-Tag correctly
- Use Meta-Description correctly
- Use Meta-Keywords keywords correctly

- Use Meta-Robots correctly
- Headline-Tags
- Page-Content
- Domain
- Path
- Code is semantic and valid

In order to know more about the rules that SenSEO checks, go to `http://sensational-seo.com/on-page-criteria.html`.

In order to analyze the performance of our web page against a particular keyword, let's follow the steps mentioned:

1. Open the web page that we want to analyze in Firefox.
2. Open Firebug.
3. Click on the **SenSEO** tab.
4. In the **Keywords** textbox, enter the keyword (for example, **book**) and click **Inspect SEO Criteria**.

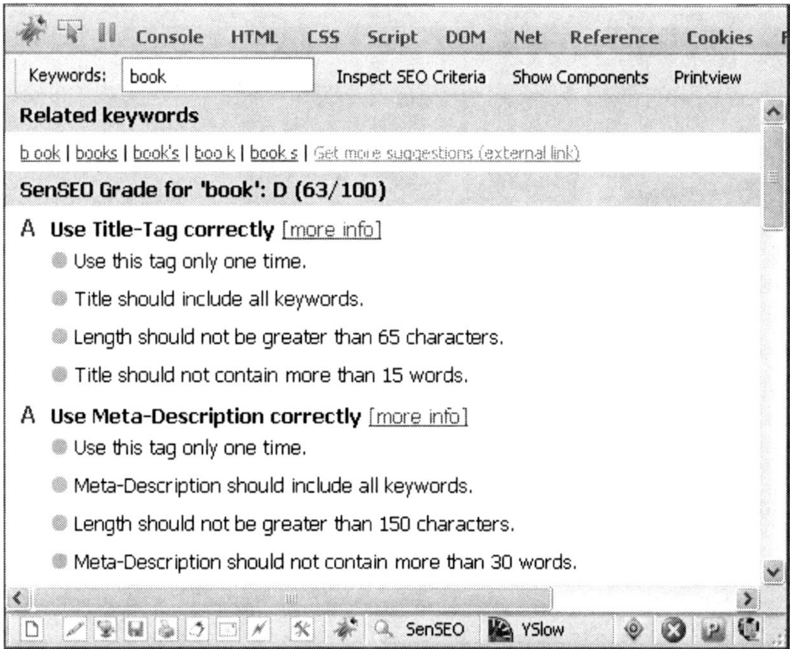

4. SenSEO will analyze the page and present the results in the same window.
5. In order to view the page components, click on the **Show Components** button.

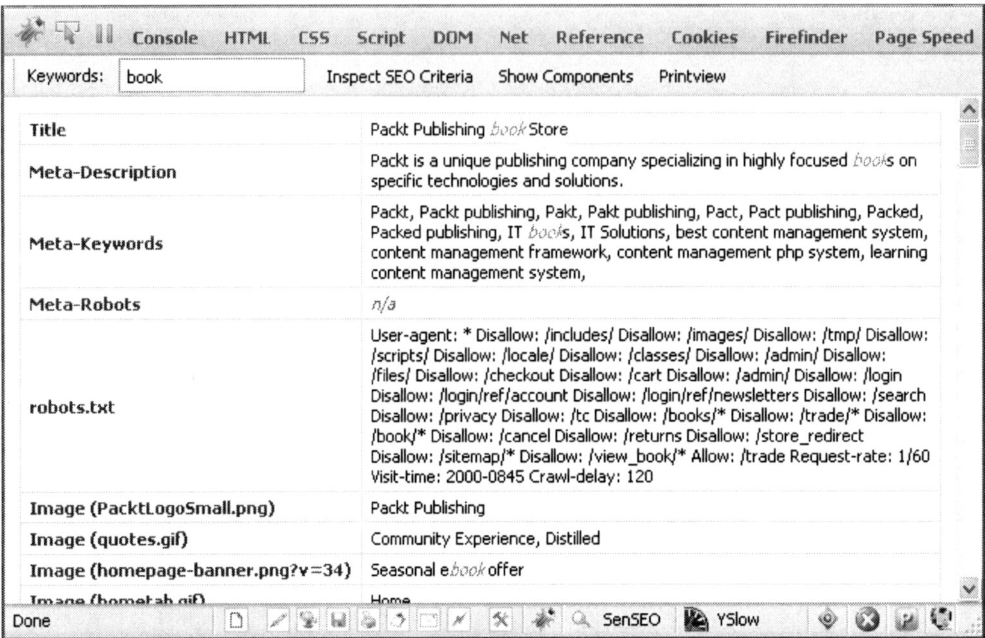

6. If we want to print the results, then click on **Printview** and the results will open in a new Firefox tab in printer-friendly mode.

Page Speed

The Page Speed extension has been open sourced by Google. In many respects, it is quite similar to YSlow; however, it is relatively new compared to YSlow. In terms of the number of rules that are checked against, Page Speed does a more comprehensive analysis. Page Speed is designed to analyze website performance and offer suggestions on how to improve page load times. Web masters and web developers can use Page Speed to evaluate the performance of their web pages and to get suggestions for how to improve them.

When we profile a web page with Page Speed, it evaluates the page's conformance to a number of different rules. These rules are general frontend best practices that we can apply at any stage of web development.

Page Speed evaluates performance from the browser's point of view, typically measured as the **page load time**. This is the lapsed time between the moment a user requests a new page and the moment the page is fully rendered by the browser.

The rules cover various steps that are involved in requesting a page and rendering the page on the browser:

- Resolving DNS names
- Setting up TCP connections
- Transmitting HTTP requests
- Downloading resources
- Fetching resources from cache
- Parsing and executing scripts
- Rendering objects on the page

Page Speed evaluates how well our page eliminates these steps altogether, parallelizes them, and shortens the time they need for their execution.

In order to run Page Speed against a web page, let's follow these steps:

To download the Page Speed extension, go to `http://code.google.com/speed/page-speed/download.html`.

1. Open Firefox.
2. Open the Firebug panel.
3. Click on the **Page Speed** tab.
4. Navigate to the web page we want to analyze and click **Analyze Performance**. Wait until the **Done** message appears on the browser status bar and the progress bar disappears.

5. When the page is analyzed, Page Speed displays the list of web performance best practices and the page's score on each one, sorted by importance/priority for this page.

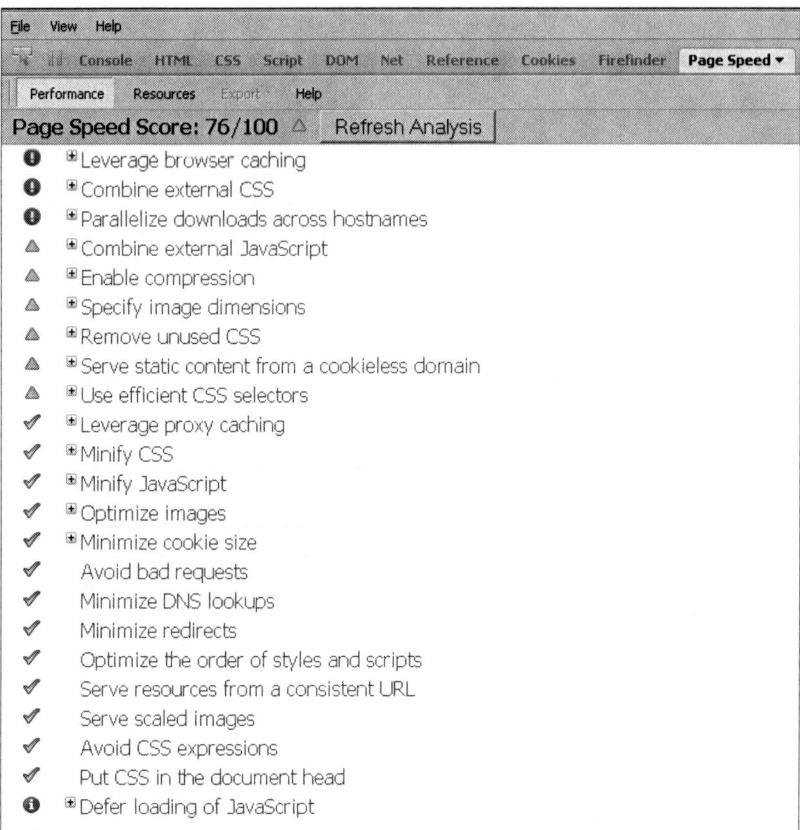

6. In the performance summary report, we can do any of the following:
    - Expand any of the rules to see specific suggestions for improvement.
    - Click any of the rule names to see documentation about each rule.
    - Click the **Show Resources** button to show a detailed list of resources referenced from this page.
    - Select **Export | Write Results in JSON Format** to export the results in JSON format.

The report generated by Page Speed groups the findings into priorities. The high and medium priority groups list elements that must be optimized to increase the performance of the website. Low priority items can still provide some performance gains, but not as much as the medium or high priority items.

The **Page Speed Activity** tab displays a timeline of all browser activities, including JavaScript processing, which makes it easier to spot scripts and elements that are increasing the loading times. The data shown on the **Page Speed Activity** tab is divided into various blocks that define events such as network latency, DNS lookups, connection establishment, and JavaScript processing.

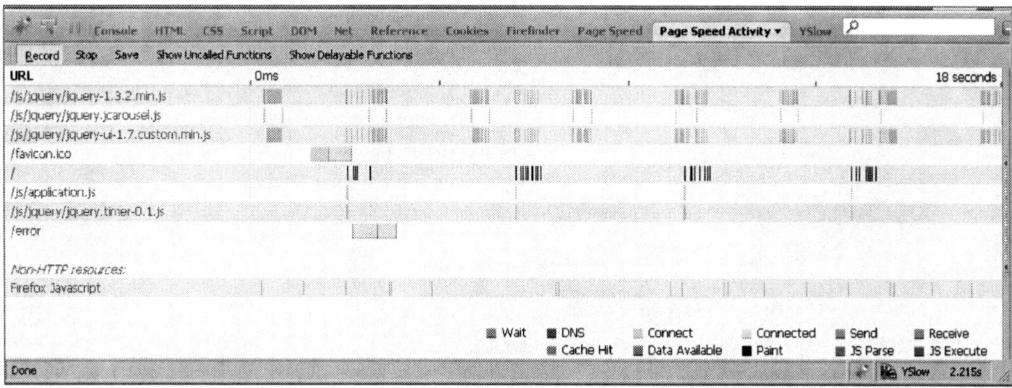

The best practices that Page Speed checks against the loading of a page are divided into five categories that cover different aspects of page-load optimization.

- **Optimizing caching**—keeping our application's data and logic off the network altogether:
    - Leverage browser caching
    - Leverage proxy caching
- **Minimizing round-trip times**—reducing the number of serial request-response cycles:
    - Minimize DNS lookups
    - Minimize redirects
    - Combine external JavaScript
    - Combine external CSS
    - Optimize the order of styles and scripts
    - Parallelize downloads across hostnames

- **Minimizing request size**—reducing upload size:
    - Minimize cookie size
    - Serve static content from a cookieless domain
- **Minimizing payload size**—reducing the size of responses, downloads, and cached pages:
    - Enable gzip compression
    - Remove unused CSS
    - Minify JavaScript
    - Minify CSS
    - Defer loading of JavaScript
    - Optimize images
    - Serve resources from a consistent URL
- **Optimizing browser rendering**—improving the browser's layout of a page:
    - Use efficient CSS selectors
    - Avoid CSS expressions
    - Put CSS in the document head
    - Specify image dimensions

In order to understand the various rules checked by Page Speed in detail and the rationale behind those rules, the reader is encouraged to take a look at the excellent documentation available at `http://code.google.com/speed/page-speed/`.

Summary

In this chapter, we looked at some of the useful Firebug extensions. There are many more extensions that are available and are very useful; however, it is not possible to cover all of them in this chapter. Firebug users should take a look at all of the available extensions.

11
Extending Firebug

In this chapter, we'll discuss the steps that can be used to develop an extension of Firebug. We will discuss setting up a development environment, file and directory structure, and some JavaScript code.

Extensions are packaged and distributed in ZIP files or bundles, with the XPI (pronounced as "zippy") file extension. Developing an extension to Firebug is the same as developing an extension to Firefox. This means that the directory structure, the files, the coding language, the style, and other things are the same for an extension of both Firebug and Firefox.

In this chapter, we'll discuss the following on extending Firebug:

- Setting up an extension development environment
- Getting started with a small "Hello World" extension of Firebug
- Taking "Hello World" to the next level

Setting up an extension development environment

To develop a Firebug extension, we first need to set up the development environment on the system. There is no difference between environments while developing an extension for Firebug or Firefox. The directory structure and files in Firebug extension are also similar to a Firefox extension. The following is an overview of what we need to configure to set up the environment for developing an extension to Firebug:

1. Create a development user profile to run our development Firefox session, with special development preferences in **about:config**.

2. Install some Firefox development extensions to our *dev* profile.
3. Edit files in the extensions folder of our profile and restart the application with the *dev* profile.

Setting up the development profile

To avoid performance degradation from development-related preferences and extensions, and to avoid losing our personal data, we can create a *dev* profile for development work, which will be separate from the default profile.

We can run two instances of Firefox at the same time by using separate profiles and starting the application with the `-no-remote` parameter. For example, the following command will start Firefox with a profile called *dev*, whether an instance of Firefox is already running or not:

- **On Ubuntu:**

```
/usr/bin/firefox -no-remote -P dev
```

- **On other distributions of Linux:**

```
/usr/local/bin/firefox -no-remote -P dev
```

- **On Mac:**

```
/Applications/Firefox.app/Contents/MacOS/firefox-bin -no-remote -P
                                                                 dev
```

- **On Windows:**
- **Start** | **Run**. Then type the following command:

```
"%ProgramFiles%\Mozilla Firefox\firefox.exe" -no-remote -P dev
```

If the profile specified does not exist (or if no profile is specified), Firefox will display the *Profile Manager* window. To run with the default profile, specify **default** as the profile (or omit the `-P` switch).

Now let's execute the command `firefox -no-remote -P dev`. If a *dev* profile already exists, then Firefox will open up with *dev* profile mode; otherwise it will prompt us to create one on the fly.

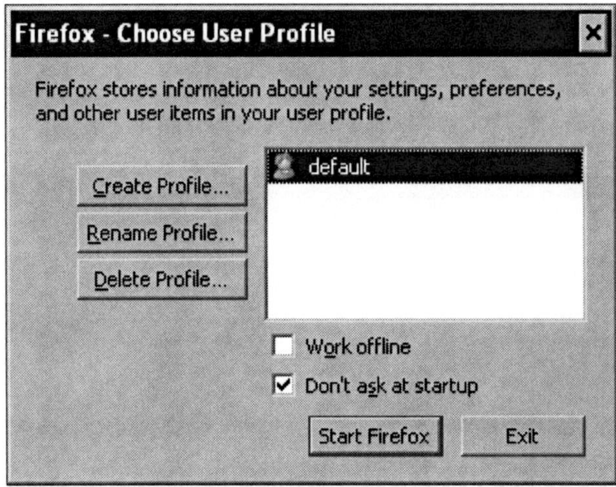

If we don't have a *dev* profile, then we can click on the **Create Profile...** button to create a new *dev* profile and follow the wizard's instructions for creating a new profile.

Development preferences

There is a set of development preferences that, when enabled, allows us to view more information about application activity, thus making debugging easier. However, these preferences can degrade the performance of Firefox, so we may want to use a separate development profile when we enable these preferences. Open Firefox with a *dev* profile, as discussed in the previous section, and change the preference settings in Firefox. Type `about:config` in the address bar of the browser.

A new page will open in Firefox where we can set our own customized preferences. There are many preferences and settings in the Firefox, so it would be difficult to find a particular preference. Firefox provides a **Filter** box which we can use to filter the **Preference Name** and find the desired preference in no time.

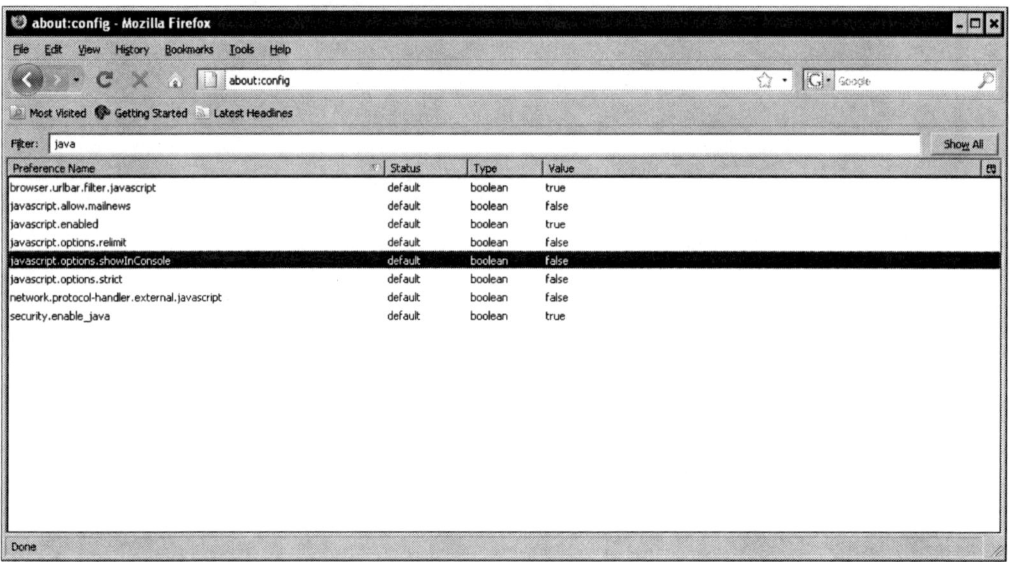

To change the value of a preference, double-click on the preference name. A small input form will appear in which we can provide/set the desired value.

Not all preferences are defined by default, and they are therefore not listed in `about:config` by default. We will have to create new entries for them.

For adding the new preferences, right-click anywhere on the page. Select **New** and we will see a submenu with the options—**Boolean**, **String**, and **Integer.** Choose any one from the menu. An input window will appear asking us the preference name and its value.

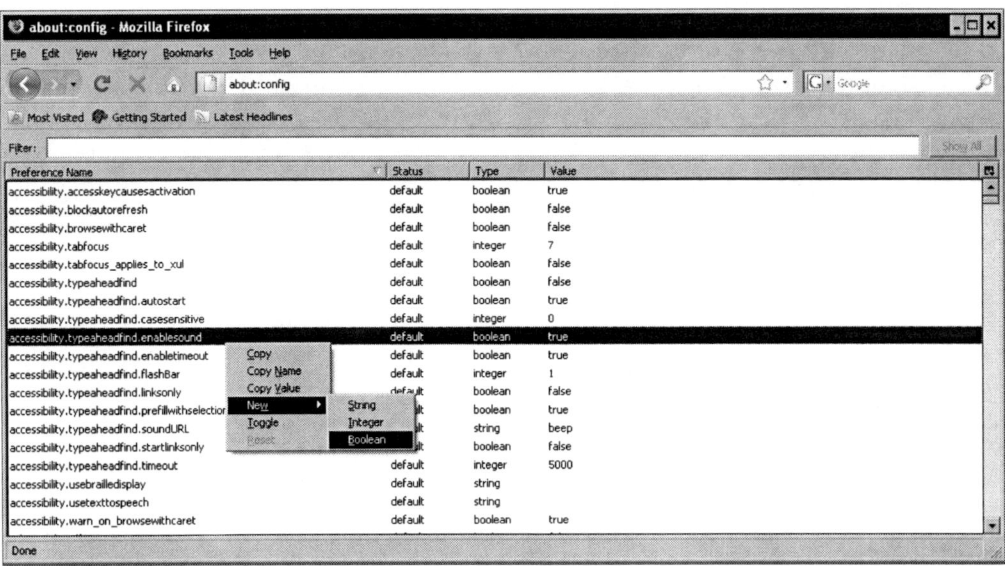

The following are the preferences that we need to set before developing an extension:

- `javascript.options.showInConsole = true`: This logs errors in chrome files to the error console.
- `nglayout.debug.disable_xul_cache = true`: This disables the XUL cache so that changes to windows and dialogs do not require a restart. This assumes we're using directories rather than JARs. Changes to XUL overlays will still require reloading of the document overlaid.
- `browser.dom.window.dump.enabled = true`: This enables the use of the dump(message) statement to print to the standard console.
- `javascript.options.strict = true`: This enables strict JavaScript warnings in the error console. Note that as many people have this setting turned off when developing, we will see lots of warnings for problems with their code, in addition to warnings for our own extension. We can filter those with Firebug's console filter options (as illustrated in Chapter 2, *Firebug Window Overview*).
- `extensions.logging.enabled = true`: This will send more detailed information about installation and update problems to the error console. (Note that the extension manager automatically restarts the application at startup sometimes, which may mean we won't have time to see the messages logged before the automatic restart happens. To see them, prevent the automatic restart by setting the Environment Variable `NO_EM_RESTART to` 1 before starting the application.)

- `dom.report_all_js_exceptions = true`: As this key is not available by default, we need to create this key. Setting up this key will log all the exceptions from inner frames. Alternatively, we can set the Environment Variable `MOZ_REPORT_ALL_JS_EXCEPTIONS`. It doesn't matter what value we set this to (it can even be `0`). If the variable exists, all exceptions from inner frames will be reported.

There are a few extensions that we might want to install on our Firefox for debugging and development purposes. The following are some of them:

- **DOM Inspector**: This is used to inspect and edit the live DOM of any web document or XUL application.
- **Venkman**: This is a JavaScript debugger.
- **Extension Developer's Extension**: This is a suite of tools for extension development.
- **Console2**: This is an enhanced JavaScript console.
- **JavaScript Command**: This is for writing/testing JavaScript on Firefox windows.
- **Chrome List**: This is for navigating and viewing files in `chrome://`.
- **Chrome Edit Plus**: This is a user file editor.
- **Extension Wizard**: This is a web-based application that generates an extension skeleton.
- **Chromebug**: This combines elements of a JavaScript debugger and DOM.
- **MozRepl**: This explores and modifies Firefox and other Mozilla applications while they run.
- **ExecuteJS**: This is an enhanced JavaScript console.
- **XPCOMViewer**: This is an XPCOM inspector.
- **JavaScript**: This shells to test snippets of JavaScript.
- **SQLite Manager**: This manages the SQL Lite database.
- **ViewAbout**: This enables access to various `about: dialogs` from the **View** menu.
- **Crash Me Now!**: This is useful for testing debug symbols and the crash reporting system.

Getting started with a small "Hello World!" extension of Firebug

Let's not waste any more time and quickly move on to developing a small "Hello World!" extension to Firebug. This extension explains how to add a new tab to Firebug.

To start developing a "Hello World!" extension, we need to set up a directory and file structure of the extension. The directory structure should look similar to the following one:

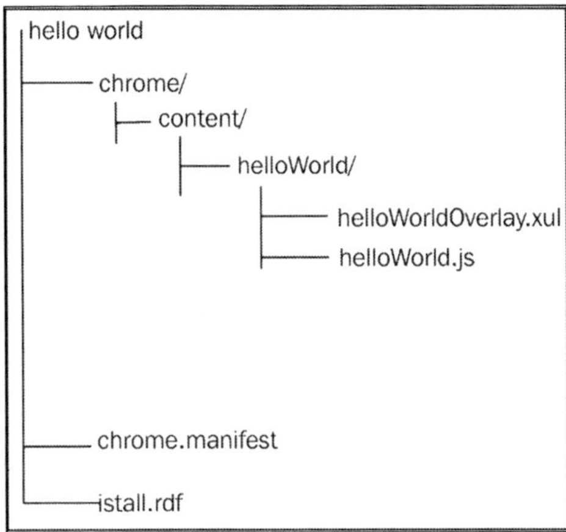

As we can see, `helloWorldOverlay.xul` and `helloWorld.js` are the main files where the actual implementation code resides. The other two files—`chrome.manifest` and `install.rdf`—are used by Firefox to install the extension.

The chrome.manifest file

The `chrome.manifest` file specifies that there is content under `chrome | content | helloWorld`. The second line signifies that the `helloWorldOverlay.xul` overlay represents an overlay for `firebugOverlay.xul`. The configuration in XUL files is called chrome registration.

[To know more about chrome and chrome registry, one can visit `https://developer.mozilla.org/en/Chrome_Registration`.]

The following is the content of the `chrome.manifest` file:

```
content helloworld chrome/content/helloWorld/ xpcnativewrappers=no
overlay chrome://firebug/content/firebugOverlay.xul chrome://
helloworld/content/helloWorldOverlay.xul
```

We can also disable the security tests that Firefox runs before installing the extension by setting the value of `xpcnativewrappers` to `no`.

The install.rdf file

The general information about the extension is placed in the `install.rdf` file. The general information such as e-mail ID, extension version, description of extension, creator, and so on, are provided in this file.

The following is the content of the `install.rdf` file:

```
<?xml version="1.0"?>
<RDF xmlns="http://www.w3.org/1999/02/22-rdf-syntax-ns#"
xmlns:em="http://www.mozilla.org/2004/em-rdf#">
<Description about="urn:mozilla:install-manifest">
<em:id>awesome@coder.com</em:id>
<em:type>2</em:type>
<em:version>0.1</em:version>
<em:targetApplication>
<Description>
<em:id>{ec8030f7-c20a-464f-9b0e-13a3a9e97384}</em:id>
<em:minVersion>0.1</em:minVersion>
<em:maxVersion>3.7.*.*</em:maxVersion>
</Description>
</em:targetApplication>
<em:name>Hello World!</em:name>
<em:description>A Simple Firebug's Extension</em:description>
<em:creator>Chandan Luthra</em:creator>
<em:homepageURL>http://www.myHomePageUrl.com</em:homepageURL>
</Description>
</RDF>
```

Let's look at the parameters used in the file:

- `awesome@coder.com` : This is the ID of the extension. This is a value we come up with to identify our extension in an e-mail address format (that it should not be our e-mail). Make it unique. We can also use a GUID.

[This parameter *must* be in the format of an e-mail address, although it does *not* have to be a valid e-mail address. (`example@example.example`)]

- `<em:type>2</em:type>` : The `2` declares that it is installing an extension. If we were to install a theme it would be `4`.
- `{ec8030f7-c20a-464f-9b0e-13a3a9e97384}`: This is Firefox's application ID.
- `<em:minVersion>0.1</em:minVersion>`: This is the exact version number of the earliest version of Firefox that we're saying this extension will work with. Never use a `*` in a `minVersion`, it almost certainly will not do what we expect it to.
- `<em:maxVersion>3.7.*.*</em:maxVersion>`: This is the maximum version of Firefox that we're saying this extension will work with. Let's make sure we set this to be no newer than the newest currently available version! In this case, `3.7.*.*` indicates that the extension works with Firefox 3.5 and any subsequent 3.5.x release.

The helloWorldOverlay.xul file

The Gecko engine behind Firefox is designed to allow us to build user interfaces using an XML-based language called **XUL** (**XML User Interface Language**). One primary objective of this language is to allow us to overlay new components by essentially inserting them into existing XUL-based applications such as Firefox. Firefox extensions make heavy use of overlays to add functionality to Firefox without needing to modify the Firefox code.

[To know more about XUL and overlays, visit `https://developer.mozilla.org/en/XUL`.]

The following XUL code specifies that the `helloWorld.js` file is to be included and it also helps the Firefox to know which JavaScript file(s) are to be executed and in which order:

```
<?xml version="1.0"?>
<overlay
xmlns="http://www.mozilla.org/keymaster/gatekeeper/there.is.only.
xul"><script src="helloWorld.js"/>
</overlay>
```

The helloWorld.js file

The `helloWorld.js` file will create a new tab on the Firebug menu bar and register a new panel with it. The new panel behaves like a container and it will be used to show the contents/results/statistics or any information that we want the end user to see.

We will notice that the actual logic is encapsulated in `FBL.ns(function() {with (FBL){.........}});`. This encapsulation is used to avoid naming collisions between local and global variables, and it acts like a namespace for our code.

The following is the content of the `helloWorld.js` file:

```
FBL.ns(function() { with (FBL) {
function MyPanel() {}
MyPanel.prototype = extend(Firebug.Panel,{
    name: "HelloWorld",
    title: "Hello World!",
    initialize: function() {
       Firebug.Panel.initialize.apply(this, arguments);
          }
});
Firebug.registerPanel(MyPanel);
}});
```

Now there is a `MyPanel` panel in Firebug that extends the `Firebug.Panel` object. The `extend()` function in the code is used for extension mechanism; through this function we can inherit the properties of any other object in the current scope. Extending the object is similar to the class inheritance. Here, in our example, inherit means that the `extend()` function copies all the properties from the first parameter(`Firebug.Panel`) to the second parameter(`MyPanel`).

There are a few name value pairs in the code. The `name` and `title` are the properties of `MyPanel` and `initialize` is a function. The `name` is used to identify the panel uniquely so that we can access `MyPanel` through the `getPanel()` function. The `title` is a display name of the tab, which will be shown on Firebug's menu bar. The `initialize` function automatically gets invoked by Firebug's framework when the panel is activated for the first time.

Now our new panel `MyPanel` is ready and needs to be registered with Firebug so that Firebug ensures that it will be properly shown on its menu bar. The `registerPanel()` function of Firebug is used to register the new panel by passing the `MyPanel` as parameter to this function.

Packaging and installation

Now we are done with this small example of Hello World! extension, it is ready to package and install. Packaging the extension is very simple, we only need to compress (ZIP) the root directory in a single zippy file with XPI as the file extension to it.

In our example, the root directory is `helloWorld`.

On Ubuntu:

```
$ cd helloWorld
$ zip -r myExtension.xpi *
```

On Windows:

- Right-click on the root directory and select the `Send To | Compressed (zipped) Folder` option
- Rename the new zipped file and change the file extension from ZIP to XPI

After packaging the extension, open the zippy file with Firefox by dragging the zippy (XPI) file into the Firefox window. Firefox will then check the version compatibility and a small window will open asking to install the extension.

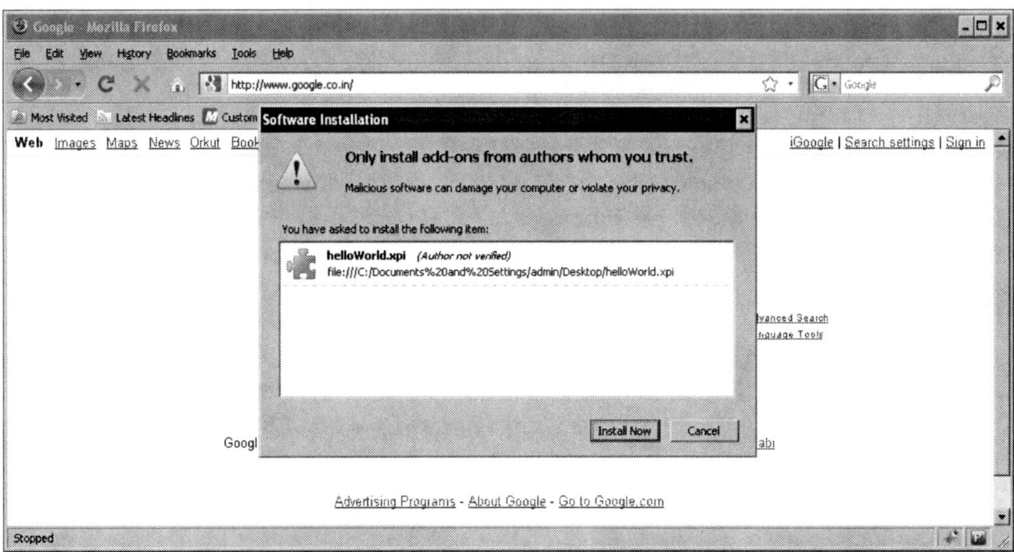

After installation, Firefox will ask us to restart it in order to invoke the extension.

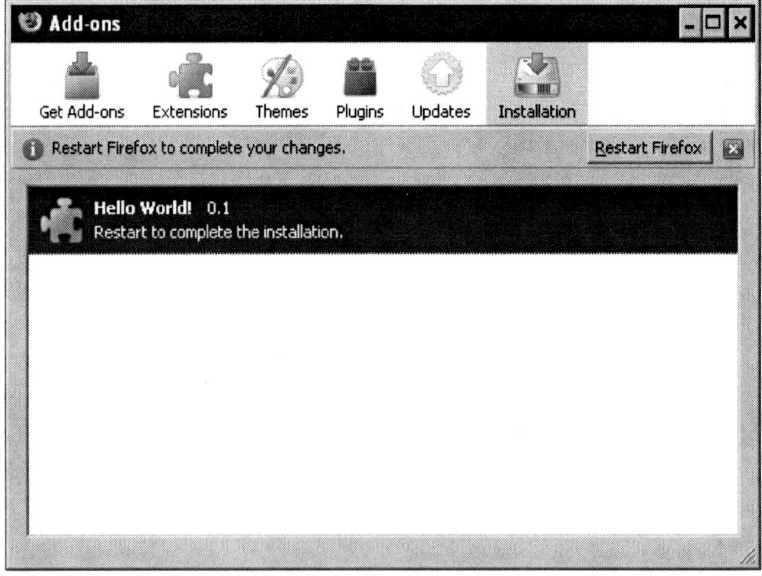

When Firefox comes up, it will inform us about the installed add-on. We can always disable and uninstall the extension from here.

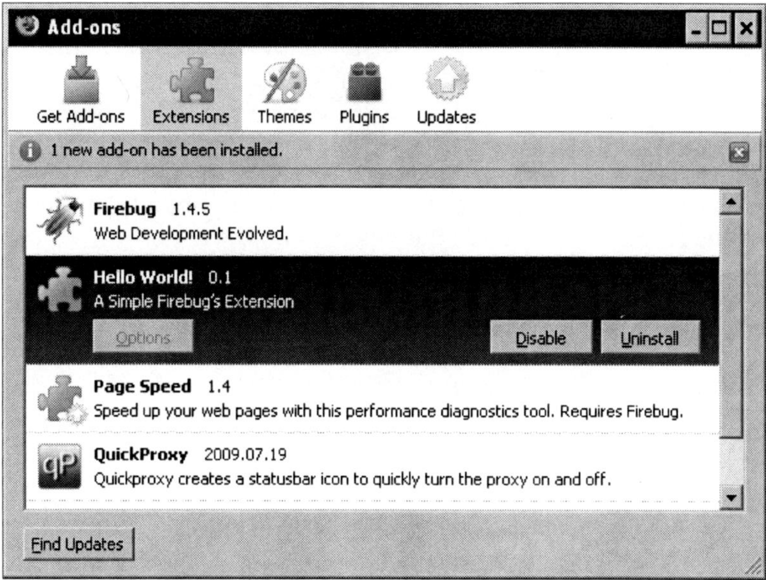

Now our test extension **Hello World!** is ready and installed on Firefox. To see it on Firebug, just press the *F12* key and we will see a new tab on Firebug's menu bar.

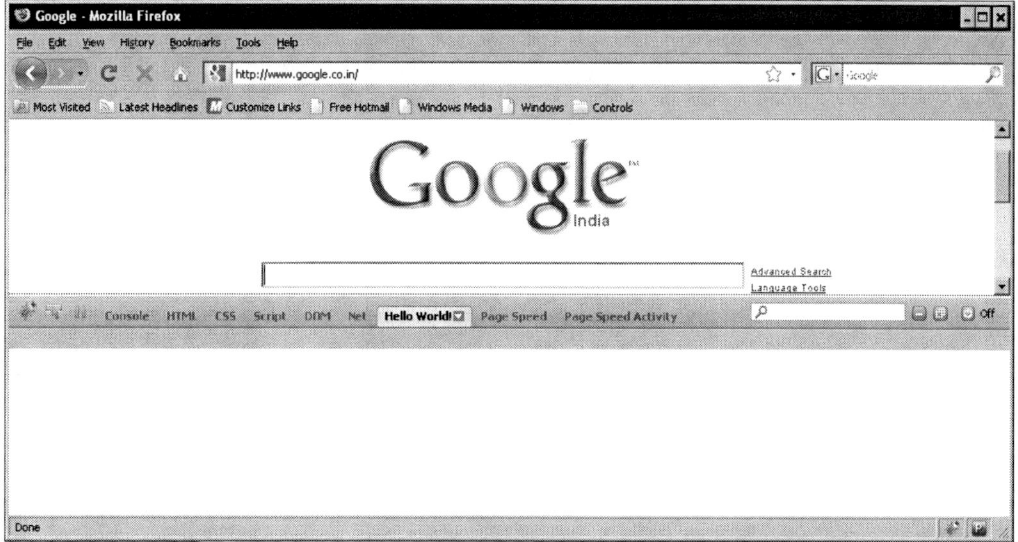

Taking "Hello World!" to the next level

Here we will learn how to attach the drop-down list of options to our **Hello World!** tab. The purpose of this drop-down list is to allow the user to set some specific preferences on the panel. Suppose the extension shows hundreds of results (like **Net** panel) and the user is interested in only those results that contain "advertisements" as a keyword. So, the options on the tab can be configured in such a way that the user can select the option and customize the results.

To display the options drop-down on the tab, we need to implement the `getOptionsMenuItems()` function in the `MyPanel` object.

There will be a slight change in the directory structure of the extension and a new file `prefs.js` will be included under `defaults | preferences`.

This is how the new directory structure would look:

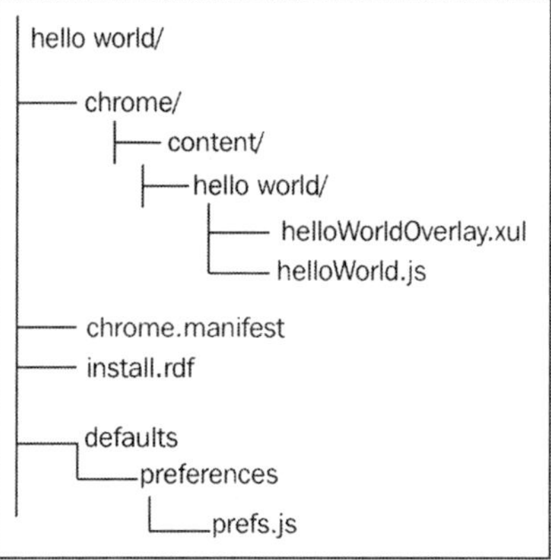

The "prefs.js" file

In spite of having `.js` as a file extension, the `prefs.js` file is not a JavaScript file. We can think of this file as a `.ini` file, which is used to inform the Firefox that `key:value` pairs written in this file are the default preferences and need to be set up on starting Firefox.

```
pref("extensions.firebug.helloworld.firstOption", true);
pref("extensions.firebug.helloworld.secondOption", false);
```

These two lines in `prefs.js` create preferences in Firefox, which can be seen by writing `about:config` in the address bar.

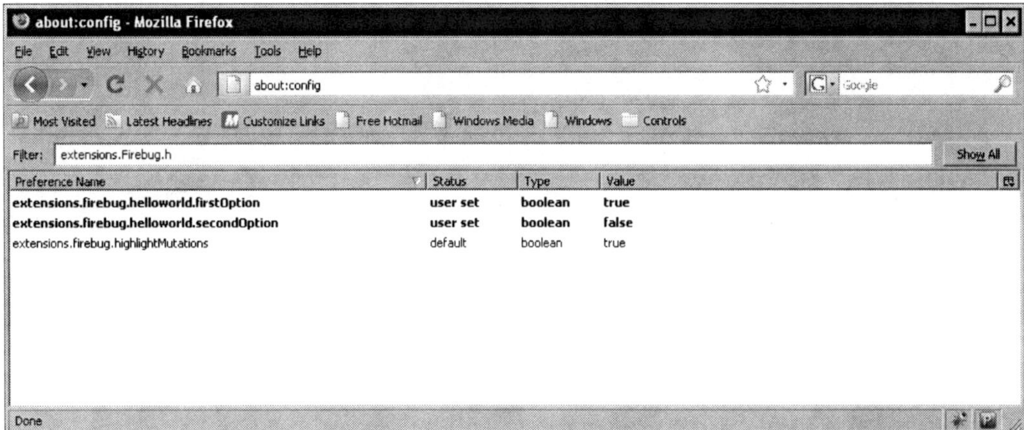

The "helloWorld.js" file revisited

Now we'll tweak our test extension's `helloWorld.js` file so that the extension is able to show both the options drop down on the **Hello World!** tab of Firebug. This will need to provide the implementation of the `getOptionsMenuItems()` function.

```
FBL.ns(function() { with (FBL) {
function MyPanel() {}
MyPanel.prototype = extend(Firebug.Panel,{
    name: "HelloWorld",
    title: "Hello World!",

    initialize: function() {
       Firebug.Panel.initialize.apply(this, arguments);
```

```
    },

    getOptionsMenuItems: function(context)
    {
        return [this.optionMenu("MyFirstOption", "helloworld.
firstOption"), "-", this.optionMenu("MySecondOption", "helloworld.
secondOption")];
    },

    optionMenu: function(label, option)
    {
        var value = Firebug.getPref(Firebug.prefDomain, option);
        return {
            label: label,
            nol10n: true,
            type: "checkbox",
            checked: value,
            command: bindFixed(Firebug.setPref, this,
                        Firebug.prefDomain, option, !value)
        };
    }
});
Firebug.registerPanel(MyPanel);
}});
```

In the code, the `getOptionsMenuItems()` function returns the list of option objects that Firebug understands and it places them on the drop-down.

The *hyphen* in the `getOptionsMenuItem()` is only for UI purposes, to display the separator between the options.

The most interesting thing is probably the implementation of the `optionMenu()` function. First of all, we are utilizing `get` and `setPref` methods from Firebug namespace:

`Firebug.getPref(prefDomain, name);`

`Firebug.setPref(prefDomain, name, value);`

The usage is quite obvious. The first parameter is used to specify the preference domain, the second specifies the preference name, and the third specifies the new preference value. The domain should be `extensions.firebug` (there is a constant `Firebug.prefDomain` for that).

Further, there is a new `bindFixed` function. Here `bindFixed()` is used to bind a method (`Firebug.setPref`) to a handler (`command`), with three parameters (`Firebug.prefDomain, option, !value`).

Now install the extension in a similar way as we did earlier. To view the extension in action we need to open `about:config` in the browser, open Firebug, and click on the **HelloWorld!** tab's option drop-down. We will see the value of that the preferences that we added in `prefs.js` file is getting toggled.

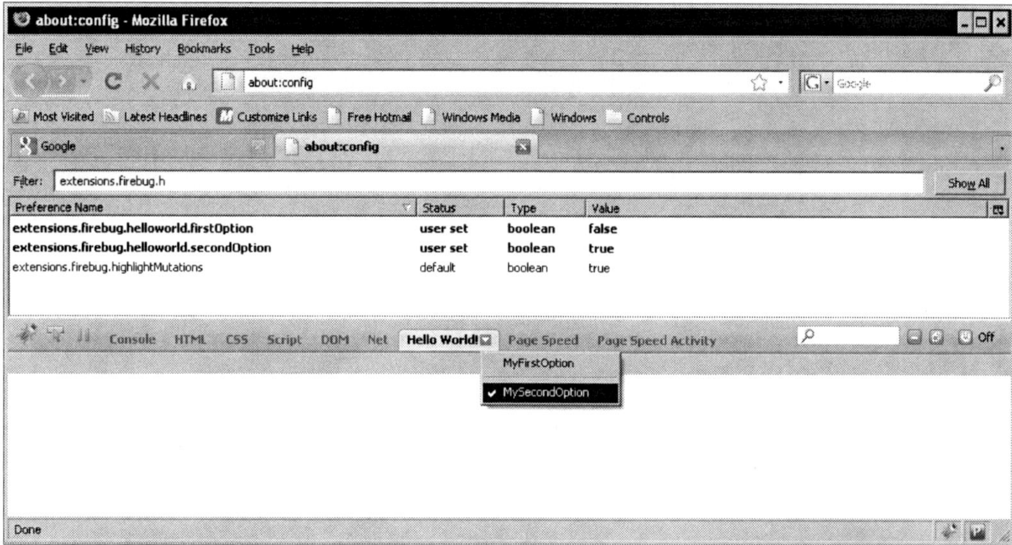

Summary

In this chapter we discussed setting up the development environment on our machines. The Firefox extensions are simply compressed files with XPI file extensions. We saw that we can restrict the extension to a particular version of the Firefox by modifying the `minVersion` and `maxVersion` elements in the `install.rdf` file.

In the development process, sometimes the browser gets crashed, which can corrupt the default user profile. Therefore, it is recommended to create a new *dev* profile for developing purposes.

There is a very good tutorial on developing Firebug extensions by Jan Odvarko (a contributor of Firebug). We suggest that you go through his blogs; you can visit his site at `http://www.softwareishard.com`.

A Quick Overview of Firebug's Features and Options

This appendix acts as a reference for various Firebug features and options. We will also take a look at some of the features that are expected in future releases of Firebug.

Keyboard and mouse shortcuts reference

Firebug provides a lot of keyboard and mouse shortcuts in order to make working with Firebug an easier and faster experience. As we become more experienced with Firebug, we will find ourselves making more and more use of these shortcuts to accomplish common tasks, instead of opening the Firebug panel and then clicking on various tabs and buttons.

The following shortcuts are divided into the various categories. Please note that these shortcuts work with Windows and Linux.

Global shortcuts

Task / operation	Shortcut
Open Firebug panel	*F12*
Close Firebug panel	*F12*
Open Firebug in window	*Ctrl+Shift+L*
Switch to previous tab	*Ctrl+`*
Focus command line	*Ctrl+Shift+L*
Focus search box	*Ctrl+Shift+L*
Toggle inspect mode	*Ctrl+Shift+C*

Task / operation	Shortcut
Toggle JavaScript profiler	*Ctrl+Shift+P*
Re-execute last command line	*Ctrl+Shift+E*

HTML tab shortcuts

Task / operation	Shortcut
Edit attribute	Click on name or value
Edit text node	Click on text
Edit element	Double-click tag name
Next node in path	*Ctrl+.*
Previous node in path	*Ctrl+,*

HTML editor shortcuts

Task / operation	Shortcut
Finish editing	*Return*
Cancel editing	*Esc*
Advance to next field	*Tab*
Go back to previous field	*Shift+Tab*

HTML inspect mode shortcuts

Task / operation	Shortcut
Cancel inspection	*Esc*
Inspect parent	*Ctrl+Up*
Insect child	*Ctrl+Down*
Toggle inspection	*Ctrl+Shift+C*

Script tab shortcuts

Task / operation	Shortcut
Continue	*Esc* or *Ctrl+ /*
Step over	*F10* or *Ctrl+ '*
Step into	*F11* or *Ctrl+ ;*
Step out	*Shift+F11* or *Ctrl+Shift+;*
Toggle breakpoint	Click on line number
Disable breakpoint	*Shift*+Click on line number
Edit breakpoint condition	Right-click on line number
Run to line	Middle-click on line number or *Ctrl*+click on line number
Next function on stack	*Ctrl+.*
Previous function on stack	*Ctrl+,*
Focus menu of scripts	*Ctrl*+press space bar
Focus watch editor	*Ctrl+Shift+N*

DOM tab shortcuts

Task / operation	Shortcut
Edit property	Double-click on empty space
Next object in path	*Ctrl+.*
Previous object in path	*Ctrl+,*

DOM and watch editor shortcuts

Task / operation	Shortcut
Finish editing	*Return*
Cancel editing	*Esc*
Autocomplete next property	*Tab*
Autocomplete previous property	*Shift+Tab*

CSS tab shortcuts

Task / operation	**Shortcut**
Edit property	Click on property
Insert new property	Double-click on white space
Focus menu of stylesheets	*Ctrl+Space*

CSS editor tab shortcuts

Task / operation	**Shortcut**
Finish editing	*Return*
Cancel editing	*Esc*
Advance to next field	*Tab*
Advance to previous field	*Shift+Tab*
Increase number by one	*Up arrow key*
Decrease number by one	*Down arrow key*
Increase number by ten	*Page Up*
Decrease number by ten	*Page Down*
Autocomplete next keyword	*Up arrow key*
Autocomplete previous keyword	*Down arrow key*

Layout tab shortcuts

Task / operation	**Shortcut**
Edit value	Click on value

Layout editor shortcuts

Task / operation	**Shortcut**
Finish editing	*Return*
Cancel editing	*Esc*
Advance to next field	*Tab*
Advance to previous field	*Shift+Tab*
Increase number by one	*Up arrow key*
Decrease number by one	*Down arrow key*
Increase number by ten	*Page Up*
Decrease number by ten	*Page Down*

Command line (small) shortcuts

Task / operation	**Shortcut**
Autocomplete next property	*Tab*
Autocomplete previous property	*Shift+Tab*
Execute	*Return*
Inspect result	*Shift+Return*
Open result's context menu	*Ctrl+Return*

Command line (large) shortcuts

Task / operation	**Shortcut**
Execute	*Ctrl+Return*

Console API reference

The Console API is very powerful for development and debugging. The following is a quick reference table for the Console API, which explains all the console functions in short:

Task / operation	Purpose
`console.log(object[, object, ...])`	Writes a message to the console. We may pass as many arguments as we like, and they will be joined together in a space-delimited line.
`console.debug(object[, object, ...])`	Writes a message to the console, including a hyperlink to the line where it was called.
`console.info(object[, object, ...])`	Writes a message to the console with the visual *info* icon, color coding, and a hyperlink to the line where it was called.
`console.warn(object[, object, ...])`	Writes a message to the console with the visual *warning* icon, color coding, and a hyperlink to the line where it was called.
`console.error(object[, object, ...])`	Writes a message to the console with the visual *error* icon, color coding, and a hyperlink to the line where it was called.
`console.assert(expression[, object, ...])`	Tests that an expression is true. If not, it will write a message to the console and throw an exception.
`console.dir(object)`	Prints an interactive listing of all the properties of the object. This looks identical to the view that you would see in the **DOM** tab.
`console.dirxml(node)`	Prints the XML source tree of an HTML or XML element. This looks identical to the view that you would see in the **HTML** tab. We can click on any node to inspect it in the **HTML** tab.
`console.trace()`	Prints an interactive stack trace of JavaScript execution at the point where it is called.
`console.group(object[, object, ...])`	Writes a message to the console and opens a nested block to indent all future messages sent to the console. Call `console.groupEnd()` to close the block.
`console.groupCollapsed(object[, object, ...])`	Similar to `console.group()`, but the block is initially collapsed.

Task / operation	Purpose
`console.groupEnd()`	Closes the most recently opened block created by a call to `console.group()` or `console.groupEnd()`.
`console.time(name)`	Creates a new timer under the given name. Call `console.timeEnd(name)` with the same name to stop the timer and print the time elapsed.
`console.timeEnd(name)`	Stops a timer created by a call to `console.time(name)` and writes the time elapsed.
`console.profile([title])`	Turns on the JavaScript profiler. The optional argument title would contain the text to be printed in the header of the profile report.
`console.profileEnd()`	Turns off the JavaScript profiler and prints its report.
`console.count([title])`	Returns the count of how many times the line of code is executed. The optional argument title will print a message in addition to the number of the count.

Command line API reference

The Firebug command line allows user-entered expressions to be evaluated in the page, similar to having scripts in our page. It is one of the most useful and powerful features of Firebug. Here is the quick cheat sheet for command line:

Command	Purpose
`$(id)`	Returns a single element with the given ID
`$$(selector)`	Returns an array of elements that match the given CSS selector.
`$x(xpath)`	Returns an array of elements that match the given XPath expression.
`dir(object)`	Prints an interactive listing of all properties of the object. This looks identical to the view that we would see in the **DOM** tab.
`dirxml(node)`	Prints the XML source tree of an HTML or XML element. This looks identical to the view that we would see in the **HTML** tab. We can click on any node to inspect it in the **HTML** tab.

Command	Purpose
`cd(window)`	By default, command line expressions are relative to the top-level window of the page. `cd()` allows us to use the window of a frame in the page instead.
`clear()`	Clears the console.
`inspect(object[, tabName])`	Inspects an object in the most suitable tab, or the tab identified by the optional argument `tabName`. The available tab names are **HTML**, **CSS**, **SCRIPT**, and **DOM**.
`keys(object)`	Returns an array containing the names of all properties of the object.
`values(object)`	Returns an array containing the values of all properties of the object.
`debug(fn)`	Adds a breakpoint on the first line of a function.
`undebug(fn)`	Removes the breakpoint on the first line of a function.
`monitor(fn)`	Turns on logging for all calls to a function.
`unmonitor(fn)`	Turns off logging for all calls to a function.
`monitorEvents(object[, types])`	Turns on logging for all events dispatched to an object. The optional argument types may specify a specific family of events to log. The most commonly used values for types are *mouse* and *key*. The full list of available types includes *composition, contextmenu, drag, focus, form, key, load, mouse, mutation, paint, scroll, text, ui, and xul.*
`unmonitorEvents(object[, types])`	Turns off logging for all events dispatched to an object.
`profile([title])`	Turns on the JavaScript profiler. The optional argument title would contain the text to be printed in the header of the profile report.
`profileEnd()`	Turns off the JavaScript profiler and prints its report.

Firebug online resources

The following are a few online references for some useful information, such as releases, issues, new features, extensions, and so on:

Resource description	URL
Firebug site homepage	`http://getfirebug.com/`
Firebug wiki homepage	`http://getfirebug.com/wiki/index.php/Main_Page`
Firebug video by Joe Hewitt	`http://video.yahoo.com/watch/111581/938140`
Firebug Google group	`http://groups.google.com/group/firebug`
Firebug issues tracking system on Google code	`http://code.google.com/p/fbug/issues/list`
Firebug internals page on Mozilla site	`https://developer.mozilla.org/en/FirebugInternals`
Firebug plugins page on Firebug site	`http://getfirebug.com/extensions/`

Features expected in future releases of Firebug

Firebug is a rapidly growing application and every new version of it has major changes as compared to the previous versions. The Firebug Working Group has some initial plans for Firebug 1.6 and 1.7, the short versions.

Firebug 1.6

In this version, Firebug will focus on Firebug extension technologies and deliver most of its new functions as extensions. The major new work will be the Swarm implementation.

A **Firebug Swarm** is a collection of Firebug extensions that are tested, maintained, and marketed together. It is a scheme for distributed development and installation, combined with centralized testing and marketing.

The Firebug development team is aiming for a release in April 2010. Some of the features can be implemented as separate extensions that could be part of the Firebug bundle.

Some improvements in this version

The Firebug team plans what will be included in new releases on the basis of discussions on the mailing list, the forums, and the community, as well as issues and bugs. Here are some enhancements and improvements that Firebug will have in its next release.

Scrolling panel tab bar

Some scrolling support is necessary as extensions often create a new panel and there is not enough space for displaying all of them.

FBTest support for Firebug extensions

The Swarm will support testing of Firebug extensions together with Firebug, but using Firebug's tests. Firebug also needs a solution for extensions to add their own tests.

Locales as extensions

Having this has two advantages:

- Users can switch back to the default en-US language
- If some strings are not translated, we can use them from the default language

Currently the string key (formatted for this purpose) itself is used as the default.

Extension points for panel buttons and main menu options

Some smaller extensions are actually harder to write than new panels because Firebug has no support for adding menu options and buttons. Therefore, some extension points will be there in Firebug for panel buttons and main menu options so that one can quickly develop a new extension.

Breakpoint column for the HTML panel

Similar to the **Script**, **DOM,** and **Net** panel, the **HTML** panel should also offer a vertical column (on the left-hand side of the panel content) in order to easily create a breakpoint. HTML mutation breakpoint creation is currently hidden behind a context menu.

Break on next CSS change and CSS breakpoints

Like **HTML**, **Script**, and **Net** panel, we can create breakpoints on the **CSS** panel. This feature will allow user to set breakpoints, which will be triggered whenever CSS change is encountered.

Options for the break on next feature (mainly a UI-related issue)

The break on next feature should have options for every panel:

- **XHR**: Break on request/response
- **Script**: Break on click, mousemove, and so on

Net panel improvements

The following are mostly issues for improving the **Net** panel reported in the Firebug issue list:

- New columns with additional information—for example, IP address (hidden by default)
- Change the order of columns
- Showing cache reads (not network communication really)

Script panel improvements

The following is a list of proposed improvements of the script panel that need to be done in this version of Firebug:

- Improve the script location menu. Group scripts (by inline, events, evaluated) and use nested menus.
- Jump from function calls to their definition.
- Jump from the ID defined in `getElementById()` to element in **HTML** panel.
- Jump from a variable name to the **DOM** panel by holding down *Ctrl* and clicking on it.
- Every variable could have a context menu entry for putting it to the watch list.

JavaScript function support

Firebug is aiming to rework on JavaScript's "function" support with new JavaScript debugging features that will show us:

- A list all of the objects that refer to a function
- The property names

Firebug 1.7

This version of Firebug is targeted to be released in September 2010. In this version, Firebug focuses on refactoring the architecture of Firebug. With this change in the architecture, the following features will be added:

- Prepare to support remote debugging for mobile and multiprocessing browsers:
    - Server side will be headless
    - Client side will have no access to Firefox data
- Allow simpler and more robust extensions:
    - JavaScript oriented loading, no **XPCOM** (**Cross Platform Component Object Model**) loader required
    - Isolation and concentration of extension code
- Clean up expedient code and clarify the implementation:
    - Relation to platform window system
    - Relation of panels and modules
    - Prepare/exploit shift to jetpack

Following are some proposed changes for Firebug 1.7:

Separate modules and panels

Broadly speaking, Mike Collins' architecture for remote Firebug puts the module code in the server and the panel code in the client (UI side). The Firebug's `context` object (`TabContext.js`) is passed over the wire between them using CrossFire.

The first step in that direction is to divide all of the source into module and panel files. For example, we might have `debuggerModule.js` and `debuggerPanel.js`. Then `firebug.js` would be divided between module dispatch and panel dispatch (`dispatchModules.js` and `dispatchPanels.js`). The API between these objects would be the remote CrossFire API.

Issue: File names versus folder names

However, it's more common to need to write with one kind of module and panel rather than all the panels and modules. Creating a subdirectory for each feature, for example, `debugger.js/module.js`, makes a lot of small folders. Any scheme where the folder is used to disambiguate makes a lot of tools hard to use because we end up with a lot of UI selections, such as `module.js` or `debugger.js`; we can't tell what it means. That is how the Firebug team ended up with `debuggerModule.js` and `debuggerPanel.js`— where a developer will follow some unambiguous naming convention. The name starts with the feature name to make it unique, and hence there is no conflict.

Components replaced by SharedObjects

Firebug currently has five XPCOM components. The Firebug team needs to create two more XPCOM modules—ECMA harmony modules and CommonJS modules. As these are all in JavaScript, the XPCOM infrastructure only exists to arrange common access between Firebug windows. By creating a single `SharedObject` XPCOM component, the amount of boiler plate code can be reduced. This will also prepare for in-place JavaScript editing and dynamic update features in future.

Issue: SharedObject API

Leverage work by CommonJS:

- ECMA harmony modules
- CommonJS modules

This will put Firebug on the same path as jetpack proposals.

As far as we know the CommonJS as well as Mozilla platform, `Components.utils.module` supports common code loading, but common object sharing is also needed. So, there may be some additional work on API.

Recode TabWatcher/DOMWindowWatcher

TabWatcher is still very heuristic and relies on Firefox idiosyncrasies that can change. Chromebug has its own watcher and even more guesses about the platform. Maybe `nsIXULWindow` and `nsIDOMWindow` lifetime event notifications will be replaced with a clean abstraction. Then we would put it in a `SharedObject`, so that only one per application is needed, and get a clean API. This will require platform support.

Sandboxed extension loading

By reapplying the module loading technology, a jetpack-like environmental wrapper for Firebug extensions can be created. The extensions will be slightly simpler because they'll just be ZIP files. The extensions would be slightly more robust too, as they would be evaluated with `eval()` in a scope that only contains Firebug.

This enhancement depends upon the Firefox improvements. When Firefox improves, only then can the Firebug team work on this enhancement.

Memory panel

Firebug will provide a new panel for its users. This is one of top features that has been requested many times, and it would certainly be very helpful for web application developers. It will show some memory profiling activity.

Apart from the preceding improvements some refactoring and bug fixing will also feature in Firebug 1.7.

Index

Symbols

$$(selector) 191
$$(selector) method 68, 69
$(id) 191
$(id) method 67, 68
$x(xpath) 191
$x(xpath) method 69
<em:maxVersion>3.7.*.*</em:maxVersion> 175
<em:minVersion>0.1</em:minVersion> 175
<em:type>2</em-type> 175

A

AJAX 119
AJAX calls
  debugging, console object used 130
Asynchronous JavaScript and XML. *See* **AJAX**
awesome@coder.com 175

B

bindFixed function 183
box model
  inspecting 65
  tweaking 65
browser cache
  analyzing 113-115

C

callback parameter 122
cd() function 141
cd() method 140
cd(window) 192
cd(window) method 72
Chromebug 172, 197
Chrome Edit Plus 172
Chrome List 172
chrome.manifest file 173
clear() 192
clear() method 72
CodeBurner
  about 159
  steps, for using 159
command line API methods
  $$(selector) 68
  $(id) 67
  $x(xpath) 69
  cd(window) 72
  clear() 72
  debug(fn) 74
  dir(object) 70
  dirxml(node) 71
  inspect(object[, tabName]) 72
  keys(object) 73
  monitorEvents(object[, types]) 76
  monitor(functionName) 74, 75
  profileEnd() 77
  profile([title]) 77
  undebug(fn) 74
  unmonitorEvents(object[, types]) 76
  unmonitor(functionName) 74, 75
  values(object) 74
command line API reference 191
command line JavaScript 16
command line (large) shortcuts 189
command line (small) shortcuts 189
CommonJS modules 197

conditional breakpoints
about 86
removing 88
configuration options, Pixel Perfect
hide overlay when inspecting 155
hide statusbar info 155
Console2 172
console API methods
console.assert(expression[, object, ...]) 81
console.count([title]) 82
console.debug(object[, object, ...]) 80
console.dir(object) 81
console.dirxml(node) 81
console.error(object[, object, ...]) 80
console.groupCollapsed(object[, object, ...]) 81
console.groupEnd() 81
console.group(object[, object, ...]) 81
console.info(object[, object, ...]) 80
console.log(object[, object, ...]) 79
console.profileEnd() 82
console.profile([title]) 82
console.timeEnd(name) 82
console.time(name) 82
console.trace() 81
console.warn(object[, object, ...]) 80
Console API reference
about 190
console functions 190
console.assert(expression[, object, ...]) 190
console.assert(expression[, object, ...]) method 81
console.assert() function 133
console.count([title]) 191
console.count([title]) method 82
console.debug() 131
console.debug() function 130, 132
console.debug(object[, object, ...]) 190
console.debug(object[, object, ...]) method 80
console.dir() function 134
console.dir(object) 190
console.dir(object) method 81
console.dirxml(node) 190
console.dirxml(node) method 81
console.error(object[, object, ...]) 190
console.error(object[, object, ...]) method 80
console functions 190
console.groupCollapsed(object[, object, ...]) 190
console.groupCollapsed(object[, object, ...]) method 81
console.groupEnd() 191
console.groupEnd() method 81
console.group() function 141
console.group(object[, object, ...]) 190
console.group(object[, object, ...]) method 81
console.info(object[, object, ...]) 190
console.info(object[, object, ...]) method 80
console.log(object[, object, ...]) 190
console.log(object[, object, ...]) method 79
console.profileEnd() 191
console.profileEnd() method 82
console.profile([title]) 191
console.profile([title]) method 82
console tab
about 16
command line JavaScript 16
errors and warnings section 17
console.timeEnd(name) 191
console.timeEnd(name) method 82
console.time(name) 191
console.time(name) method 82
console.trace() 190
console.trace() method 81
console.warn(object[, object, ...]) 190
console.warn(object[, object, ...]) method 80
Crash Me Now! 172
CrossFire API 196
CSS
tweaking 58, 60
CSS development
about 55
cascading rules, inspecting 55
colors, previewing 57, 58
images, previewing 57
CSS editor tab shortcuts 188
CSS element
inspecting 55, 56
CSS files
modifying 30-33
viewing 30
CSS inspector 29

CSS properties
enabling/disabling 60-62
CSS rule
editing 59
CSS stylesheet
box model, inspecting 65
box model, tweaking 65
delete <property> option 64
disable <property> option 64
edit <property> option 64
inspecting 62
new property option 63
new rule option 63
CSS tab
about 29
CSS files list 30
CSS inspector 29
CSS, modifying 30-33
functions 29
searching, within 65
CSS tab shortcuts 188

D

debug(fn) 192
debug(fn) method 74
development preferences, extension development environment
about 169, 170
setting 171, 172
value, changing 170
dir(object) 191
dir(object) method 70
dirxml(node) 191
dirxml(node) method 71, 72
dock view, Firebug modes 12
Document Object Model. *See* **DOM**
DOM
about 91
constants, filtering 93, 94
functions, filtering 93, 94
inspecting 91, 92
live modifications, viewing 128, 129
modifying 96, 97
modifying, auto-complete used 97
properties, filtering 93, 94
Domain Specific Languages. *See* **DSLs**
DOM and watch editor shortcuts 187
DOM attributes
adding 100-102
removing 98, 99
DOM editor 96
DOM inspector 91
DOM Inspector 172
DOM tab
about 36
functions 36
working 37
DOM tab shortcuts 187
download speed, web resource
finding 117

E

ECMA harmony modules 197
errors and warnings section, console tab
about 17
descriptive errors 19
informative errors 19
JavaScript commands, executing 19
status bar error indicator 18
ExecuteJS 172
extend() function 176
Extension Developer Extension 172
extension development environment
development preferences 169, 170
development profile, setting up 168, 169
setting up 167
Extension Wizard 172

F

features, Firebug 1.6 193-195
features, Firebug 1.7 196-198
Firebug
about 7
closing 11
console.groupEnd() function 141
console.group() function 141
console tab 16
CSS tab 29
DOM tab 36
features 7, 9

highlight changes feature 43
history 8
HTML source, viewing 41-43
HTML tab 20
inspect functionality 48
installing, on FireFox 10
installing, on non-Firefox browsers 10
keyboard and mouse shortcuts 185
magical cd() function 137
modes 11
need for 8
Net panel 106
net tab 38
opening 11
script tab 34
search box 50
shortcut keys, configuring 143
source, modifying 44

Firebug 1.6
about 193
features 193, 195

Firebug 1.7
about 196
features 196

Firebug Extensions
about 147
Chromebug 172
Chrome Edit Plus 172
Chrome List 172
CodeBurner 159
Console2 172
DOM Inspector 172
ExecuteJS 172
Extension Developers Extension 172
Extension Wizard 172
Firecookie 151
Firefinder 155
FireQuery 157
for, analyzing performance 118
JavaScript 172
JavaScript Command 172
MozRepl 172
Page Speed 162
Pixel Perfect 153
SenSEO 160
Venkman 172
XPCOMViewer 172
YSlow 148

Firebug Google group
url 193

Firebug internals page on Mozilla site
url 193

Firebug issues tracking system on Google code
url 193

Firebug Lite
about 10
using, on non-Firefox browsers 10

Firebug modes
about 11
dock view 12
window mode 12

Firebug online resources
about 193
Google group 193
internals page on Mozilla site 193
issues tracking system on Google code 193
plugins page on Firebug site 193
site homepage 193
video 193
wiki homepage 193

firebugOverlay.xul 173

Firebug.Panel object 176

Firebug plugins page on Firebug site
url 193

Firebug site homepage
url 193

Firebug Swarm 193

Firebug video
url 193

Firebug wiki homepage
url 193

Firecookie
about 151, 152
features 152
functions 152

Firefinder
about 155
features 156
steps, for using 155

Firefox
Firebug, installing 10

FireQuery
about 157

features 157
functionality 157

G

getOptionsMenuItems() function 180-182
getPanel() function 177
GET/POST request 125-127
GET request 124
headers tab 124
JSON tab 125
response tab 124
getScript() function 131
global shortcuts 185
groupedOutput() function 142

H

Hello World! extension
about 173
chrome.manifest file 173, 174
drop-down list, attaching 180
helloWorld.js file 176
helloWorld.js file, revisited 181, 182
helloWorldOverlay.xul file 175
installing 177-179
install.rdf file 174
packaging 177, 178
prefs.js file 181
starting 173
helloWorld.js file 176
helloWorldOverlay.xul 173
helloWorldOverlay.xul file 175
highlight changes feature, Firebug 43
HTML editor shortcuts 186
HTML element
attribute, editing 23
breakpoints, setting on 52-54
editing 24, 25
events, logging 26, 28
finding, on web page 51, 52
HTML inspect mode shortcuts 186
HTML source
copying, for HTML element 52
HTML source, Firebug
viewing 41
HTML source, modifying
about 44
attribute, adding to HTML element 46
HTML attribute, modifying 45
HTML element, deleting 47
HTML element source, modifying 47
HTML source panel
about 21
options 22, 23
HTML tab
about 20
events, logging 26, 28
functions 20
HTML element, editing 23
HTML source panel 21
HTML tab shortcuts 186
HTTP headers
examining 112

I

iFrames 137
iFrame code 138
inspect functionality 48
inspect(object[, tabName]) 192
inspect(object[, tabName]) method 72
installation, FireBug
on FireFox 9
on non-Firefox browsers 10
install.rdf file 174

J

JavaScript 172
JavaScript code
debugging, with Firebug 83-85
JavaScript code navigation 102, 103
JavaScript Command 172
JavaScript debugging
about 82
conditional breakpoints 85-88
with Firebug 83
JavaScript development
command line API methods 67
console API methods 79
JavaScript Object Notation. *See* **JSON**

JavaScript profiler
about 77
columns and description 78, 79
JSON 122

K

keyboard and mouse shortcuts
about 185
command line (large) shortcuts 189
command line (small) shortcuts 189
CSS editor tab shortcuts 188
CSS tab shortcuts 188
DOM and watch editor shortcuts 187
DOM tab shortcuts 187
global shortcuts 185
HTML editor shortcuts 186
HTML inspect mode shortcuts 186
HTML tab shortcuts 186
layout editor shortcuts 189
layout tab shortcuts 188
script tab shortcuts 187
keys(object) 192
keys(object) method 73

L

layout editor shortcuts 189
layout tab shortcuts 188

M

magical cd() function 137
monitorEvents(object[, types]) 192
monitorEvents(object[, types]) method 76
monitor(fn) 192
monitor(functionName) method 74, 75
MozRepl 172
multiline command line 70

N

Net panel
about 106
browser queue wait time 110
information 107, 108
load-time bar color significance 108, 109
request, breaking down by type 110, 111
net tab
about 38
columns 38, 39
functions 38
network monitoring 106
non-Firefox browsers
Firebug, installing on 10

O

optionMenu() function 182

P

page components
inspecting 48
page edit
inspecting 49
page reload
inspecting 50
Page Speed
about 162
rules 163
Page Speed Activity tab 165
Page Speed checks
best practices 165, 166
Pixel Perfect
about 153
configuration options 155
features 153
steps, for using 153, 154
prefs.js file 181
printMe()function 140
profileEnd() 192
profileEnd() method 77
profile([title]) 192
profile([title]) method 77

R

registerPanel() function 177
request/response headers 120-122
rulesets, YSlow
Classic (V1) 149
Small Site or Blog 149
YSlow (V2) 149

S

script tab
about 34
breakpoints, subtab 35
functions 34
stack, subtab 35
watch, subtab 34
script tab shortcuts 187
search box, Firebug 50
SenSEO
about 160
features 160
rules 160
steps, for using 161
setPref method 182
SharedObject API 197
shortcut keys, Firebug
configuring 143
SQLite Manager 172 172

T

TabWatcher/DOMWindowWatcher 197

U

undebug(fn) 192
undebug(fn) method 74
unmonitorEvents(object[, types]) 192
unmonitorEvents(object[, types]) method 76
unmonitor(fn) 192
unmonitor(functionName) method 74, 75
URL parameter 122

V

values(object) 192
values(object) method 74
Venkman 172
ViewAbout 172 172

W

web application performance
analyzing 105
web application performance, analyzing
browser cache, analyzing 113
HTTP headers, examining 112
network monitoring 106
requests, breaking down by type 110
XMLHttpRequest monitoring 116
window mode, Firebug modes 12

X

XmlHttpRequest
GET/POST request 125
request/response headers 120
tracking 120
XMLHttpRequest
monitoring 116
XML User Interface Language. *See* **XUL**
XPCOM components 197
XPCOM modules 197
XPCOMViewer 172
XUL 175

Y

YSlow
about 148
components tab 150
features 148
grade tab 149
rulesets 149
statistics tab 150
tools tab 151

Thank you for buying Firebug 1.5: Editing, Debugging, and Monitoring Web Pages

Packt Open Source Project Royalties

When we sell a book written on an Open Source project, we pay a royalty directly to that project. Therefore by purchasing Firebug 1.5: Editing, Debugging, and Monitoring Web Pages, Packt will have given some of the money received to the Firebug project.

In the long term, we see ourselves and you—customers and readers of our books—as part of the Open Source ecosystem, providing sustainable revenue for the projects we publish on. Our aim at Packt is to establish publishing royalties as an essential part of the service and support a business model that sustains Open Source.

If you're working with an Open Source project that you would like us to publish on, and subsequently pay royalties to, please get in touch with us.

Writing for Packt

We welcome all inquiries from people who are interested in authoring. Book proposals should be sent to `author@packtpub.com`. If your book idea is still at an early stage and you would like to discuss it first before writing a formal book proposal, contact us; one of our commissioning editors will get in touch with you.

We're not just looking for published authors; if you have strong technical skills but no writing experience, our experienced editors can help you develop a writing career, or simply get some additional reward for your expertise.

About Packt Publishing

Packt, pronounced 'packed', published its first book "Mastering phpMyAdmin for Effective MySQL Management" in April 2004 and subsequently continued to specialize in publishing highly focused books on specific technologies and solutions.

Our books and publications share the experiences of your fellow IT professionals in adapting and customizing today's systems, applications, and frameworks. Our solution-based books give you the knowledge and power to customize the software and technologies you're using to get the job done. Packt books are more specific and less general than the IT books you have seen in the past. Our unique business model allows us to bring you more focused information, giving you more of what you need to know, and less of what you don't.

Packt is a modern, yet unique publishing company, which focuses on producing quality, cutting-edge books for communities of developers, administrators, and newbies alike. For more information, please visit our website: `www.PacktPub.com`.

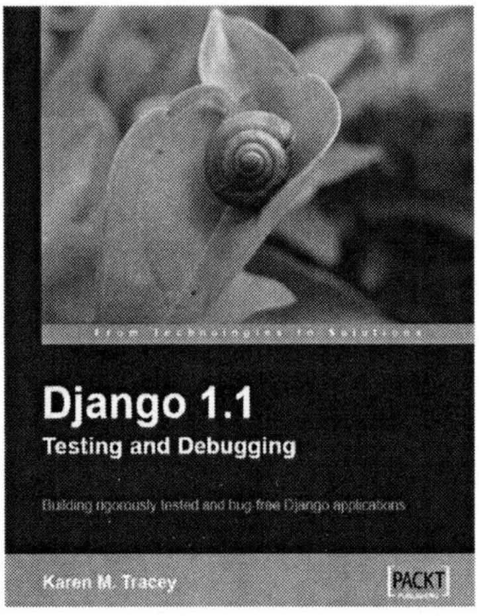

Django 1.1 Testing and Debugging

ISBN: 978-1-847197-56-6 Paperback: 430 pages

Building rigorously tested and bug-free Django applications

1. Develop Django applications quickly with fewer bugs through effective use of automated testing and debugging tools.
2. Ensure your code is accurate and stable throughout development and production by using Django's test framework.
3. Understand the working of code and its generated output with the help of debugging tools.

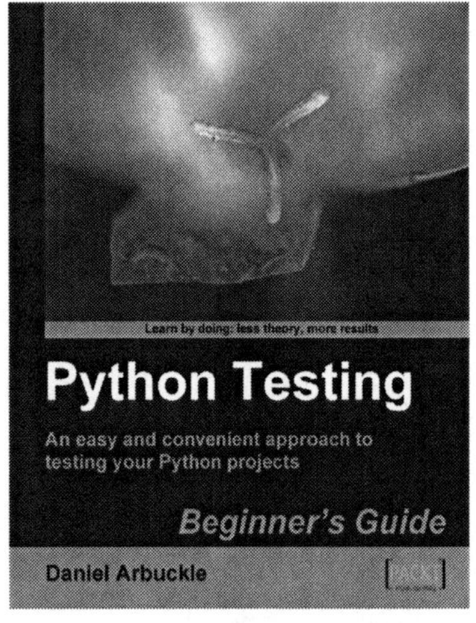

Python Testing: Beginner's Guide

ISBN: 978-1-847198-84-6 Paperback: 256 pages

An easy and convenient approach to testing your powerful Python projects

1. Covers everything you need to test your code in Python
2. Easiest and enjoyable approach to learn Python testing
3. Write, execute, and understand the result of tests in the unit test framework
4. Packed with step-by-step examples and clear explanations

Please check **www.PacktPub.com** for information on our titles

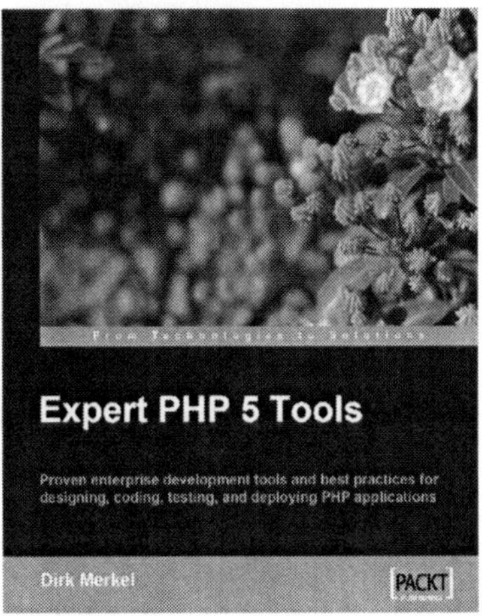

Expert PHP 5 Tools

ISBN: 978-1-847198-38-9 Paperback: 480 pages

Proven enterprise development tools and best practices for designing, coding, testing, and deploying PHP applications

1. Best practices for designing, coding, testing, and deploying PHP applications - all the information in one book
2. Learn to write unit tests and practice test-driven development from an expert
3. Set up a professional development environment with integrated debugging capabilities

-

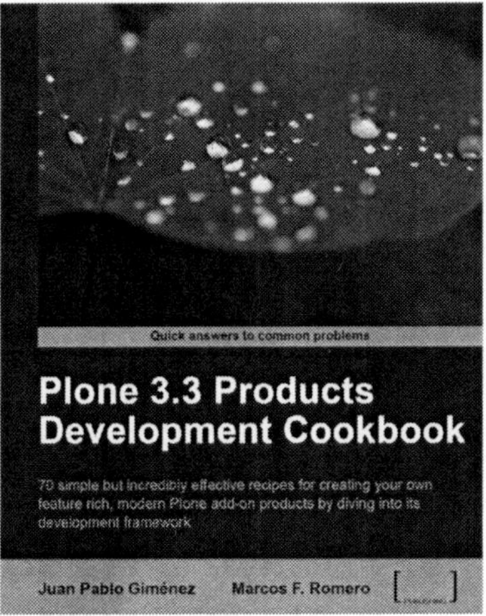

Plone 3.3 Products Development Cookbook

ISBN: 978-1-847196-72-9 Paperback: 380 pages

70 simple but incredibly effective recipes for creating your own feature rich, modern Plone add-on products by diving into its development framework

1. Create custom content types, add utilities, and internationalize your applications using Plone products
2. Manage site installation, configuration, and customization with code instead of manual actions that are likely to be forgotten
3. Guarantee your code operation and performance by including automatic testing and caching techniques

Please check **www.PacktPub.com** for information on our titles

Breinigsville, PA USA
15 December 2010
251491BV00003B/10/P
9 781847 194961